# Thank You For Yesterday

## A CROSS-CULTURAL ADVENTURE

## Kate Ellis

Full Court Press
Englewood Cliffs, New Jersey

*First Edition*

Copyright © 2020 by Kate Ellis

All rights reserved. No part of this book may be reproduced or transmitted in any form or by any means electronic or mechanical, including by photocopying, by recording, or by any information storage and retrieval system, without the express permission of the author, except where permitted by law.

Published in the United States of America
by Full Court Press, 601 Palisade Avenue,
Englewood Cliffs, NJ 07632
*fullcourtpress.com*

ISBN 978-1-946989-71-0
Library of Congress Catalog No. 2020909674

*Editing and book design by Barry Sheinkopf*

"We have been wearing our write dresses
Far too long—squeezing into spotlit  silk, chiffon
The color of nothing."
	—*Helen Mort*

# Contents

| | | |
|---|---|---|
| I | Far Rockaway, 2016 and 2003 | i |
| II | Adoption, 1993-97 | 19 |
| III | Green Card, 1998–2003 | 157 |
| IV | The Big Tree, 2003–07 | 237 |
| V | Epilog, 2016 | 307 |

*Far Rockaway, 2016 and 2003*

# 1

The weekend after Hillary Clinton was defeated by Donald Trump, I was sitting in my kitchen listening to Kate McKinnon accompanying herself on the piano and singing Leonard Cohen's "Hallelujah" on *Saturday Night Live*. When she finished the song, she turned to look straight into the camera and said, "I'm not giving up, and neither should you."

"That was a nice ending," my long-time friend Marcia said when I spoke to her the next morning. "But it will be a while before Hillary has nothing on her tongue but hallelujah."

"Will she ever?"

"Well, I think about times when it all went wrong in my life, and when I look back, I'm not a bit sorry I did what I did. And I'm sure that's true with you, too."

"Like what are you thinking about?" I asked, hoping to hear about something that had happened to her. But she turned the conversation toward me.

"Well, you came to New York to study dance with Martha

Graham and people like that. But then you got into that little five-person company and felt miserable, so you went back to school and ended up a professor at Rutgers. I did the same thing, and it got me teaching at Medgar Evers."

"Yes, we both have that in our histories. I remember a while back standing on the corner where that studio was, and when I saw trucks demolishing it to replace it with some expensive apartments, I started to cry."

"It was a beautiful place," Marcia said. "With that peaceful garden in the back. But what about your marriage to—what's his name, your Nigerian?"

"Foley," I reminded her. "And even with everything that happened, I have to say I'm still glad I married him, and stayed married to him for ten pretty interesting years."

"We've both lived good lives," Marcia said, and she was living proof that a good life didn't have to include a husband. It was a belief that I held for most of my adult life, and though I like to think I'm free of it now, it was an inheritance from my mother that was difficult to dispel. When I left my first husband in the Seventies, the women's movement was in full bloom. It had introduced the title Ms. so that a woman's marital status was not the first thing you knew about her. But the wish to be married rather than single was so deeply imprinted on my psyche that when a handsome Nigerian woodcarver wanted to marry me in 1993, I did not hesitate to say yes.

It was a marriage with lots of space in it. We were together in the States for part of the year. I joined him in Nigeria when I wasn't teaching, for three months every summer, a month every Christmas, and for two sabbatical leaves. I loved living in two places at once, and I thought he did too. I was welcomed immediately into his extended family, and I'm still welcomed even now that the legal bond that tied me to him, and therefore to them, is now broken. Perhaps they hoped that I would still bring them money from America, and I've done that. But I still think there was more to their welcome than a wish for financial support.

I had to be pushed to end that marriage, and the person who pushed me was Sara, a friend who does my taxes. My first venture into matrimony was with a fellow graduate student who gave me a son who in turn gave me three thriving grandchildren. Kevin's father was the smartest person in our cohort at Columbia, and I wanted to marry a man who was smarter than me so I wouldn't have to play dumb around my husband the way my mother had to do in order to keep her flagrantly unfaithful husband tied to her legally.

But I'm also no longer married to the Nigerian woodcarver, twenty years younger than me, that I met in his country in 1993. Nevertheless I am glad that I spent ten years going back and forth between our two countries, legally joined to a vast extended family whose members still claim me as theirs. I still sometimes put on the wrappers, blouses, and head ties in the brilliant colors and patterns that are part of that country's vibrant everyday life. It's been more than a decade since the arrangement that brought these clothes into my closet came to an end. But hearing Leonard's song got me thinking back over that time in my life.

It began in 1993 when I traveled to Nigeria and met the man I married a year later. He impressed me, not just with his easy smile and his expertise when he danced with me in the courtyard of the art school where he taught carving, and where his carvings were on display. These were tall, elegant figures representing the deities of Ifa, the traditional Nigerian religion that preceded the Christianity there. His father and grandfather were carvers also, along with several of his brothers.

It took a full decade for the marriage to come to an end. But while it lasted, we lived in my Manhattan apartment for part of the year, and I joined him in Nigeria when I wasn't teaching, that is, for three months every summer, a month every Christmas, and two sabbatical leaves that lasted for six months. I loved having a home in two places at once, and I thought he did, too.

I was welcomed immediately into his enormous extended family, and they still consider me family even though the bond that tied me to them no longer exists. Perhaps they hoped that, as their son's wife, I would always bring them money from America. And I was happy to do that when I came to Nigeria on my own, five years after the marriage ended, on a grant to make a film about dancing in Nigerian church services.

I had to be pushed to end it, and the person who pushed me was Sara, a long-time friend recommended to me by a fellow writer, who does my taxes every year. So in 2003, ten years after Foley and I met in Osogbo, where he taught his family's tradition of woodcarving at an art school, I had to tell her that, for the second year in a row, I had no paperwork about my husband's income. Like me, she is the one with the money in their marriage. Her husband works with her in the office, but it's her office, and the building where they live above it is hers, too. When she told me that she gives him cash for the tab before they go into a restaurant, I suspected that Foley would not like it if I did that instead of quietly paying the check myself.

"You know, Kate, you can't file again jointly without information from Foley," she said. "So you'll have to do this as a married person filing separately, and it'll cost you quite a bit more. Where is he now, anyway?" She sounded concerned, not judgmental.

"I really have no idea."

"And this is okay with you?"

"I don't know. When we got married, we agreed, or I thought we did, to live apart as well as together. It was the kind of marriage I wanted. Not being joined at the hip."

"Looks like you got more of that than you bargained for."

"Well, you know me, I like being alone," I said. "Maybe more than most people. I used to tell people that I had the freedom of being single and the security of being married. And I liked it. But I don't like being abandoned, and that's how I feel now."

"This is serious, Kate," Sara said, turning away from her computer screen and looking directly at me. "I've known you for longer than you've known Foley, and it worries me that you're putting up with this. Why are you doing it?"

"Well, I like spending time in Nigeria. And I guess I also like being married more than I like being single. In fact, that's an understatement."

"So you think you need to be married in order to be happy?"

"I know I'm not supposed to think that. I call myself a feminist, after all."

"What does that word mean to you now?"

"Well, I got hired at Rutgers to bring a women's studies program to Rutgers, and we got one. But then Kevin's dad sued me for custody, and his lawyer read in court some of what I'd published, claiming that I was a man hater so I shouldn't have custody of our male child. "

"But he didn't win, right?"

"Thank goodness. It was a horrible year, though." I can see Sara's hands on her keyboard and the wedding ring on her finger. In my eyes, a plain band on that finger—in the subway, for instance—is a visible sign that somebody loves you, someone who will be waiting for you when you get home. The promise to be with you till death do you part isn't taken all that seriously any more, but it's there in the background nevertheless. Someone has chosen you to play a defining role in their life, not just in the present but in a future that awaits you both. Perhaps I came to connect marriage with home because, when I came home from school, nannies and maids were there but never a parent wanting to know how my day had gone.

"But this isn't being married, Kate," Sara said firmly. "Being legally tied to someone whose source of income you don't know is very dangerous. Let me give you the number of a lawyer. And a private detective, too. Then you can file as a single person starting next year. It will be more expensive, but you have to do it."

"Okay, but what can a detective do? You know that Nigerians are very evasive."

"Exactly. That's why you need one."

Sara opened an address book and retrieved the phone numbers she had promised. We then went through the information she needed, and I was about to stand up when she looked up and asked, "How much older are you than Foley?"

"He doesn't know his exact date of birth, but there's about a twenty-year age difference. I know that's a lot, but I've always been with men who are younger than me."

"Maybe so, but I don't think many women would marry a man that much younger. Not to mention a guy from—"

"Well yes," I said, leaning back in my chair. "Lots of people think I'm crazy. Are you saying that I should have been more careful? Like I should look before I leap?"

"No, I'm saying something different. In fact, it looks to me like your life has been a whole series of risks, and good for you. You've done things that a lot of people wouldn't do."

"Like what?"

"Well, coming to New York by yourself, for starters."

"That's true. I didn't want to be a debutante. Or to marry a guy who'd gone to the prep school that was paired up with my girls' school, which is what most of my classmates did."

Just then the phone rang, and Sara picked it up. "I'm sorry, Kate, but my next client is here," she said as she hung up. "This is my busy time, you know. But we can get together and talk after April 15, okay? In the meantime, you need to make these phone calls."

On the way home I thought about my escape from the debutante world of Toronto that had loomed before me as I was growing up. It started with those "not-out" parties that my parents and their friends held over the Christmas and Easter holidays. The boys wore tuxes and we girls had to have a new full-length strapless gown every year. We carried a dance card on ours wrists, and the number of dances reserved on these cards was a register of our popularity, the predictor of future happiness. I think that's a horrible idea now, and I may have thought so then. But I saw no alternative to going through the motions. My favorite dress was dark green net, strapless, with a spray of white flowers at the waist. But it wasn't only these dances leading up to the big one at which you came out. There was the life that followed it: the Junior League and various charitable committees that I would join, as my mother had done. I would attend these meetings while my husband was at the well-paid job that would give us a house and a summer place, along with two cars, some maids and a nanny. Sara was right. Getting away from all that was the beginning of my real life.

A few days before my appointment with her, I had walked into my apartment as the phone was ringing. When I picked it up, a flat male voice intoned, "Is Fun-so there?" and I knew it was a collection agent. Everyone calls my husband Foley, but his full name, Folorunso, is shortened to Funso. In Yoruba, his native language, an "s" is pronounced "sh". Of course these agents don't know that, but their mispronunciation always annoyed me. They'd been calling off and on for a year, and I usually hung up, fearful that their thuggish cohorts would appear and take everything I own. Whom could he owe money to, and how much? Judging from the persistence of these callers, it must be a lot. I'm very careful about money myself, having absorbed, at my boarding school and at home, the biblical idea that from those to whom much is given, like an education at this expensive school, much shall be required.

But talking about him had always been a feature of the relationship that I enjoyed, and still do. When I tell strangers that my husband is Nigerian, they are always curious, though I think I know what's behind that curiosity. Nigeria, where one in four Africans live, is also known as the place from which faxes and emails arrive, persuading gullible people to hand over their bank information in expectation of huge rewards. But it's also the home of a flourishing arts community that most Westerners don't know about, but that I got to know well. I'd always deleted those predatory emails and felt perfectly safe, but maybe Foley had gotten mixed up with some of their senders who spoke Yoruba. He and I could never really talk about money. It was a forbidden topic in my household growing up. So I was never good at it, and now it looked like it was too late.

Usually when these collection agents called, I felt like screaming: Why do you keep calling me? I have no idea where he is. And anyway, what business of yours is that? I didn't tell them that my husband is descended from a long line of Nigerian woodcarvers. That ancestry was one of the things that impressed me about him, along with the way he looked at me when we were dancing together. It was this dancing that really sealed the deal for me. But he hadn't a clue about how the American legal system works. And the sporadic jobs he had usually involved standing in silence for hours, guarding something that had once belonged to somebody else. So why were they after him? Could they be from one of several banks whose offers, addressed to him, of cards with high credit allowances, still come into my mailbox?

But this time I collected myself enough to ask the annoying voice of the debt collector a question: "Do you have another address for him besides this one?"

"5707 Shore Front Parkway," came the agent's brusque answer. "Number 1404."

"Do you have a phone number, too?" I asked, and I wrote it all down. From the address it had to be near the ocean, but where? Then, after hanging up the phone, I summoned the courage to call the number I'd written down, only to get the mechanical male voice that used to come with cheap answering machines, announcing that "the person you have called is not available."

But at least I had an address and a phone number to give to the detective. So I took a deep breath and called the number Sara had given me. His name, Skip, struck me as an odd name for a detective, whose job is to look for people who have skipped out of view. But something in his voice reassured me, so I gave him the address and phone number the collection agent had given me, as well as the phone numbers of Foley's two brothers who, like Foley, had come to this country with the visitors' visas I'd helped them to get. I also had a string of other numbers from his driver's license, green card, and Social Security card. "The area code tells me he's living out in Brooklyn or Queens," I added. "But that's all I have to give you."

"I never close a case till I've found the person I'm looking for," Skip said. His confidence lifted my spirits, and I was glad I had not hung up on that collection agent.

I spent the next week coming to terms with the prospect of a second divorce initiated, like my first one thirty years ago, by me. My mother's greatest pride had been staying with my father in spite of infidelities he didn't try to hide, though in reality she had no other option. She'd married a wealthy, handsome man who became a popular politician, and she lived surrounded by nannies and maids in the house his grandfather had built. Marrying a man like him had been her only goal, so keeping him was her only measure of success. Besides, a divorce would have ruined his career, and how would she have supported herself? And where would we three girls have gone? "Don't come running home to mother the minute things go wrong," she said in 1965 as I was putting on her mother's white cotton wedding dress with its rows of tucks and buttons. Then I took my father's arm and walked slowly up the aisle of a flower-filled Episcopal church, to Purcell's "Trumpet Voluntary."

Her message was clear: Stay married no matter what. She was probably only repeating what her own mother had said to her when she got married, but though everything I had learned as a feminist academic told me that a ring on your left fourth finger is not an automatic key to happiness, this knowledge had not been enough to dislodge her spell: You can't be happy unless you are secure, which means that you must be married. Perhaps happy is not the right word since she was unhappy and denied it with every breath. But wearing that ring means that someone has promised to keep you secure till death do you part, to stand by you into the future so you don't have to face it alone. It gives you a long-term "we of me." The times that I've been single have tended to be lonely, so the spell has had lots of reinforcement. For my mother, and probably for her mother as well, staying married meant not looking too closely at what one's husband was doing when he was not with you. Maybe I didn't subscribe to that program, but it looks like I have lived it anyway.

I remember my grandmother as cold and judgmental, not someone to run home to when you were hurt or disappointed. "A lady is known by the way she folds her towels" was a favorite saying of hers, and I remember her pronouncing it several times. That memory may account for the fact that I always fold my towels (and everything else) very neatly, and I suspect that my mother did, too. But those chilly words also tell me why my mother didn't want to hear any details from me when I told her that things had gone wrong. Feminism has been at the center of my teaching ever since I started out at Rutgers in the Seventies. But had it rubbed off on me? Many of us who joined the women's movement then did it in order to be different from our mothers. We introduced a gender-neutral salutation, for instance, so that a woman's marital status was not the first thing you knew about her, though my mother had been proud to occupy that space. When I left my first husband, a brilliant man who, I now know, was on the Asperger's spectrum, my women friends stepped in to support me while my mother looked away. But we were challenging gender prescriptions that had been honored for centuries and can't be changed by an individual act of will. I was younger then, of course, and we didn't really know what being single in a culture that was still highly patriarchal could mean. But my mother's belief did not disappear, leaving me tethered to a past that wasn't even mine and fearful of giving my heart away. Yet a married woman does not fear the future: It's a belief that I still hold. Where did I get this conflicted idea if not from her?

A few days after that 2003 visit to Sara, the phone rang again, and to my surprise and relief it was not another collection agent but Skip. "I have some information," he said, "about the address you gave me. It's an apartment in Queens rented under the name Komolafe. Does that name ring a bell for you?"

It did, but I didn't think that this detective would want to hear the whole story. "It's the last name of a woman who was a student at the art school in Nigeria where I met Foley," I told him before hanging up. I then went on the internet to find out how to get to Shore Front Parkway, and the following Saturday found me on an A train bound for Far Rockaway with an address and apartment number on a slip of paper in my pocket. I didn't tell the two students who rent rooms from me to help cover the maintenance on my apartment where I was going, since they would probably tell me I was crazy.

Maybe I am a bit crazy. I'd never been to the end of the A line. Maybe what I'd find would upset me and I'd regret making the trip. But another part of me let me know that I needed to see what was out there, and looking back, I'm glad I yielded to my desire to see what I saw.

I'd changed trains at Columbus Circle, and the A raced past local stops as it charged into Lower Manhattan. But as we moved under the East River and into Brooklyn, a mechanical announcement let me know that, that weekend, the A would be running locally, pulling into one white-tiled station after another, their walls water-stained and splotched with almost illegible ads. I was glad I had brought the briefcase, sitting at my feet, filled with papers from my students on a novel whose heroine, Moll Flanders, became a criminal out of desperation but ended up in America, repentant and rich. Perhaps my husband had similar visions of his American future. The "rich" part anyway.

Finally the A train came up from underground, stopping at the Aqueduct Raceway and then at Howard Beach. This is where a gang of white youths killed a Trinidadian boy in 1986 for the crime of being on "their" territory. It's also the station where you can catch a bus to JFK airport, so it's the last stop where white passengers predominate. The surge of the Atlantic became faintly audible in the distance as I peered out through the train's dirty windows. We clattered past two-story pastel houses with barn-shaped roofs, some close enough to the water to have docks right outside their back doors, each with a small boat anchored to it. What was I hoping to learn from taking that long trip on a day with no sunshine? When I asked Skip about the phone call he had made, he had told me that the person answering the phone said that Foley was "not around." That annoyingly vague expression is used all the time in Nigeria, telling you nothing about the person you are looking for, like where he went or when he'll be back. "Who answered the phone?" I'd asked him. "Male or female?"

"It sounded like a little girl," he had said.

By now the aluminum-sided houses were behind me. Tall brick buildings, squared off like those in a child's drawing, lined up in the distance against a gunmetal sky that threatened rain. I never imagined that there would be so many tall housing projects so close to the water, but those buildings look like taller versions of the Frederick Douglass housing projects two blocks from where I live on the Upper West Side. If this was where my husband chose to live, he was far away from the places that have kept me in New York since I crossed the Canadian border straight out of high school forty years before. Riverside Park and Central Park a few blocks on either side of me. The Met Museum, and just about everything in it. The Cloisters. Carnegie Hall, where I ushered when I first came to the city to be a modern dancer. What could be going on here, I wondered, that would draw him to such stark surroundings?

The three other riders still in my subway car were black, and two of them were women. As I smiled at them, I wondered if I looked out of place to them in my green suede coat with a fur collar, my battered briefcase stuffed with papers resting on the floor next to my feet. The third was a teenage boy who slouched in his seat, his wide-legged jeans slung low on his hips below an oversized leather jacket. He got up and shuffled toward the door, keeping his head down, and got off one stop ahead of mine: Beach 60th Street.

As I walked toward the turnstile, the sight of a cluster of young black men at the top of the stairs, laughing loudly in their black head wraps, told me that this was an area where white people are probably as much of a rarity as they are in Nigeria. If it had been dark out I might have been nervous walking past them, but I sensed that their laughing presence probably gave Foley a sense of familiarity that I could never offer. No one with Foley's skin color lives in the building to which I would return, though my co-op board says it has never excluded buyers on the basis of race. My husband's friends always admired my apartment with its picture-lined hallway and paneled dining room, just as my American friends do. But when we two were alone, he'd sometimes tell me he was going down to the lobby to "play" with one of our three doormen, the only other black men on the premises. Perhaps I should have taken that as a warning that something was wrong, but I did not.

When Foley first came to the States to visit me, before we were married, a Jamaican man named Bartholomew was our daytime doorman. He and I did the Times crossword puzzle in the lobby on days when I was not teaching, he supplying the "guy" words from sports while I contributed the literary references. When my neighbors teased me about our rapport, I insisted that crossword puzzles are a great way to ward off Alzheimer's. I knew that Bartholomew had several children and a girlfriend, so the presence of a handsome African in my life allowed me to enjoy a mildly flirtatious rapport I might not have risked had I not been "taken."

Bartholomew's lilting accent was part of his charm, but we could talk politics too. He told me during the O.J. Simpson trial that O.J. was "guilty as sin," and when we heard the verdict over the radio he kept on the desk in our lobby, we were both appalled. Foley had no history with O.J., and this was just one of many things I couldn't talk to him about. I see now that I had more in common with Bartholomew, who'd lived in the States for years, than I did with the man whose presence in my life would lift me out of the state of single womanhood that was making me miserable and into a place where I could speak about "my husband."

Perhaps I might have seen this lack of common experience as a sign that trouble was on the horizon, but I did not. The truth is, I did not want to go back to being single, so I was not on the lookout for problems. Quite the opposite, in fact. What I learned from my marriage I learned the hard way, and perhaps there is no other way. Our histories shape the way we see the present, and ours unfolded at opposite ends of a very wide economic spectrum. The deities in his religion are part of a world of invisible presences that includes one's ancestors. They see things that we cannot, and can therefore help us in this life. It has never occurred to me to attribute such powers to my ancestors, but one of them came to this country just before the Revolution, for reasons I will never know.

So perhaps he guided the leaps I've taken, not knowing where I would land.

After pushing through the turnstile, I approached the woman inside the token booth and asked her, though the transparent barrier, for directions to Shore Front Parkway. Her black hair was streaked with gray, pulled back in a tight bun that went well with her rimless glasses. "What number?"

"5707 Shore Front Parkway. I know it's a tall building because the apartment I'm looking for is on the fourteenth floor." The fact that the collection agent had unwittingly given me this indispensable information struck me as a piece of unanticipated good luck.

"Well, 59th Street is at the bottom of these stairs. So turn right and you'll be walking along Shore Front Parkway."

I thanked her, and when I reached the street I looked out at the dull brown ocean in the distance. A woman in a trench coat was standing at the intersection. Her dreadlocked hair reached almost to her waist, and she hugged a large shopping bag against her chest. "I'm pretty sure it's over this way," she said when I approached her with my address. "I'm heading that way too, so I'll go part way with you. You're lucky it's not in the Edgemere projects back there. It's not really safe for a lady like you to be walking around there by yourself."

I don't remember feeling a bit unsafe, though. In fact, I had a growing sense that my mission was going well, that helpers were showing up just when they were needed. That's the way Joseph Campbell describes a hero's journey. My African-American friend Marcia told me that this fearlessness comes from my privileged upbringing: never having to go without something I really wanted for lack of money. What Sara said about my willingness to leap before looking comes with a belief that a safety net will be there for me when I land. But when I joined the antiwar movement as a Columbia student in the Sixties, I learned that, for Karl Marx, the ruling class was the enemy. The class into which you are born shapes the way you see the world, he said, so I kept quiet about my family and its support for the war we were taking to the streets to end. My father and two uncles, World War II vets, believed that North Vietnam should be "bombed back into the Stone Age." One uncle was blinded in combat, and the other led his regiment, the Queen's Own Rifles, as part of the D-Day invasion of Normandy. So at home I didn't talk about going to Washington again and again and gathering with thousands of people to shout, "What do we want? Peace. When do we want it? Now."

At home we didn't talk about money either. So a history of silence kicked in around Foley and his friends, who could live for at least a year on what I pay to live in my apartment for a month. Then there is the fact that I'd never met a black person till I came to the States. Our British nannies and maids were white, and so was everyone in my boarding school. Nevertheless my belief that the forces in charge of the world I live in are on my side lets me enjoy going to places where I don't fit in, and that's how I felt as I looked over my shoulder at the projects my companion was referring to. "You got the number of the person you come to see?" she asked. "That filling station over there has a pay phone you could use."

"I want to surprise him," I said as we followed the sidewalk that curved away from the elevated subway rattling above us. On my right, a vacant lot that had probably once been a basketball court filled the space beside us, its cracked surface guarded by a chain-link fence.

As we walked under the overhead subway tracks, my guide spotted a mailman coming out of one of the buildings. "Mailmen always know where everything is," she said. "Let me go ask him."

"Hey, sister, what you doin' back here?" he asked with a grin. "I thought you moved." I've always envied this familial way that black people talk to each other, but not to me.

"Yeah, I moved," she said. "But my aunt's still here, and I'm bringing her some stuff. This lady here is looking for 5707 Shore Front Parkway."

"That's it over there," he said. "Over here's even-numbered buildings."

"So this friend don't know you're comin' out here?" my Virgilian guide asked as we made our way under the tracks and across the street.

I thought for a minute about how much I wanted to tell her. "He's Nigerian."

"Why didn't you say so? That gray building over there is where all the Nigerians live. If he's Nigerian, I'll bet that's the place you're looking for."

Then she hesitated, looking down at my briefcase, then back at me. "You're not some kind of lawyer, are you?"

"Me? Not at all. I'm a teacher. This stuff in here was written by my students."

"A teacher, huh? What subject?"

"English."

"Oh boy, not my good subject. Okay, be safe now," she said with a smile, and I thought about the fact that I'd never heard a white person tell another white person to be safe.

Past the vacant lot, I came to a metal door marked 5707. Just as I reached it, a boy of about fifteen let himself in. I followed him to the elevator, and we waited for an uncomfortably long time. Finally the door opened and he, his bike, and I entered the metal-lined cabin. When we stopped at the first floor another boy, wearing a bright red hoodie and thick glasses, joined us, and they chatted in English until they arrived at their respective destinations. Their parents must have come here from Nigeria, but they looked and talked like regular American kids.

By the time I reached the fourteenth floor, I was alone. When the elevator opened, I stepped out into a space between two rows of doors, each painted a dark burgundy. They were quite close together, so the living area behind them had to be quite small. Facing me was another set of doors, closer together. In Nigeria, toilets and showers are shared by everyone on the floor of an apartment building, so I assumed that this building followed that pattern. Of course this tall elevator building was nothing like the two-and-three-story apartment buildings I'd seen in Nigeria. But if Nigerians were the dominant group and Yoruba the dominant language, then these tightly packed living spaces with their shared bathroom facilities were about as close to the way Foley lived in Nigeria as anything he could find this side of the Atlantic.

As I moved close to 1404, I heard voices from a television set, and live voices too, so people were home. If I were to ring the bell in front of me, the whole mystery of why he had moved out here would be resolved in a stroke. But I didn't want Foley to know that I was looking for him in this apartment rented under the name Komolafe, a woman I had met in Nigeria. Even standing where I was, I was courting a discovery that I didn't want, since there was nowhere to run, nowhere to hide, if the door opened. The elevator once more took its time coming, pinning me anxiously to where I stood. I felt relieved when its metal door finally closed slowly, not quite willing to acknowledge, just then, that my suspicions about the world my husband had left me to live in had proved to be all too true.

"Did you find what you were looking for?" The woman at the token booth smiled at me when I paused for a moment before moving through the turnstile and up the stairs to the subway platform that would take me back to Manhattan and to the apartment I loved, filled with books and plants and pictures on the walls, a refuge I'd assembled in the years before I met my husband and where he simply could not create a life for himself.

"Yes," I said, and it was true. Sara had given me, not one phone number, but two, and I would tell her the next day that I'd called her lawyer friend. The long, winding road between Far Rockaway and my apartment was a measure of the distance between the places my African husband and I could call home. Out of a fear of losing that part of my life that I loved so much, I had not been willing to look below its appealing surface. But here it was before my eyes.

*Adoption, 1993-97*

# 2

My African journey really began in 1980, two decades and change before that long ride out to Far Rockaway. I had just been awarded tenure by the English Department at Rutgers and had moved into the city from New Jersey. The rent was low because my apartment was in a drug-ridden neighborhood near Columbia University, my alma mater, at the height of the crack epidemic. The influx of crack brought more guns onto the streets.

But that wasn't the only danger in the city just then. The owners of apartment buildings were trying to flush out the elderly residents who had lived for years in rent-controlled apartments, so they could sell these apartments as co-ops. They scared them by firing doormen and superintendents, breaking the locks on front doors, anything that would make these undesirable elders feel unsafe. Our building had just been bought by an owner who was part of this unsavory cadre. We still had a super, but our doorman was gone. My boyfriend at the time had some experience as a tenant organizer, and we in the building had launched a rent strike against our new landlord.

A few days before Christmas, I was coming home alone from a

party and heard footsteps following me into my lobby, footsteps I still hear sometimes when I come home late at night. I was gripping my key in my hand when one of them held a gun to my head. The other one unzipped his pants and said, "Suck this." I did what he said, gripping the handle of my pocketbook the whole time. As the two of them turned toward the door, the one I had fellated grabbed the pocketbook, and I hung on. His friend pointed his pistol at me and fired, and off they ran into the night with the pocketbook. I hardly knew what had happened at first, though I now know that the bullet ran right through my body. Shock does that to you. But I was glad I had taken out my key. Pressing my hand to my chest, where blood began oozing through my coat, I made my way over to the row of doorbells and rang for the super who, fortunately, had not been fired. He came right up from the basement and supported me as we walked down the stairs o his apartment. His wife called 911, and two medics came quickly with a stretcher. They wrapped me in a tight Velcro vest that had been first used, I learned later, in the Vietnam War I had so vehemently protested in college.

I must not have fully understood what had to me happened because, when the super's wife said she would go and get Kevin, my son, I told her not to wake him up, I was that sure I would be back soon.

Once Kevin got in the ambulance with me, we sped up Broadway to St. Luke's Hospital, his hand in mine, till I was put in a gurney and wheeled to a room where nurses cut through my favorite purple sweater and a doctor opened a place in my chest, with no time for an anesthesia to take effect, and inserted a chest tube. I screamed with the pain, but what I protested most was the ruin of a beloved, hand-knitted purple sweater.

I don't know how many hours later I woke up, still breathing, in the ICU. "Your son is here," a nurse told me. "And his dad is here with him."

"Good lord, he came all the way from Boston? How long have I been here?"

"I don't know," the nurse said. "But your parents were here, too."

"Where are they now?"

"I think they said they were going home."

"Home? They live in Toronto." Later I would ask myself why they had left before I was out of the ICU. If it had been Kevin I would slept on the floor next to his bed if the nurses would let me. But my mother could not let herself have the feelings that would drive me to do this.

During my two-week stay in a regular hospital room, friends from far away called and those nearby came to see me. *They* were glad I'd survived, and I'm convinced that it was their concern for me that had pulled me back into life. As for my parents, they did come back to New York when I was ready to go home, no longer attached to my gurgling lung machine, and we spent the weekend in a suite at the Plaza Hotel with windows that looked out onto Central Park. I can't remember what we did, but I asked my mother to buy me a new pocketbook. I wanted a large one like the one with the novel in it that I had just finished teaching. When she came back with one that looked like a horse's feedbag, I didn't say anything. Instead I found the receipt from Saks in the bathroom wastepaper basket, and my friend Marcia returned the purse for me and brought me a store credit.

Before she left for Toronto my mother gave me the Christmas check my sisters and I got every year, minus the price of the purse. Had she been able to tell me how glad she was that I was alive, she would have had to acknowledge that the outcome of that awful night might have been different.

What I now see, all these years later, is that my parents didn't just leave New York while I was still in the ICU. They fled. Having a child die before you do has to be the worst nightmare that we humans can face. I think about that every time the parents of another victim of another mass shooting appear on television with their story of how they are coping. So my parents couldn't stay near me as long as that possibility was alive. They had to get home as soon as possible to a world where a maid brought my mother her breakfast in bed. Tucked into the side of her breakfast tray, with its boiled egg and glass of squeezed orange juice, was a notebook in which she wrote the menu for dinner that night and the list of groceries that needed to be ordered.

Over time I've come to see that she and my dad were not loving because their parents were not loving. It was not the way you were a parent in the affluent world of the early twentieth century into which they were born. You sent your children to boarding school, and I have nothing but happy memories of my time at my boarding school in Ottawa. It was coming home for the holidays, to boys and dances, that had me decide that I needed to get away from that world altogether.

What I have also come to see since then is that New York was going through a really bad time in that decade. The crack epidemic was gathering steam, and robbery, murder, and violent crime generally spiked as a result. Black males were denounced, in headlines and on television, of "wilding" in Central Park, and anger against them rose to a crescendo after the brutal assault and rape of Trisha Meili, the Central Park jogger, in 1989. Subway cars covered in graffiti were forced to stop for fifteen minutes when someone pulled the emergency brake that hung at one end of each car, and who would do this other than a black male who wanted to assert his power over the rest of us? Fear for one's safety rose up from cracks in the sidewalks.

The rent was low when I moved into my apartment in 1980, and when I bought it at the end of the decade the neighborhood was still considered a bad one because it was twenty blocks below the lower edge of Harlem. I've been told that the pay phone on my corner was used, in the days before cell phones, by drug dealers. Gentrification has changed that, so despite what happened to me, I'm very lucky to have moved in when I did.

"I hope they catch whoever did it," people invariably said. But I knew that wouldn't happen, and looking back, I'm just as glad they didn't suffer the fate of the Central Park "Gang of Five." The police had come to my hospital room and asked me to identify them from pictures in a lineup, but though I never had any of the flashbacks that are signs of PTSD, I completely erased their faces from my memory. My strongest feeling was not anger at them but gratitude toward the doctors who kept me alive. Even now, I never hear an ambulance siren without remembering the one that came for me. Letting myself into the building with my key now, I can sometimes hear footsteps behind me.

But when something makes me happy, I think *this might never have happened.* I got to see my son graduate from high school and then college, get married, and become a father. Then I went to Africa and learned things that I could not have learned in any other way. The doctors and nurses who saved my life spent more than eight hours with me in the operating room, keeping going when they might have given up. Had the bullet gone close to my spine, or through the side where my heart is, I might be paralyzed or dead, and I never would have done any of these things.

I must be a lightning rod for physical disasters that repeatedly call up my powers of recovery. They let me see things I could not have seen had these disasters not occurred, starting with the departure of my parents from the hospital. There was the head-on collision on a Nigerian road that happened when I went there for the first time on my own, leaving Foley to stay out his visitor visa while I checked out his country, which would become mine by marriage. That collision left the car a total wreck and me with nothing worse than a broken wrist. "Unbelievable," people said. "You should go to the junk yard and see that car." I did pass out when it happened, and the driver of the car carried me to a nearby hospital, where I learned that Nigerian hospitals don't have good x-ray machines and don't supply their patients with food. If you don't have a family nearby, I don't know what you do. I spent the rest of that summer in an uncomfortable cast from my knuckles to my armpit, and my wrist had to be broken again and set properly once I got back to the States.

Then, a few years ago, I was coming home from teaching an evening class at Rutgers when I was hit by a driver going so fast that the kind man who was going the other way and stopped to help me get up could not catch the number on his license plate. I was bleeding pretty heavily from the place where my head hit the road, and he produced some paper towel that I held against the bleeding. He then offered to take me to the local hospital, but I insisted on getting on the train I usually took. Perhaps it was my memory of earlier visits that had me so determined to go back to the place where my life was saved after the shooting, and where my son was born. The conductor checked in with me at each stop, telling me he would have called an ambulance if I'd lost consciousness. I didn't know about Natasha Richardson, the actress who'd injured her head while skiing, thought she was perfectly fine, and then died shortly afterwards. But *he* must have heard that story because, when we reached Penn Station, he guided me to the Eighth Avenue exit and put me in a cab that drove me to the hospital. There the doctors stapled the wound on my scalp and I went home the next morning, high on Percoset.

How could I not think of these narrow escapes as miracles? What power had kept me alive? My answer was not the judgmental God I'd learned about growing up, but one who had a future in mind for me. There was more for me to do in this life, and I needed to find out what it was. While I was still in the hospital, recovering from my gunshot wound and plugged into a lung machine that bubbled quietly day and night, Marcia, who'd been my friend since we were both studying dance with Martha Graham, told me about a cousin who'd grown up with her on Chicago's South Side. "She was shot in the head," Marcia told me, perched on the edge of my bed. "Then they put her into the trunk of a car. She needed huge amounts of therapy, physical, mental, the whole works. But once she got through that, she began to have a life she would never have led had this horrible thing never happened."

"I want that to be so in my life, too," I told her.

"It will," Marcia said. "I know you, girl."

To the surprise of my friends, I moved back into my apartment, not willing to give my landlord the eight rooms he wanted to sell. We ended our rent strike, and I sued the landlord for criminal negligence, winning $150,000. Later that year, I met an African-American couple who ran programs for inner-city young people living in the same drug-ridden world as the two kids who'd come after me. It seemed to me that a higher power had brought them into my life just then, and I started volunteering in their organization. I don't know how they found the kids we worked with, but in addition to workshops on Saturdays over several months, we visited their homes. I could see that there was no quiet place for them to do their schoolwork, and the boys were often drawn into the drug world of their neighborhood, whose pull was greater than anything we could offer. All this let me know young black males, not only as sources of violence to themselves and others, but as kids who dealt on a day-to-day basis with a world very different from my son's. I was not the only white volunteer, but I was conscious of entering a culture that was not mine.

I still wonder why I experienced none of the reactions to trauma that are now called PTSD. Perhaps it's because I had never met a black person until I came to New York. I grew up in an all-white part of Toronto where, if I had stayed, I would have had to "come out," as my parents called it, dancing in a chandelier-lit ballroom with a prep-school partner who would probably have been as unhappy to be there as I was.

My sense of safety comes from that world. But I also had to get away from it, and to find a family that would not have left me in the hospital till I was out of the ICU. I know that African-American children do not grow up in a world free of pain and loss. But they call each other brother and sister. They tell one another to be safe. As a volunteer mentoring inner-city young people, I was often the only white person in the room, and this put me on the side I wanted to be on in this country's racial divide. When I first got my job at Rutgers, I moved into a black neighborhood in New Brunswick, preferring it to the surrounding white suburbs. We did get robbed there, but my six-foot, three-hundred-pound neighbor Amos told me to get a dog. Once we did, we never got robbed again. Amos also helped me get into my car when I had locked my keys inside, and pulled up the hood at a moment's notice when I couldn't get it to start.

But here I was in an eight-room apartment in a neighborhood that has become a lot more expensive since I moved in and therefore out of the reach of more and more people. I had a job I loved with tenure, so I had no financial worries. My son had just married a terrific woman and was starting a new chapter in his life. I still look younger than I am, and I'm pretty vain about that.

But none of these blessings helped when it came to dating. I was wary of marrying another academic, and men who were not in that world often found my profession intimidating. "An English professor, huh? Not my good subject." I'm not sure where sex appeal comes from, but I don't think I've had it in abundance, starting as a teenager. Recently divorced men my age were looking for a younger woman. And having a teenage son who was critical of the men I saw was not an asset either. So despite my good job and nice apartment, I missed the support of a partner. My first husband, a fellow graduate student, had smoothed the way for my entry into academia, where I was the first tenure-track woman to be hired in my department. But he had not followed me to New Brunswick, or even into academia. Most of all, I missed being part of the kind of community that the antiwar and women's movements had given me. But now those communities were gone.

I'd never been to Africa. Never even thought of going there. Yet it was the back story of all the people with whom I was now spending my weekends as a volunteer. So when the offer came, I jumped at the chance to create a new chapter in my life's story.

I arrived in Nigeria in August, when the rainy season produces ferocious but short-lived daily downpours. I had not been much of a traveler up to then, since I didn't like to think of myself as a tourist. But you can be whoever you wish to be when you are on your own in a foreign country. I'd been to London and Paris, and as I walked along those streets by myself, I would imagine myself at home in those magical but unfamiliar cities. I did read what was said in the guidebooks about the sights I visited, but only after being there. So, true to form, I didn't read up on Nigeria before taking off. I wanted to rely on my own first impressions, not receive them filtered by those of others. Perhaps this whole story would be quite different had I consulted some of the many books on Africa that I have read since that first trip. But, quite intentionally, I did not do that. My son teases me about not distinguishing the world as it is from the world as I want it to be. This was never more true than on my many trips to Nigeria.

Before we left New York, my guides, Max and Felicia, told us about their friend Nike Davies, our hostess, whose invitation letter we needed in order to visit her country. "It's not pronounced like the sneakers," Max said to us once. It's NEE-KAY." As a young girl from Ogidi, birthplace of the famous Nigerian author Chinua Achebe, she'd married a well-known artist named Twins Seven and become an artist herself. Polygamy is still accepted in much of Nigeria. But when Twins brought younger wives into their household, Nike left him and was shunned by her fellow Nigerians. Undaunted, she set up a center in nearby Osogbo to teach young Nigerian women and men to make and market the traditional arts of batik and bead painting, metal sculpture, and tall, imposing wood carvings of the deities of their Yoruba religion. Without her art, and the community she created around it, she would probably have slipped back into the poverty that is acute for Nigerian women with no husbands. I admired her even before she greeted us at the end of a three-hour drive from the Lagos airport in one of the yellow vans she had sent to pick us up after a long wait at the luggage carousel for the sight of our bags lurching toward us. While we waited, one of our teenagers took out his camera and was about to snap a picture when two soldiers brandishing AK-47s swooped toward him, almost knocking the camera out of his hands. "Not here," one of them said. "You don't do that here."

"Hey, we're not in Kansas anymore," Max said with a smile meant for all of us.

The drive to Osogbo added another three hours to the eleven we had spent in the air, so I was in anything but good spirits by the time we pulled up in front of Nike's gallery, a two-story building set back behind plastered walls covered with Keith Haring-like dancing figures. But when the driver honked and a set of wrought iron gates opened to let us drive up to a two-story building with a red tile roof and a porch supported by carved wooden poles, I felt a welcome rush of energy. A woman who had to be Nike came toward us wearing a long, flowing batik garment with a matching head-tie twisted and tucked into an elaborate shape. Behind her, several young men in brightly colored pants and tops were beating drums and shouting "Welcome!" in English. Nike then ushered us into the gallery itself, where batik t-shirts, bead paintings, and tall wooden carvings were laid out for purchase in rows, on tables, or hung on the walls: Things to take home, so you could show your friends that you'd been to Nigeria. I was beginning to feel glad that I'd made this trip as we got back into the van and were taken to Nike's house a short distance down the road, where a meal of chicken and fried plantains awaited us.

After we ate, the ten of us settled into the guest house behind Nike's white two-story home, where we fell into a welcome sleep.

The next day, after an American-style breakfast of scrambled eggs and toast, we were driven back to the gallery. There the drummers appeared again, along with a group of traditional masqueraders from the town who entertained us, under a blazing sun, with acrobatic feats that showed off their wildly layered costumes. After the performance, a dozen students of both sexes, wearing the multicolored batik fabric they had learned to make at the school, drew us visitors into a circle, and while the drummers continued to fill the air with their pulsating beats, one of them would draw one of us into the circle to dance. Having studied dance as a vocation, I was happy when one of them, a good-looking man with close-cropped hair, broad shoulders, and a winning smile, chose me not once but twice. His name, Nike told me, was Foley. He came, she said, from a family line of woodcarvers going back several generations and was one of the school's stars.

At breakfast the next morning our conversation, over more scrambled eggs and toast served in Nike's long dining room by several of her female students, turned to the subject of who among the young men we had seen the day before was hot.

Someone asked, "What about that carver? The one who danced with Kate. Is he married?"

"No," Nike said, perhaps too quickly. "He's available, girls, and one of you who's looking for a husband should check him out. In fact," she added gleefully, "I think Kate is the one he likes."

My first reaction was to be embarrassed. Was everyone making fun of me, the oldest member of the group? I was annoyed, or perhaps simply confused. But I did notice, when we gathered in the courtyard again two days later for more dancing and drumming, that he picked me out again, and I was the only visitor with whom he danced.

I had no idea why he was choosing me. But after a divorce followed by a decade of looking for a mate back home, it felt good to be sought after rather than wait for a man to call me back. Drawing on my years of modern dance training, and the dancer's body I'm proud to have kept, I stamped and shook my fanny with a confidence that mirrored his. We did this well together: A good sign, I thought. My first husband had hated to dance, and none of my dates since my divorce shared my enthusiasm for swing dancing. Foley obviously loved to move to a beat, and as we showed off our well-matched skill to the applause of those watching, I thought of what Marcia had said about having a life I would never have had if I had not been shot. Perhaps that life was beginning already. I couldn't just come here on my own, though. Max had made that clear on the drive from the airport. A white woman would need somebody, by which I knew he meant somebody male, to protect me.

After that first outing, Nike's students started chanting, whenever they saw the two of us together, "Katie, Katie, *iyawo* Foley." *Iyawo* is a Yoruba word that applies to a woman in any male–female relationship. We Americans make precise distinctions between a female friend, a casual girlfriend, a more serious girlfriend, a new wife or one of many years. In Nigeria one word, whose root, *iya*, means mother, covers them all. Whenever I heard it, I saw myself being invited into a vibrant community that wanted me to be happy, an invitation I gladly accepted. Perhaps it took away whatever residue of trauma that still lingered from my being shot by those two boys. I would marry for that. Why not? I would help him, and he would do the same for me. It would not be a one-sided relationship for either of us.

It was also true that wanting a second home was part of a long history that I had brought with me to Africa. Growing up in a large, pillared house in Toronto where the vacuum cleaner always seemed to be running, where unmarried British nannies and maids lived on the third floor while we three children lived in the back of the second, I conjured up scenarios of escape. There was nothing overtly wrong in our household that could be noticed, by us children or anyone else. I never heard loud words, and there was certainly never any violence. At the same time, I never saw my parents act affectionately toward each other, but then I didn't really see much of them at all. They went to parties in evening clothes, and when they entertained at home they would gather with their guests around our grand piano in the drawing room and sing songs from Broadway shows and from the First World War like "The White Cliffs of Dover." I can still hear my father belting out, probably after a few too many drinks, "When Irish Eyes Are Smiling," and he did appreciate my skill at the piano. But because of it I never learned to read music, and like other people I know, I disparaged what came to me easily. Daddy was handsome and told jokes that made everyone around him laugh, so he was always the center of attention, at least until he got too old to turn everyone around him into an admiring audience.

I don't know if this helps to explain why, at a very early age, I began to develop a double life in my head. I was the person that everyone saw, going through the routines of my day. But the person I was in my head was a little girl who had achieved stardom. Inspired by Elizabeth Taylor in *National Velvet,* my first imaginary second self was a child movie star. Then ballet lessons and the sight of my teacher's toe shoes led me to *Theater Street,* the autobiography of Tamara Karsavina, a "baby ballerina" and the youngest member of Diaghilev's Ballets Russes. So I began a second life in my head as a baby ballerina, living not just in two places but as two people at once. One of them was a star whose parents did all they could to support her stardom. Psychologists call this "dissociation": *The person you see in this body is not the real me.*

It's a coping strategy that can set a person up for problems later in life.

Something about this dreamy split personality of mine must have annoyed my sisters because we fought constantly until I was sent to an Anglican boarding school in Ottawa, where I became the school's top student and my double life, not needed while I was surrounded by supportive teachers, fell away. From there I moved back home and went for a month to the University of Toronto, where my parents had met. What they wanted for me was the popularity and partying they remembered with fondness. But I didn't like fraternity parties, and "petting" didn't turn me on, as it apparently did most of my girlfriends. I could tell that my lack of popularity disappointed my parents, so I hid in my room for the better part of the weekend. I knew I did not want to be a wife and a member of the Junior League like my mother. So when all the girls I had gone to school with were about to "come out," I announced that I wanted to move to New York to study modern dance. I imagined myself, not just a dancer, but a choreographer. "If you fail, you can always come home," my mother told me when we said goodbye at Toronto's Union Station. I could tell that she assumed that I would fail, and I knew I would never come back, no matter what happened in the future.

My first new home was The Rehearsal Club, a New York residence for girls down the street from the Museum of Modern Art. This city had always been my luminous Mecca, and moving there allowed me to put an international border between my old life and my new one. I left maids and evening meals with my family at a long, candle-lit dining room table. Several years of studying with Martha Graham, Jose Limon, and Merce Cunningham got me into a dance company headed by James Waring. I'd worked hard for it and must have assumed that I would be happy when my efforts were rewarded. But those three gay men, and one other woman, never became the away-from-home family I'd hoped to find. Instead I was hit by a devastating dose of depression and spent three months getting all sorts of treatment for it. After that, I danced in one performance and then went back to school, first to the Columbia School of General Studies and then to its graduate program. There I met a man very different from the one now being presented to me as "hot"—a brilliant fellow student who married me in an Episcopal church with both our families present. I was three months pregnant, and he wanted to be a parent as much as I did.

I was also twenty-nine, an age considered pretty much over the hill in those days. I'd been engaged briefly once before to a man my parents could not have taken into their family. His father ran an Arabic newspaper, and he was a poet who took too seriously Baudelaire's injunction to "be drunken always." My graduate school boyfriend had just the right background: Main Line Philadelphia. And he told me I was smart.

In the graduate seminar where I met him, I was one of two women in a class of seventeen. The other woman, Vicky, was married, but being single, I kept remembering my mother's words about men not liking women who are smarter than they are.

But the whole point of being in graduate school was to impress our professors, and I couldn't do that unless I spoke up. Once I was "taken," I could I finally offer up my ideas without fear, and the arrival of our son Kevin the following November brought me the happiest years of my life. My husband's M.A. thesis on Andrew Marvell was brilliant, and in its acknowledgments he is grateful to his wife, without whose support he could not have written it. I now had everything I wanted: a husband, a baby, and a future in academia. I loved him for giving me all those things, and I still do.

Fatherhood threw him back, however, into a painful childhood with a mother who was in and out of mental hospitals. A piece of him broke, and he failed his orals. He withdrew from school and into his childhood fantasy of being a racing car driver, and spent his days reading *Road and Track* and *Car and Driver*. Something devastating had happened to the man whose brilliance I had looked up to, and he became a stranger to me. "I hated being in school," he told me, meaning that he hated being the man who'd released me from my mother's fate by being smarter than me.

"You're the one who needs a therapist," he'd say when I urged him to get help.

I had to choose between staying with him, which meant that I could not continue to shine where he had failed, or ending the marriage and taking Kevin with me. I kept going, more determined than ever to pass my orals with distinction, which I did. But we were no longer allies working toward a shared future, the one he had emboldened me to step into. So after four years, some of them very happy, he got his own apartment while I threw myself into the antiwar movement and then moved to New Brunswick to become an assistant professor at Rutgers, the first woman in my department to get hired on a tenure track.

I spent years after that asking myself if I could have pulled him out of a darkness that I only later came to understand as the other side of the brilliance I so admired, a condition we came to know as Asperger's syndrome. But you can't help someone who insists he doesn't need help, and he didn't want it. Especially not from me. As for giving up academia and remaining with him, I still think I couldn't be happy, or even all that good at any other line of work.

I had spent the 1980s volunteering in Max and Felicia's organization. We worked with teenagers like the ones who had almost killed me, and it felt like a natural way to move beyond that attack. The two of them liked to refer to everyone they worked with as their family. Sister Sledge's "We Are Family" was the signature song we loved to dance to when all of us, adults and teens, got together. I was not the only white person in the group but one of two or three, and being in that situation gives me a feeling of being special. So when this couple invited me to travel with them to Nigeria with three of our teenagers, I was delighted that they had chosen me. It meant that I was not, in their eyes, the chilly white person I'd been raised to be but more like an honorary African-American. Growing up and going to boarding school in Canada, I hadn't met any black people. I hadn't studied the American Civil War in school, or learned about Canada's role in the Underground Railroad. But the moment I set foot on the red soil of Nigeria with the sun blazing overhead, it was as if the second home that I'd imagined as a child was there, waiting to receive me.

On my first Sunday, I did something that confirmed my belief that Nigeria was where that home should be. Behind Nike's house, a dirt road led to a village with a small, white church whose tolling bell regularly woke me up. That Sunday I managed to slip away while my fellow visitors were still asleep, and to follow the sound of the bell. As I ambled along, I listened to the wind in the palms above me and the swish of wheels on the paved road behind me that ran past Nike's house. Occasionally a car would approach, and I'd step into the ditch beside the road to let it pass. Since everyone in Nigeria greets one another, the driver would nod to me with a *"Bawo ni?"* or its English approximation, "How're things?" Then I'd answer him with the Yoruba phrase I'd learned, "Dada ni," letting him know that things were fine with me. The morning air felt cool on my face as I drew closer to the sound of the bell, passing tin-roofed houses set back from the road behind stretches of swept red dirt. Scrawny, almost naked children ran up to me and grabbed my hand. Then they retreated, giggling and shouting, *"Oyinbo! Oyinbo!"* This word means not just a white person but any stranger.

The church service had started by the time I got there and lasted for a good three hours more. I sat on the crowded women's side in the back, where children squirmed and babies slept, tied on their mothers' backs by lengths of patterned cloth knotted above the women's breasts. The men's section was only about half full. After a hymn sung in Yoruba whose English version I knew, the church's priest, wearing a clerical collar and a white surplice over the ankle-length black garment that priests wear, began a sermon that would last for over an hour. But its length was not the only feature that distinguished it from the sermons I'd heard back home. When this man shouted out the name and verse of a book of the Bible, the parishioners grabbed their bibles, and the first one to find it stood up and read it aloud.

After half an hour of this, I was wondering when I could gracefully leave, but I'm glad I did not because the best part of the service came after the regular ceremony has ended.

A member of the congregation walks to the front of the church, turns to face it, and speaks briefly. I learned later that they are asking for a blessing: a new baby, a new job, a recently deceased family member. Then someone else sings out a phrase that everyone knows. The petitioner's friends join in as they sing, dancing up the aisle and kneeling in front of the altar. The minister then recites a prayer, and the friends sing again as they dance back to their seats.

Half a dozen people did this the day I was there, and I went back again the Sunday before we left. It all took place in Yoruba, so I didn't understand what was said or sung. But this way of relating to God called out to me, perhaps because I had been a dancer before I went into academia. It was a pull I did not want to resist, a way of doing church very different from the formal scenario that Episcopalians adopted, going methodically through the Book of Common Prayer set forth by Thomas Cranmer before he was beheaded by "Bloody Mary" Tudor.

When I joined my fellow travelers for a late breakfast in Nike's dining room, I didn't tell them where I'd been. Because I loved being alone in that unpredictable part of the world, so near the equator, where the cries of roosters call the day up out of darkness, I decided to walk back along that road two days later. As I was putting on the sandals I'd learned to leave at our front door, Nike came out onto her porch. "I'm going for a walk," I told her. "I like being outside here when the sun is barely up."

"Would you like company?" she called out, and I told her I would.

"That's a lovely town," she said when I told her my destination. "Its name is Erin-Osun. You know that Osun is the patron goddess of Osogbo?"

"Someone told me that. The goddess of fertility, right?"

As we walked along the rutted road lined with low, bushy trees, she asked me how I liked Africa. But then she turned the conversation in a direction I did not anticipate. "Felicia tells me you are not married."

"Not right now," I told her.

"Do you want to marry again?" Nike continued.

"Well, sure." I shrugged. "Do you have someone in mind?"

"Yes, I do," she said with a wide, winning smile. "It's that carver."

One feature of Nigerian marriage arrangements involves an *alarina*, a friend of one or both members of the potential pair. The person acts as a go-between and undertakes to find out how the two parties feel about one another, a much better procedure than going to a singles bar or packaging yourself on the internet. Though she barely knew me, Nike played that role in bringing Foley and me together. What she did know, from my own mouth, was that I taught at a university. She'd been to the States often enough to know that professors can invite African artists like herself to exhibit their work to their colleagues and students. Knowing this, I began to see her as my partner in making me part of a couple, a wish I had but felt ambivalent about acknowledging.

So I began to see "that carver" could be a real alternative to the dating I had not enjoyed back home. I could tell that he was younger than me by a good many years, but we were both thin and energetic and the same height, and later we discovered that we could wear the same size in jeans. But that age difference only made his interest in me all the more attractive. The quality in him that made the attraction mutual was a contagious joy that I liked being near. I'd not seen myself as a middle-aged woman who'd go to Africa out of a wish for a hot sexual encounter. But perhaps Nike saw me this way. I knew then that she saw in an arranged marriage, so to speak, a source of Rutgers-sponsored invitations to the States, not just for Foley but for her children and students.

On my side I told her just enough to let her fill in a few details. I did keep a few secrets, however, in particular about a serious battle with depression that I'd waged in my twenties and its continuing role as a state I wanted to avoid. I also wanted to make sure that neither she nor Foley would find out that I was over fifty, with a married son—an old woman by African standards.

As I later found out, she kept a few secrets from me as well.

On our second Sunday in Osogbo, I avoided, not only my fellow Americans, but Nike as well, and followed the rutted road to the church behind her house. I was glad to be going there by myself and took my seat on the women's side. Since I was familiar with the Anglican prayer book from my time at my Canadian boarding school, I was able to tell where we were in the service.

But finally the singing and dancing for which I had come took over. This time I was clear about what I found so compelling. The dancers were using their bodies as part of their worship. In the Western church this inclusion of the body in worship has always been severely restricted. In the twice- daily chapel services at my all-girls school, we were not allowed to sit with our legs crossed or our knees apart. Our bodies had been formed in sin, so official Christian doctrine told us. But, apparently, expression of our ineradicable sinfulness hadn't caught on in this part of the world, and I wanted to find out why.

That afternoon, the group went to the gallery and, catching sight of Foley, I asked what he'd been doing that morning. "I went to my church," he said simply.

"What kind of church?"

"Christian," he said. "My father had us all baptized in Catholic church. But now I go to a different one. Much smaller."

"Maybe I can come with you sometime," I said. I told him that I, too, went to church back home, though I didn't tell him about being shot and how that horrible event had made me grateful for being alive.

I also didn't tell him that I'd begun to think that I wanted a mate who worship with me. But his churchgoing added to my impression that a divine plan had brought us together. In America, my return to churchgoing had begun in the inner-city neighborhoods I entered thanks to Max and Felicia, my guides to this African adventure. I went to black Baptist services in Harlem full of abandoned singing and shouts of "Amen!" I loved the warm welcome I received, obviously a visitor from another part of the world. But I began to feel a need to return to the rituals connected to my own ethnic history, and I had started attending an Episcopal church in my neighborhood, founded in the early nineteenth century, whose Tiffany windows my ancestors would have admired had they sat in its pews.

At the end of a service there, an elderly man sitting next to me said, "My dear, you have a lovely voice. Why don't you join the choir?" I kept thinking about his remark in the weeks that followed, and, realizing that singing was something I'd always loved to do, I went up to the choir loft after the service and asked what I needed to be able to do to join the volunteer choir. "Can you carry a tune and stay on pitch?" the choir director asked me, and handed me a hymn book open to one I knew. So began a journey that would continue into my marriage and beyond it.

"Can I count on you," Nike asked me that afternoon, "to write invitations, using your Rutgers letterhead, to bring our students to the States to give exhibitions of their work?" She must have told Foley that I had agreed to do this; a few days after that, he showed up at the gallery carrying a pillow and a sheet and asked me to come for a walk with him. I knew I didn't want him to "go all the way," as we called it in high school. I didn't want him, or anyone he would talk to, to see me as an "easy American woman." But I was curious about his skills as a lover, so we just held each other and kissed, and that got me excited and looking forward to more. By that time, I'd promised to invite him to visit me in the States, so he took my no in the present to imply, quite rightly, a yes in the future. I was not in love with him in the way I'd learned from the top hits and show tunes I'd heard growing up. In fact, I was rather afraid of that state, perhaps because I associated it with my mother's refusal to leave my father no matter how much he hurt her. And the one time I'd been taken over by a desire to be with a man who made me come every time, the pain I felt when he left me for a younger woman was almost more than I could bear. But now I saw my life taking a new, unforeseen turn with him in it, and I began to think that he wanted the same from me. He was handsome and charming, and, seeing in these attributes the makings of a good husband, I know now that I was more like my mother than I was willing to admit at the time. And Nike was obviously interested in our getting together.

She and I now began most of our days with a walk while it was still cool. On one of these, she told me that Foley was the grandson of a famous carver whose work was in the African art collections of museums in my country. "If you go upstairs in the gallery, you'll see some of his carvings." When I did that, a student explained that the large pieces depicted Yoruba deities surrounded by the animals sacred to them. I had never seen anything like them, and all of us Americans were impressed. I assumed that some were Foley's. But I didn't see any names, so I had no idea which ones might be his, and he was never there when I was.

I did ask him about his grandfather, though. "My father is a carver too," he said. "And some of my brothers." I didn't ask him how many brothers he had, though Nike had let me in on the fact that his mother was the last of his father's eight wives.

"And you want to carry on the tradition?"

"Yes, I do." Here was a man with a vision for his future as an artist. So he would want some space between us in which he could pursue it, just as I did. This was something we had in common, a hoped-for future for ourselves that included a supportive partner. I was already seduced by the vibrations of a continent I was hearing through my mosquito netting as I fell asleep in Nike's fan-cooled guest house. I loved the palms whose sinuous trunks upheld a starburst of spiky foliage against a pearl-white sky. I sensed that I would miss the constant sound of drums that came from somewhere out of sight, and the sight of women wearing brilliant colors and carrying huge baskets on their heads with such ease. Perhaps this place could be the setting for the happy double life I had imagined as a child, when I had augmented my ordinary life as the child of my parents with Tamara Karsavina's childhood as a Russian "baby ballerina."

At one point during our walks, Nike confided to me that she was ditching her British second husband, David Davies, and was seeing the Police Commissioner of Osun State. Felicia had told us all about Nike's marriage to her first husband, a well-known Nigerian artist with the odd name of Twins Seven Seven. "She didn't like it when he collected other wives," Felicia said. "But that's the way that a man here lets people know that he's a success. And rich."

"So a woman without a man to protect her has a really rough time here," Max added. Apparently David spent a lot of time in England, so Nike was probably more on her own than she liked. She had two young daughters by David and three older children with Twins. So I asked her, as one mother to another, whether either of her sons was moving in the direction of matrimony. "Not yet," she said. "Marrying here is very complicated."

"So I've heard."

"But it's good if you are with the right person," she said, giving me a knowing smile.

So it looked like I might be acquiring, not only a husband, but a woman friend who was happy with her own life and happy to help me to enter a new phase in mine. We discussed the invitations she wanted me to write on my Rutgers letterhead—documents needed by her students and her three grown children to get visitor visas to the States. I would be taking a risk, since I wasn't really sure what I could do for her students. But I'd worked hard to get tenure, so why not use that secure position to help people whose economic future was more precarious? And how else would I get to see Foley on my home territory? So I was delighted by her eagerness to play the *alarina* for us. She was doing something for me, and I was simply reciprocating.

During our final week, Foley and I went on our first and only "date" to a bar in Osogbo. We sat on stools at the bar and watched a soccer game on a fuzzy black-and-white television set above us. Foley played soccer with his friends, but he couldn't explain what was happening on the screen, and I didn't press for details. Obviously we lived in two very different language worlds. I didn't mind the lack of conversation, though. I was happy simply being in his radiating presence, especially when he took my hand firmly as we walked back out into the crowded street. More of that was just what I needed.

Other people had shared my intellectual interests. My former husband had been impressed by my mind, and for the first years of that marriage I'd had everything I wanted: a supportive husband, a child, and a future where I could be smart. But his brilliance had turned out to be one aspect of his Asperger's, so when he failed his orals and I passed mine with distinction, our shared future disappeared. Now *here* was a man with an ability to be happy even under difficult circumstances, and I saw this ability magically rubbing off onto me.

Finally our three weeks were up, and we were on our way back to the airport. Foley drove one of Nike's vans, and she arranged that I would sit next to him. Felicia objected to this. She never approved of what later developed between Foley and me, perhaps knowing more than I did then. But Nike insisted that I stay where I was, and, happy to be the recipient of her maneuvering, I settled next to Foley on the passenger side. To the extent that we were able to overcome our different levels of competence with English, we discussed the visit that my invitation letter would facilitate. Could I help him find ways to make money conducting carving workshops in New York and at Rutgers? He had been to Detroit for Black History Month the previous year, and a friend of Nike's had apparently helped in that way. I had a small circle of African-American friends, one that included my guides Felicia and Max, their volunteers, and a few Rutgers colleagues. Not really knowing what I was promising, I said, "I'd be happy to help."

Then one of our tires had a blowout. We all screamed as the van rocked back and forth, but Foley guided the ricocheting vehicle to the right edge of the road. He put branches behind it to warn the oncoming traffic, and changed the tire with a speed and skill that left me quite in awe of his vibrant, take-charge masculinity.

When we arrived at the airport I went with the others and checked in. Then I went back to the car in the parking lot and sat with him till it was almost time to board the plane. There is a canteen beyond this lot, and I bought us some bean cakes and sodas. I told him about the Cloisters, the museum that houses some extraordinary wood carving, and talked up New York as a great place for him to sell his work. "I would like to see that museum," he said; I promised him that we would go there together.

On the plane ride home, I thought about something my new daughter-in-law had said to me at her wedding reception: "Maybe something like this will happen to you now." I'm sure I shook my head at the time, but the thought obviously stayed with me as I put in my application for a semester's leave from my job that would start in the upcoming spring, ostensibly to do research on Africa. This coming together felt like a work of larger forces. Perhaps it was even the next step in a divine plan, something that would never have happened had I not been shot.

# 3

Nike Davies' house, a two-story white building surrounded by flowering pink bougainvillea, is protected by a high wall edged with broken glass across the top and a guard at the wrought iron gate. We two were sitting on her open porch, drinking tea one hot, equatorial afternoon when I raised an issue that friends in the States had cautioned me about: the importance, for an African man, of having sons. "You know I already have a son," I told her. "And I won't be having any more. Foley has no wife and children now, didn't you say?"

"That's true," she said without a moment's hesitation.

"Well, I don't want a second wife brought in later on to do what I can't do."

"Not all African men are domineering patriarchs," she said, a smile blossoming below her high cheekbones and dark eyes. This formed a smooth segue to her favorite topic, the police commissioner, who was also an unusual African man, she assured me. A widower with three grown children, he had a household full of servants and uniformed officers to drive his many well-maintained cars. I'd met his children a few times, two boys and a girl, all in their twenties. They struck me as spoiled and empty-headed, with no future plans beyond enjoying the life their father's wealth enabled.

Nike's comments about Foley as my future husband reminded me of the efforts he had made to cook and clean for his friends when they stayed with us; not one of whom had picked up a broom, a sponge, or a dish towel. He hadn't officially proposed, but he'd started referring to me, when speaking to his friends in my presence, as his wife. "I know he doesn't insist on being waited on," I said. "But how does it follow from that that he doesn't want children?"

"He has so many brothers and sisters," Nike said. "So he doesn't feel a need to add more children to his family. If anything, he thinks there are too many already."

"How many wives does his father have?"

"Eight altogether, I think. Four are still alive."

"Well, I love being a mother. It's definitely the best thing I ever did, and I think that Foley would be a terrific father. I've seen him play with some of the children here and he's really great. So I've been thinking about adoption."

"Really?" Nike's face brightened. "I think I have the solution for you. One of our students is a young woman who has just had a baby without a husband."

I was surprised at how quickly she came up with this solution. I'd donated money back in the States to an organization that intervened in the lives of African children whose parents had died of AIDS, so I had been thinking of one of them. "But wouldn't it be better," I said, "to adopt a child who has no parents?" Nike looked puzzled. "From an orphanage, I mean? You know, a place that takes in children whose parents have died." I had recently read about the plight of AIDS orphans in Uganda, and I assumed that there would be some in Nigeria as well.

"When that happens," Nike said, "an auntie or a senior sister will take the child into her own family. Some of our students have been taken in like that. You should talk to them."

"I'd love to," I said. "But they're not all orphans, are they?"

"Sometimes it's just not enough money, so they go to live with a relative who has more. When there are many wives, it makes trouble for the children. Foley's mother is his father's last wife, so her children are at the end of the line. And he is her only son."

"I can understand that," I said, rather at a loss for words. The organization whose website focused on AIDS orphans operated mainly out of Uganda, but I'd heard there were many orphans in Africa, especially places where there were wars between opposing tribal factions. I didn't see myself taking a child out of its birth culture, though, but rather drawing me further into it.

"And you know," Nike went on, "many parents here would be glad to have one of their children raised in America. There are so many opportunities for them there that we don't have here. Let me bring this baby to you. Her name is Funmilola, and she's a lovely baby."

Nike was right. Funmi was a lovely baby, with soft black hair and a dimple in one cheek. Yet the first time I saw her, tied on her mother's back, she burst into tears. "Don't worry," said Nike. "Some children react that way because they've never seen a white person."

She was right about this, too. Children I had seen as I walked along the road by myself would call me "*Oyinbo.*" They'd run after me and try out the English they've learned in school: "How are you? Nice to meet you," to which I'd reply with the Yoruba greetings I'd learned: "*Bawo ni? Ki ni oruko re?*" This last request, asking for their names, always produced gales of laughter, either because my pronunciation of their tonal language was so inaccurate or because of the unexpectedness of a white person speaking it. But sometimes a child would run away screaming, and his companions would laugh at that, too.

This was one of many instances in which I have come to see how being white in Nigeria is totally different from being a white person at home. For me growing up, there was nothing to notice, like the fish that is not aware of swimming in water. That's not true in New York, but it certainly describes the Toronto where I grew up. In Nigeria the differences have mainly to do with gender, where women are valued for their strength, that is, for their ability to work lifting heavy loads or pounding yams by thrusting a wooden pestle into a pile of peeled, cooked yams in a large wooden basin. Polygamy gives a man as many of these strong bodies as he can take on. My thin frame, straight red hair, and sunburn-prone skin are seen as liabilities, or at best as interesting curiosities. I don't need, and therefore don't have, the upper body strength to carry pails filled with water or to balance a basket or a stack of wood on my head. I can't grind peppers on a grinding stone, because the peppers will sting my delicate white fingers. I need company to shop, because I can't bargain. I might be an object of pity but for one thing: I come from America and so, in their eyes, I have money, vast amounts of it. Wasn't this the very label—being rich—and the life it involved, that I'd worked so hard to run away from?

I intuited these assumptions about me mainly from Nike's female students, who included me in the female activities of shopping and cooking. They made it difficult to read other people's reactions to me, and right from the start this was a problem in my relationship with Funmi's mother. Kehinde Komolafe spoke almost no English, so I had to rely on others to interpret what she said and did. When Nike introduced me to her as the woman who wanted to deliver Funmi to me in America, she was all smiles. When I told Foley, over the static-filled line to New York, about my talk with Nike, he sounded pleased, too. "Whatever you want, I will be happy to do it."

"Would you not prefer a son to a daughter?" I asked.

"No. If you love Funmi, I will love her too."

"Are you sure Kehinde wants Funmi to grow up with us in America?"

"Why not? There is no chance in Nigeria for children like in the States. You are doing good for her. I am coming to Nigeria soon."

"All right, we will give her a chance," I said, happy to embrace a role that is so central to the Nigerian concept of womanhood. Was this not one more instance of Nike helping to bring about something I wanted? With her knowledge of Nigerian ways I felt really happy to be on the receiving end of her friendship. Why would I not trust her?

Foley arrived in May, and we moved into a small room in a building not far from the gallery, where Nike's poorest students lived. I had assumed that he would set about securing a nice house for the two of us, perhaps one with the carved wooden balconies that I admired in town, remnants of colonial times. But he seemed not a bit interested in that plan, and I, who had been happier at boarding school than living at home, enjoyed staying in that dormitory and cooking an evening meal with the other residents, most of whom were women. There wasn't much in the way of privacy, but then there isn't much privacy anywhere in Nigeria.

I didn't ask Foley how life had been for him in New York without me, assuming that, because he had now told me several times that he loved me, he was not looking for another woman in America. Perhaps I just didn't want to know what he'd been doing, and he didn't ask me any questions either. I don't know what I would have answered if he'd asked. My belief that I was loved silenced a cloud of unanswered questions. He'd never actually told me so, but lying in his arms in the morning after doing something with me the previous day, he'd say, "Thank you for yesterday," a phrase that I took to be his Nigerian way of putting his feelings for me into words. Now that he's gone, it's become a mantra for me, a prayer to the deity I thought we shared.

Foley's ability to charm children was on full display when he was with Funmi, carrying her on his shoulders or throwing her up in the air. He repeated his comments about limited opportunities for Nigerian children, and a friendship I had formed with Abike, one of his many cousins, lent support to what he said about Kehinde's wishes for her daughter. Abike was the first wife of Segun, one of Nike's carvers, and the mother of six of his children. But

Segun now had a second wife, Jemilat, a much younger woman. He had moved into her family's compound, and a baby was about to come from that marriage. Traditional polygamy is supposed to give the first wife an honored position in the household. But once an economy moves from farming to wage-earning, the family with multiple wives can become a battleground, as the children of each wife fight for their share of the family's diminishing resources. This must have been the case with Foley's father's eight wives, with his mother, the last wife, getting the short end of the stick.

After I was back in New York, I heard that Segun had taken Abike's six children, who were legally his, into his new household, where his new wife was close to delivering a baby. But that spring they were still living with their mother and were, as far as I could tell, a happy though fatherless family of seven. I visited them several times, bringing ingredients for a meal that I would help cook and then eat with everyone. From the markets lined up along the dirt road between the highway and Abike's flat I bought tomatoes, onions, peppers, bouillon cubes, some rice and beans or a yam, and a pineapple if I saw one. I didn't mention anything to Abike about Funmi, and in fact nothing was really settled between Kehinde and me at that point.

But one day, a week after Foley's arrival, one of Nike's students told me that Abike was angry with me. I at once took a taxi to her house, and when I got there she was talking to one of her neighbors, a woman married to another of Nike's artists. Abike shooed the children away, and the three of us sat on wooden stools in her living room, the neighbor serving as intermediary and translator.

"She say she hear you bringing a little girl with you to States," the neighbor said. "You promised her you would bring her son there."

"I never said that. Which son are we talking about?"

"Demola. The youngest one. The one who love you."

"I hope they all love me," I said. "Because I love all of them. But I never said anything about Demola coming to the States. Abike must have misunderstood me."

Demola was the most demonstrative of Abike's children, running up to me when I arrived and wrapping his thin arms and legs around me when I sat down. The two women talked for a while, Abike looking back and forth between me and her friend. Finally the neighbor asked me if I loved Demola. "Of course I do," I said. "Absolutely I do." I looked for the child I had carried on my back, his thin legs wrapped around my waist. "But I can see that he's completely attached to his mother. I couldn't imagine separating them. I hope you can say this," I said to the neighbor, "in a way that Abike can understand."

"I don't know. She don't understand you now."

"But she must know that Segun would never let me take a child of his to the States. He knows I come here and he doesn't like me. A father owns his children here, right?"

"Yes, that would be a problem," the neighbor acknowledged. "He is the father."

"I'm so sorry," I said, taking Abike by the shoulders. "I love all of you. Please don't think I don't." I saw skepticism in the faces of both women. But just then Abike's eldest daughter burst in the door with a stream of Yoruba addressed to her mother, and I gave her a hug, too. Then the rest of the children returned, and Abike cut up the pineapple I had brought for all of us to eat.

"Will you come back to see us again?" the daughter asked.

I looked over at Abike, who was smiling at her daughter. "Sure," I said. "I like eating with you and your family."

I rode back in a taxi, feeling sad and confused. Why could I imagine separating Funmi from her mother but not Demola from his? I now think that Abike believed I would bring her to the States along with Demola. But that would mean leaving her other children, and why would she want to do that? A cousin of hers asked me, shortly after that visit, if Abike could work in the States looking after children. Like so many women in impoverished parts of the world, she must have seen her choice as one between staying with her children with no income and leaving them in order to contribute to their survival.

"She speaks too little English," I told him. "No one would

leave their children with someone with whom they can't have a conversation."

My visit to Abike that afternoon clouded my perception, not just of our friendship, which I think we repaired before I went back to the States, but of how things stood between Kehinde and me. Perhaps she would be in a better position to marry if she would not be bringing a child fathered by another man into the marriage. Kehinde's fellow students were already referring to me in front of her as "*iya* Funmi," Funmi's mother, and to Funmi, on her mother's back, as "*omo* Katie."

"Is she not upset at the prospect of losing her daughter?" I would ask them when Kehinde was not around. But they always insisted that she was happy sending her daughter to such a good place. When I pressed Foley, he said the same thing.

No one seemed to have any doubts about my ability to replace Kehinde, a woman half my age. And I confess I did not have serious doubts either. Being a single mother struggling to get tenure at a large state university had not been easy, but I had done it. Then there was my sister Ellen, whose severely troubled middle son had gotten an equally troubled young woman pregnant. Ellen had won custody of this baby and I'd had never seen her happier. Several of the teenagers I'd mentored in New York were being raised by grandmothers after the parents had died of AIDS or overdoses. Perhaps I should have worried, but I didn't.

At the end of my seven-month stay, in August 1994, I traveled with Foley, two of his younger brothers, and several other members of Nike's school to Osi, his birthplace, for our engagement ceremony, a ritual that Nigerians see as just as important and irrevocable as a wedding since it represents, not two individuals, but two families getting together.

"You don't change your mind after that ceremony," Nike's oldest son, Olabayo, told me as we waited by the side of the road for Foley to pick us up in the 1978 Datsun Bluebird that I'd bought from a friend of his for two hundred dollars. As his father's eldest son, Olabayo has tribal marks, three lines cut into each cheek, as a sign of his position in the family. An American girlfriend of his had ended their relationship after this ceremony, and the disapproval that followed fell, not only upon her, but upon him, too. What made me sure I was not going to do that? he wanted to know.

"I don't plan on backing out," I told him. "Why would I?" On the drive home, with three of us squeezed in the front and five in the back, I asked him what had happened between him and the unfaithful girlfriend.

"She said she didn't really know me," he said, shaking his head as if he still didn't grasp the basis for her objection. That night I thought about what he had said. Did I know Foley? In Rogers and Hammerstein's *The King and I,* Anna sings about getting to know the King "day by day."

Foley and I never went through that day-by-day process. We did not have the shared vocabulary to tell each other about the lives we had led in the years before we met, which is where so much "getting to know" happens. I could never imagine what growing up in Osi had been like as a child of his father's eighth wife. And my refusal to become a debutante and leaving Toronto would have been equally incomprehensible to him. But I saw him as a man who would give me a future that I wanted, just as my first husband had done: I would be a married woman with a second home in Africa. I was grateful for that gift, and determined to hang onto it despite what my friends began to see as obvious deceptions. And was I not giving him what he wanted, a second life in the States?

Foley's father presided over his son's engagement ceremony from a chair on the porch of his two-story house, surrounded by his family and fellow villagers who encircled the central courtyard of his compound, some of them drumming. The houses in that part of Osi are built in the "old style," with mud-covered walls and no electricity or running water. I remember kneeling next to Foley and putting my head on the ground in front of the throne-like chair on which his father sat, bald and smiling. But the most unforgettable moment of the day was going inside the house, with Foley's sisters and female cousins and his father's four still-living wives, for a ceremony that gave me a Nigerian name, Aduke, meaning "She Who Is Cared For." All I remember is clasping the outstretched hands of one after another of these elegantly dressed and head-tied women of all ages, none of whom spoke a word of English. Coming from a family that frowned on any public display of feelings, I could not imagine my mother and sisters treating each other like that, let alone an outsider. Being taken into so welcoming a family was the high point of my entire visit that year, and I still look back on it in that light. Whatever became of this marriage, I would always have this to remember.

Of course Foley's mother was one of these women. She actually looks a bit like me, with a thin, angular body and prominent collarbones. But I have never seen her without the head tie that sets off her chiseled face and hides her hair. Her steady gaze, from eyes so dark that the pupil is not distinct from the iris, reminds me of Rembrandt's portraits, whose subjects look, not at you, but past you into a great distance. I've never caught her eye or seen her smile, and since liking a person is usually shown, where I'm from, with eye contact and a smile, I have no idea what she thought of me as her son's wife. Nor would anyone I know there understand my question if I did ask it. "Of course she likes you," they would say.

When I returned to Nigeria with Foley the following summer to get ready for our traditional wedding, Funmi no longer spent most of her time on her mother's back. We set up a system in which Kehinde would bring her daughter to the gallery, or to the dormitory where Foley and I were once again staying. Then Kehinde would slip away to the school's work area to make batik cloth with her fellow students on rows of long tables. The handover was never smooth, but after an initial tantrum on Funmi's part, she managed to turn her attention to me.

Nigerian mothers usually have too many things to do in the course of a day to play with a small child one on one. But I had, if anything, too little to do. So I gave Funmi the free run of my cosmetic case and colored pens. She enjoyed transferring things from one container to another and would pour the contents of the packages of ground nuts I'd bought into the mug from which I drank tea and then, with my help, put them back.

She liked the tea I made for myself, so I got her a small cup to hold her own weaker version, and we thoroughly enjoyed our tea parties. Sometimes she led me, along several twists and turns of a rutted road, to where she lived with her mother, her uncle, his wife, and a daughter Funmi's age. Clearly my prospective daughter was smart and strong-willed, with a natural sense of direction that I do not have. She would flourish, I felt sure, in my part of the world, where independence in women is to be encouraged and applauded. At least that was the state of affairs I was aiming to bring about in my Women's Studies work at Rutgers.

Funmi was not a bit demonstrative, but her cousin always ran up to me as soon as I appeared, and sat on my lap. "Why don't you take her, too?" asked Kehinde's aunt, who lived in the house. "She's obviously very attached to you."

"Let's take things one at a time," I said, as I enjoyed the little girl's attention, which had nothing to do with what I did for her or was promising to do. She simply took to me from the start, and I would have felt a lot less conflicted had she been the child Nike had "found" for me.

Yet Funmi had her charms as well. She had an alert, businesslike expression on her face that reminded me of some of my own baby pictures. Unlike my younger sister Ellen, I was not an adorable baby. "Say something nice to Cathy, too," my mother would say when people cooed over Ellen. So I enjoyed playing with her even as her elders sometimes disapproved of what I let her do. I had begun to learn to count in Yoruba, and taught her the equivalent numbers from one to ten in English. I drew a stick figure and labeled parts of the body in English and Yoruba as a way for us both to learn new words. I sprayed her with cologne and let her squeeze my bottle of hand lotion, which I would smooth onto her arms, legs, and face despite warnings from some of the other women that she would surely break something if I allowed her to play with my things.

At that point, my only conflict with Kehinde—and as it turned out, with her culture in general—came over the issue of hitting. One day when Funmi saw that her mother had disappeared, she bit me on the arm when I picked her up. Did I beat her? Kehinde wanted to know when she met us on the porch of the gallery and one of her friends told her in Yoruba what had happened.

"No. She calmed down after a few minutes."

Her friend spoke to her again, and then said to me, "But you must beat her."

Then another woman chimed in. "If you don't do it, she will always bite you like that."

"I don't think so," I said to all of them. "Let's just see what happens, okay?"

Even Foley agreed that I should have given Funmi a few solid whacks. It was, he said, the Nigerian way. Funmi did not bite me again, as I was sure she would not, but the tooth marks that turned into a bruise on my arm were the occasion for much joking and several lectures on a subject that would shadow my subsequent efforts to adopt a Nigerian child. I once walked out of a restaurant when I saw a man hitting his young son. I was less courageous when, on one of the few times I went with Foley to his church, I sat frozen while a small girl was severely beaten because she was "possessed" of the Devil.

While cultivating a bond with Funmi, I was also making arrangements for our traditional wedding, for which I had brought five hundred American dollars, along with a round trip plane ticket for Kehinde that I'd bought from my Nigerian travel agent in New York, since no one in Nigeria accepts credit cards. Nigerian weddings are immense public events, so it's impossible to calculate who will show up expecting to be served one—or sometimes several—meals. As July turned into August and the big day approached, I bought white cloth with a woven-in pattern to be made into outfits for Foley, Kehinde, Funmi, and me. It was Nike's idea to do this, and I was happy to make a gesture that included the two of them in our "family." I also decided to get extensions braided into my hair, a visible sign, I thought, of my membership in the family. The woman I went to had never dealt with straight hair like mine, and when I looked in the mirror after she pronounced the job done, I burst into tears. Thin braids hung limply on either side of my face because the woman had not put them in tightly against my scalp. She then sprayed them with hair spray, but that only turned the braids into a rigid helmet against my head.

"They look fine," Foley said.

"Please take them out," I implored the woman, but that was not so easy, since she first had to use hot water to get the hair spray out. Once my hair was back in place, tied in a twist behind my head, the Commissioner showed up with a heavy, expensive headdress that he said was "traditional." He urged me to buy it and wear it, but I held my ground, and Foley's sister Julie finally turned a stiff swatch of printed cloth into a head tie over my now-invisible hair.

The ceremony took place in the courtyard adjoining the roofed-in workspace where the students turned white cloth into batik. It could not have been more different from the one where I walked down the aisle of an Episcopal church on my father's arm, with Purcell's "Trumpet Voluntary" coming from the organ. Standing behind a long table with Foley and me, Nike, the Commissioner, and Foley's two oldest brothers—both of them older than me—passed dishes of honey, salt, kola nuts, and palm wine to one another, each symbolizing an aspect of a marriage: honey is sweet, salt gives flavor, and so forth. Nike had told me that she and the Commissioner would stand in for my side of the family, and I was delighted that they wanted to.

Kehinde and her daughter were not part of the ceremony. But the two of them are conspicuous in the photographs and in the video that one of Nike's students made. It features a performance by a troupe visiting Osogbo for the Osun festival that took place the next day, the women wearing grass skirts, cotton tops, and cowrie beads, the men bare-legged and bare-chested. After this came a moment that Foley had not warned me about. "You don't have to look if you don't want to," he said, and I turned my back as two people held the legs of a dog that was sliced in half with a machete, dogs being sacred to Ogun, the god of carvers. If the cut did not come clean, Foley told me, the marriage would not continue. Ours went fine, he told me as I continued to look off into the distance.

Several rambling speeches followed these performances. Then Foley and I got up to dance to a brass marching band with a huge drum. As the two of us danced, everyone followed a Nigerian wedding tradition by plastering our foreheads with *naira*, the Nigerian currency that Kehinde collected and gave me periodically. Conflicted as I was about this custom, I was glad to have the *naira* since I'd run out of money and could not get any more. And I loved dancing to this band. Swaying and twirling in pairs, it was not African dancing or American dancing but an international way of moving your body that lifted your spirits. He and I were a spectacular duo as we showed off non-stop in the glow of everyone's admiration.

Exhausted from being the focus of so much attention for so many hours, I headed home around four, leaving my husband with what I assumed to be a throng of well-wishers, and drifted off to sleep, enveloped in happiness. I don't know how long after that Foley showed up and drew me toward him as we both succumbed to exhaustion.

I flew home a week later to get ready to teach, leaving Foley to bring Kehinde and her daughter, whose visas had come through thanks to my letter on Rutgers stationery, and whose passports I had paid for out of the money I brought for the wedding. Everyone insisted that Kehinde wanted to stay only for a few weeks, to see where her daughter would be living and to help her get settled. They could both sleep on a fold-out couch in my living room for as long as Kehinde stayed with us. But since Nigerian children usually sleep in a room with their parents, I also bought a single bed to put in one corner of Foley's and my bedroom. I then went to a toy store in my neighborhood and came home with an African-American doll with tight black curls. The next time I went out to New Brunswick I bought a teddy bear with *Someone From*

*Rutgers Loves Me* on its red t-shirt.

No sooner was everything in place on my side than I got a call from Foley. "The father found out about it," he said. "He says the child belongs to the father, so he has taken Funmi."

"Even if he never acknowledged his child?" I fumed. "Or did anything for her?" I'd heard this stated as a fact from Nike, who had served as my intermediary for such information. "How *dare* he do this to her!" I sputtered, too shocked and heartbroken to say more.

"He says Kehinde is taking *his* child to the States to kill her and sell her body," Foley shouted over our poor connection. I've heard this accusation since then. Nike had insisted that other members of an African family take in children whose parents die, or are too poor to look after their many children. So legal adoption, being almost impossible, is equated in people's minds with selling. From there it is hardly a stretch to believe that Americans buy children for their organs.

"So there's nothing you can do?"

"No," Foley said. "I will see you in two weeks."

I kept my voice as steady as I could, and I hung up before starting to cry. I never thought to doubt the truth of Foley's words, or to look behind them. His story about the father fit with what I knew about Nigerian fathers. They do have control over their children in his country. But if that man had never acknowledged Kehinde as his wife and Funmi as their child, what would be his motive in keeping Funmi from coming to sleep on the extra bed in our room?

"Why would he care?" I asked Foley when he appeared, as he said he would, two weeks later.

"He is a very wicked man," was his answer, as if that adjective explained everything. This was not the first time he had used it, nor would it be the last. Back then I took this assessment of fellow Nigerians as evidence that Foley stood apart from that wickedness. But if "that man" explained the fact that Funmi was still in Nigeria, there was still the matter of the round-trip plane fare that appeared prominently on the credit card statement that was waiting for me when I got home. Later that week I went down to the travel agent from whom I had bought the ticket to ask for a refund. "We'll have to see if the ticket was used," he said, looking me straight in the eye. "Nigerians can be pretty tricky people."

"Is that where you grew up?"

"Yes, I did. And so did most of my customers. Things there don't work the way they do over here." I wanted him to be specific, but just then one of these customers walked in, and I took it as my cue to leave.

When the agent called two days later, he told me he could get me a refund only on the second half of the round-trip ticket I'd left with Kehinde. "Airlines don't like to give refunds," he said. "So this was the best I could do."

"So the first half was used."

"Yes."

"Can you find out who did that?"

"Not after the person has traveled. I'm sorry."

He knows that I've been ripped off, I thought as I got back on the elevator.

When I got home, Foley was watching a wrestling match that appealed, I suppose, to some part of his heritage that I don't share. Nigerians laugh a lot more than people I know here, and he found the clowning of these long-haired, muscle-bound males incredibly funny, whereas I was not amused. "The travel agent only gave me a refund for half of the ticket I got for Kehinde." I said, positioning myself next to the TV screen.

"I don't know about that. Maybe airlines don't give more."

Why did I not see what this agent had to have seen, that I was not only being ripped off but lied to? Years later, when the marriage was obviously not going well, Foley said, quite offhandedly, that all Nigerians are liars. As a Nigerian, he could say what I, a privileged white woman, came to conclude only hesitantly and reluctantly. Perhaps I should have pressed him that first time, but the fact is that I wasn't ready to throw a curve ball into our marriage. Looking back, I see that once again I was more like my mother, a woman who refused to throw in the towel no matter what, than I was willing to admit.

At one point when I was caught up in preparing for our Nigerian wedding at Nike's gallery I hadn't been able to find Kehinde, but when I asked her friends where she was, they'd answered with the usual evasive Nigerian phrase. She was simply "not around."

But it had never occurred to me, until my conversation with Skip, that something might be going on between her and Foley behind my back. I never saw the two of them together, and Foley didn't flirt the way Nike's son Olabayo did, so I simply wondered where she was.

My son likes to remind me that, unlike him, I assume that the way I want things to be is the way they are. I've told him that he is right, and in this case what I wanted was to stay married. So I did what my mother did when her new husband told her he had met someone else. I clung to my belief that Foley was not a liar and made myself a cup of tea. When he joined me in the kitchen, I said, "I'm hungry. Do you want to go to that Chinese restaurant where they serve free wine?

The wine took some of the edge off my disappointment about Funmi, but not enough to let me slip into sleep alongside Foley, who always fell asleep quickly. So I got up and went into the pantry, where I keep a bottle of white zinfandel just for this purpose, and poured myself half a glass. I thought about my mother's need for a drink to fall asleep. Was I on my way to becoming like her in spite of my determination not to? I had left for New York by the time her alcoholism kicked into high gear, so I never really saw her at her worst.

I had had one conversation about it with my father, though, and he'd told me he felt powerless to stop her. "I just know," he'd said, "that if I tried to cut her off, she would, you know—" he'd drawn a hand horizontally across his throat.

"What makes you think that?"

"She keeps saying that drinking is the only thing that makes her happy."

I had not wanted to ask him what it was that was making her unhappy, so I'd just hugged him and said, "I guess you gotta do what you gotta do."

Walking back into my bedroom, the glass of wine in my hand, I wondered what disappointment she was trying to delete. When I became a mother, she sent me a bunch of my baby pictures, so I know I was not the pretty child she must have been hoping for. They show me as hefty and unsmiling, not lithe and perky like the offspring of her friends who joined me in my playpen. She must have hoped that my arrival would heal the breach my father's taste for multiple women had begun to create. It didn't, of course. By the time she died in a nursing home, visited only by my sister Ellen, who lived in Toronto, she could boast of having been married for over sixty years. On the door of her room in that place was a photograph of the celebration of their fortieth anniversary—he in a set of tails, she proudly wearing her mother's Worth dress, which she had put on to walk down the aisle. Her wedding pictures, which stood on the almost unused grand piano in our drawing room, show a radiant smile on her face and four bridesmaids on her right.

They both had their reasons for staying together no matter what. He was a politician and, as I have said, marital discord in those days would have ended his career. And she, a mother of three with no marketable skills in a world where women didn't work, had nowhere to go. From an early age I was determined not to be like her, making marriage my only goal in life. But I see now that part of her lives on in me. I never became an alcoholic, but I shared her determination, at least for a while, to keep my marriage going. Yet even had I been suspicious of Kehinde, there was simply no Nigerian that I trusted to tell me what was going on. Had I called Nike to tell her that this particular student of hers had taken off with Funmi upon arriving in New York, she would have bemoaned the unreliability of her students. Some of them had stolen things from her house, she'd told me more than once. It had upset her to dismiss them, but what could she do?

This derailing of my plans might have forced me to ask why, at my age, I would want to mother a child from a culture so different from mine. One answer was that I wanted to relive the happy part of my marriage to my first husband thirty-some years earlier. But I also must have sensed, even then, that coming home to me and my apartment with its books and plants and Early American furniture would never be enough to draw Foley into my world again and again. We had too little to talk about. An African child would be part of his world, making us a family rather than just a couple, though in fact I had never really expected him to be a reliably present parent. That would be my job, as it had been with Kevin. I would need help, of course, but I was sure I would get it, just as I did then.

Raising an African child would strengthen my ties, not only to Foley, but to the sisters and brothers, husbands, wives, and friends who'd welcomed me at our engagement ceremony and wedding. Coming from a culture and a social class where people keep their distance from outsiders, how could I resist? So it never occurred to me that Funmi would not flourish under my care. We'd have a happy life together, partly in New York and partly in Nigeria. Had I not done well with Kevin, now married to a wonderful woman? I knew I would try again if given the chance.

# 4

I did get another chance a year later, but by then my friendship with Nike had started to unravel, pulled apart by tensions that I had not picked up on earlier. She had made the arrangements for our traditional wedding, and had stood in, along with the Commissioner, for my absent family. They'd assured me that they were my best friends in Nigeria. To hold up my end of the friendship, they expected me to write the invitations that I had promised to produce on my Rutgers letterhead for people whose names began emerging periodically out of my fax machine.

One weekday when I was not out teaching at Rutgers, Nike's son Olabayo called me to ask if I would pay for the airfare for some of her students.

"Air fare? How many are you talking about?"

I heard him speak to his mother in Yoruba before coming up with a number. "Six."

"Are you *kidding?*" I shouted into the receiver, quickly calling up the price of my last round-trip ticket and multiplying in my head. "That's more than five thousand dollars. What makes you think I have that kind of money to hand over to people I don't even know?"

"That's the Commissioner," Foley told me. "People say that he is her husband now, and that gives him the right to Nike's money. She listens to him now, and she does what he says."

"But why would they assume that I have so much money?"

"They are wicked people," he said. "They want to hurt us." When I asked him what he meant, he said, "Because I have success." That didn't make any sense to me, and when I pressed him, he didn't explain. I now think that "success" meant marrying an American woman.

They must think I'm a multimillionaire, I thought, living in her two-story house with a guard at the gate and two yellow vans with the logo of her school painted on the side of them, Nike was a rich woman herself. I wondered if Foley and his friends saw me in the same light, but I dismissed the idea. It felt better to embrace his scenario, which pitted the two of *us* against *them*. Besides, I didn't want to erase my sense of Nike as a friend. The six names on this first list belonged to people Foley knew. I have no idea how they mustered the cost of their air fare, but they apparently expected me to pay for everything once they got here, arriving at my door with no money to cover even their taxi fare from JFK. Of course I would not stiff these drivers for their sixty-dollar tab, and I don't think anyone ended up sleeping on the street. But after that incident, I had my husband's permission, when anyone called from JFK expecting us to put him up, to say that he should find another place to stay.

"Kate, you need to keep your wits about you dealing with these people," Marcia said when I told her about Olabayo's phone call. "Just be careful, sweetie, okay?"

We did take in Baba Sunday, a member of Nike's gallery whose program in the Virgin Islands had been wiped out by a hurricane. He slept in the living room for three months, unable to return to Nigeria until he had made back the cost of his plane fare by selling his batik clothing. I knew that people with visitor visas were not supposed to make money, but I doubted that the transactions of my visitors could be traced, and I bought a few of Baba Sunday's batik outfits myself. While he was here, he cleaned our apartment several times, bringing my wary roommates to see him as a positive addition to our household.

But for anyone else I took a stand, and Foley and I became allies against anyone trying to burden our marriage with demands that we could not, and would not, meet. I saw this as a bond that could not be broken, though I knew the stand put Foley in a bind. Sleeping on someone's floor is common in his world, so why should I not extend such hospitality to visitors to my country? I'd slept like that whenever I'd gone to Foley's village. Then there were the owners of the small shops where I stocked up on tea, sugar, powdered milk, and other small items, who would ask me to "help" a family member. Getting a son into Rutgers was a frequent request, and this would mean, not only taking care of his paperwork and tuition, but taking the boy into my house for the duration of his education. These petitioners sometimes spoke of a relative in the States, but my letterhead would apparently open doors that would be closed even to those with stateside families. I couldn't explain that a word from me would not open the doors to Rutgers, or any other place.

I expected that Nike's lists of names would diminish over time. But in fact the opposite happened. Her second fax had twice as many, only a few of their names recognized by Foley. I warned Nike over a static-filled phone connection that I couldn't write that many invitations at once. Then a third fax, with more than twenty names, arrived just before Christmas.

"Who are these people?" I asked Foley

"They are from the Commissioner," he said. "Don't invite them."

"Why would he want people to come here?"

"Drugs," Foley said simply. "The Commissioner is very rich from that."

"Maybe they're running an invitation business," I said. Foley was hearing from friends that the P.C. (as he was called) had taken over the school and was demanding from the students proof that they had no criminal records, documentation that they were too poor to supply, even if it was available. Whatever lay behind these escalating demands, we wanted no part of it. "They are not happy," Foley said several times, "because I have success. Because of you," he would always add, and I came to see how, in a world of scarcity where there is no hope for a better future, success can be seen as a zero-sum game: *More for you means less for me.* As a result, suspicion, and the lying that covers it up, run high in his part of the world.

For Foley, having success meant, first of all, finding places to sell his carvings. Most of my African-American friends were volunteers in Max and Felicia's organization, to whom I was eager to show off my new life and the hunky guy now at its center. This sounds like I saw Foley mainly as a prize to show off, and that's not entirely wrong. But it was mutual. I was his passport to success, but all this meant that we never really got close to one another. That being the case, I turned my dining room into a gallery where my friends could admire and buy the wares that had traveled across the Atlantic in many bulging suitcases. The owners of these pieces needed to make back the cost of their air fare, or what was the point of their coming to the States? For them, America was a place where "big money" flowed freely, and they were expected to return with lots of it in their pockets. I had no idea how deeply this idea would enter into not only my life but Foley's, and the pressure on him that came with marrying a woman from the land of plenty.

Of course I wanted Foley to have success. But that meant being able to travel freely without having to get an invitation each time. This required a green card, which in turn required getting married at City Hall. But before taking that step with him I had to do something I had never intended to do. For more than three decades I had resolutely clung to my Canadian identity, even to the point of risking deportation each time I got arrested protesting the Vietnam War and later Reagan's secret aid to the Nicaraguan *contras.* In fact, given how strongly I felt about America's wars in distant places, I had never even considered becoming a citizen.

However, you can't get a green card by marrying another green card holder. So once back in the States after our traditional wedding in Nigeria, I took the first step in that process, getting fingerprinted and then waiting while my arrests at demonstrations were checked out. Then came the list of questions testing my knowledge of American civics, and I, who always pride myself on doing well on tests, was elated to get all ten right.

That fall, Emmanuel, a younger brother of Foley's—same father, different mother—had gotten a visa to come to the States using one of my invitations, and he moved in with Foley and me. The two of them would go down to Philadelphia during the week to work for a Nigerian man who owned a furniture factory that employed them, they said, as carvers. We cooked a second Christmas dinner for the half dozen Nigerians who were now living in Brooklyn and New Jersey thanks to my Rutgers letterhead. Foley made fried plantains and yams bought from an African grocery store in Brooklyn. I made a turkey along with a salad that only I ate, much to the amusement of all the Nigerians, who kept reminding me that only goats eat "leaves."

Work in New York for people who lack schooling was a problem that marriage to an American would not solve. As long as I knew where Foley was, and as long as he was doing something he enjoyed, I was fine with this arrangement. In both my marriages, as I have tried to make clear, having someone I could refer to as "my husband" meant a lot to me, and people wanted to know the whole story when I told them that this one was from Nigeria. The curiosity the story aroused, and my pleasure in telling it, led me to take a step that I had never been willing to take before. I began to see my African adventure unfolding in written form, with me growing intellectually and spiritually as I moved back and forth between my two homes. So by the time Emmanuel arrived I had applied to the New School, which was launching an MFA program in creative writing. Perhaps writing my story would help me understand the combination of intense spirituality and rampant corruption, joyous laughter and omnipresent scarcity—the long lines for fuel in a major oil-producing country, for instance—that I found disturbing but Nigerians apparently did not. Sure, fights broke out when people cut into those lines. But I'll never forget driving to a party with Foley and learning that half the people there did not have enough fuel to get home. But they still danced up a storm into the wee hours of the morning anyway.

I wanted my story to have a happy ending, and not only for me. Perhaps a bit of Nigerian optimism had rubbed off on me. But I really thought that if I could move back and forth across the huge gulf that separated my world and Foley's, perhaps others could do so too and the distance between them would shrink. So I was determined to show that it could be done.

I had always imagined myself a writer as well as a teacher, and had done enough writing to get me tenure. But I did not put money down on this identity of "writer" until my husband expressed delight that I was planning to write "our story."

One day as winter turned into spring, Foley told me, a few weeks after my acceptance letter from the New School arrived in the mail, that he had landed a carving commission in Zimbabwe and planned to spend the summer there.

"Will they pay you?" was the first thing I asked.

"Oh, yes," he said, flashing his incandescent smile. "Big money."

"And they'll pay your air fare too?" He nodded, and I could not help but be glad that he was being paid to do carving, since only one of the pieces he had brought to the States had sold, bought by a Rutgers colleague who had been born in Ghana. Perhaps he could use some of the money he would make in Zimbabwe to set up a small studio in New York. I had married an artist, and I saw this commission placing him firmly on the road to an artist's life.

He went back to Nigeria in May to make arrangements for this, leaving his brother and me to follow him when my semester ended. Like his older brother, Emmanuel was always willing to help out around the house, and one evening he was standing at my kitchen sink, washing our dinner dishes, when he announced that he had just learned that his girlfriend in Nigeria was pregnant. He sounded upset, and I distinctly remember him saying, "I don't want to marry now. I want to come to America." Of course a solution came to me right away. "Perhaps Foley and I could adopt this baby," I said. "That way, he or she would still be part of the family. Isn't that the way you take care of things like this in your part of the world?"

Emmanuel was enthusiastic about the idea and took it as a given that his child would be a boy. "In America he would get education," he said. "You know, that's what's holding me and Foley back. We don't have education."

"There are plenty of good schools in New York that he could go to," I assured him. "Education is the business I'm in, after all."

Emmanuel and I had tickets for different airlines, so on a muggy day in mid-June, I let him out of our cab at the Delta terminal, where he would have a stopover in Amsterdam, and went on to British Airways, my favorite for transatlantic travel. I loved the shops at Heathrow and the accents of the pilots that connected me to my English nannies, to A. A. Milne and Beatrix Potter on the shelves of our nursery in Toronto, to the residue of colonialism that lingers in Nigeria in the form of the malted chocolate drink Bournvita, Schweppes bitter lemon, Pears soap, and Digestive Biscuits sold in places that double as drugstores and small supermarkets. I know that these products are the residue of Nigeria's colonial past, where Africa was simply a source of raw materials and a market for British goods. But knowing that does not erase my fondness for them.

Then there is the way the Nigerians I know speak with a slightly odd British accent, which was certainly part of Foley's charm for me. If this sounds like my relationship with Foley was all about surfaces, I have to say that this was true. I may have put an international border between my New York life and Toronto, but the signed photographs of Queen Elizabeth and Prince Philip hanging in our front hall link my Anglophile past to that of the

Nigerians who still bought the made-in-England items that I remembered from nursery meals and bath times.

Another pleasure provided by Heathrow is that, once I have changed into the blue-and-white *adire* wrapper and blouse that I always wear to arrive in Nigeria, I can go over to the waiting area for the plane to Lagos and join passengers wearing bright African prints, including some *adire*. "I see you have been to our country," one of them will say in the slightly British accent I find so appealing. "You are wearing our cloth." And given that all of us have time to kill, a conversation will often bubble up.

"Yes, I've spent quite a lot of time there."

"You love Nigeria?"

"Oh, yes, I really do."

"Do you go there on business?"

"No, my husband is a Nigerian man. So I feel like I belong there."

This always produces bright smiles, and the dialogue will sometimes spread to neighboring seats. I am asked what he does and where we live, and launching into my narrative about "my husband," I feel a sense of security. The words open a door to a community I could not have entered except by marriage. So losing it, and the identity that went with it, was really hard, and I delayed that loss until it was absolutely impossible to keep on hanging on. Even now, with Foley no longer in my life, I often ask cab drivers with African names, or people wearing African clothes, where they are from. And when they reply I tell them, simply for the sake of the dialogue that opens up, that my husband is Nigerian. It's an identity I haven't been willing to consign to the trash bin.

Arriving in Lagos on a June morning in 1996, married traditionally in Nigeria but not yet legally in my country, I felt a sense of homecoming as I followed the mostly African passengers through the Murtala Mohammed airport. A smiling Foley appeared behind the barrier outside the Plexiglas doors of the airport, a visible sign of a welcome home that still felt unfractured despite what had happened with Funmi. After hugging me and grabbing my suitcase, he mentioned a headache, so I gave him a drug I offer to anyone there who asks: Excedrin. On previous trips, I'd developed a reputation for benevolence based in part on dispensing handfuls of this caffeine-laden painkiller. Of course it's no cure for the malaria from which they suffered intermittently. But it did provide a respite from the hunger, fatigue, or simple frustration that I sometimes felt, feelings I imagined I shared with them.

Emmanuel's flight was not due for another hour, so Foley and I made our way to the canteen at the edge of the parking lot. I am not an adventurous eater, and traces of the anorexia I suffered from in my teens still linger in my system, meaning that I've never been able to put aside the idea that starchy food damages your body by weighing it down. The core of the Nigerian diet is pounded yams and *fufu*, made from cassava. Cassava can grow in cracks of a sidewalk, I'm told, and has no nutritional value. So these traditional foods still call up some of my long-held prohibitions. In Osogbo I eat mainly rice and beans, which make a complete protein. I also love fried plantains and bean cakes, and found some of both of these at the canteen, along with a Sprite to wash them down.

"Tell me about this job in Zimbabwe," I said to Foley as we sat down on two plastic chairs surrounded by vendors and their brightly dressed customers.

"I don't know much about it," he said. "I'm supposed to go to Harare in two weeks. I have my ticket."

"Perhaps I could come and visit you there. I'd love to go to another African country."

"That would be good. When I go there, I will try to arrange it." This was about the extent of our conversation about a time in his life that I didn't think to question,

"What has happened to Kehinde and Funmi?" I asked, sipping on my Sprite.

"They are not around," Foley said, using that favorite Nigerian expression that delivers no information. "Kehinde took Funmi to her family in the north." Rather than doubt his story, I was glad that Funmi's alleged father had not separated this mother and daughter, and gave no more thought to their whereabouts.

"So you like the idea of our adopting Emmanuel's child?"

"Yes," Foley replied without a moment's hesitation. "You know, this baby will be the first born in our family since my father died. So one of his names will be Babatunde." I had read a book on the Yoruba religion that has spread from Nigeria to the Caribbean, so I knew about ancestors who return as a newborn family member. I'd never given much thought to my own ancestors, and certainly not to the belief that they continue to guide you from the invisible but always present realm they inhabit. But the idea that I could be reincarnated as the first female member of my family to be born after I died struck me as a great way to imagine immortality. Perhaps I could return as the daughter of one of my son's grandchildren.

When Emmanuel arrived, we all got into a Peugeot that Foley had borrowed, our ancient Datsun having died. The two brothers sat in the front while I stretched out across the vinyl back seat and fell asleep.

As we pulled up to the one-story cinder-block house that Foley had rented for himself and two cousins, Emmanuel asked him when he was leaving for Zimbabwe.

"In two weeks. Emmanuel will take care of you when I am gone," Foley added to me, beaming his winning smile at each of us.

"Of course I will," said Emmanuel. "Kate always takes good care of me, so I can do the same for her." He then headed off on foot to find his girlfriend, Sade.

Our house that summer had three bedrooms and a small living room furnished with an upholstered couch, matching stuffed chairs, and the TV set that even poor families seem to manage to acquire. Foley does not own a home, so his living arrangements are erratic and uncertain, but not expensive. He told me that rent for a year on this place was 300 dollars, probably a typical rent. So I never risked telling him that my mortgage cost six times that every month, not including the maintenance fees covered by my roommates.

He often said that he wanted to build an enormous house in Osogbo for his family, including me. But money was not the only obstacle to carrying out this plan, as I would slowly learn. The cousins with whom we shared the house must have been told of our adoption plan, because they immediately referred to the unborn baby as *"omo* Katie," Kate's baby, just as everyone had done with Funmi. "I have to say I hope it's a girl," I told them. "I have a son, you know, so it would be really nice to get to raise a daughter."

After I had slept for several hours, Foley and I made our way along a rutted dirt road that led, between pastel cinder-block houses set back from the road, to a small room off a dark central hallway in the two-story building where Emmanuel and his girlfriend were living. A trace of acne on her heart-shaped face made her seem very young to me. She looked neither pleased nor upset when I followed Foley through the blue-and-yellow curtain that hung over their door and stood next to her smiling boyfriend and his brother. I sensed that I might never really know what feelings were hidden behind her shyness and our shared inability to understand each other's language.

The walls of the couple's one room were painted a pale green, and their possessions were piled in boxes against them. A bed, two stuffed chairs, and of course a TV took up most of the floor space. This room lay off a corridor that ran the length of the building, lit by a single bare lightbulb and leading to a shared toilet, shower, and kitchen at the far end. Sade sat propped up on the bed with a pillow behind her shoulders. She certainly looked far along.

"When is the baby coming?" I asked her.

"August," said Emmanuel, who seemed eager to be the intermediary between us.

Conversation was clearly not about to flow, so we four stared at a drama on TV for a while before Foley and I got up to say goodbye. "How do you think Sade feels about all this?" I asked him on our walk back to our house.

"She feels fine," Foley said in a nonchalant tone that signaled to me that, as far as he was concerned, trying to probe her feelings, not to mention his, was a waste of time. I suspect that more people around the world feel the way he does than the way I do. If you live many to a room and the cohesion of the community is more valued than its individual members, then expressing your feelings can be disruptive of family or communal unity and is therefore something to be avoided. When we in America do this, it's because we believe that by speaking up we can alter the situation in which we find ourselves. But if someone's circumstances have no apparent way of changing, why would anyone want to develop a behavior for which there would be no practical use, and might even be frowned on?

Figuring out the feelings of the Nigerians I got to know was a skill that I was much less able to employ than I realized at the time. Foley said that Sade's parents were strict Muslims, so perhaps they were not pleased with their daughter's pregnancy. "She graduated from high school," he said, "and she started at a technical college." This must have imposed a financial hardship on the rest of her family, so perhaps their displeasure now had to do with the interruption of an education they could barely afford, one that might enable Sade to rise above their situation and help them out. I also wasn't sure how Muslims felt about "mixed" marriages, and wondered if Emmanuel's Christianity could be an obstacle.

Since I spoke little more than the Yoruba used in the lengthy greetings that begin all conversations in Nigeria, I was often isolated in the midst of others. This was particularly true the night that Sade, Emmanuel, Foley, and I went to visit Sade's family, she perched on Emmanuel's lap as we piled into the taxi with one or two strangers.

A squawking chicken flew away from us as we stepped over the cement drainage ditch at the side of the road and approached a group of houses that I'd seen many times from the window of a car on the way to and from Nike's elegant dwelling. Our destination was one of those buildings, whose streaked, moldy walls, rusted tin roofs, and paneless windows spoke of the stark poverty of those who lived in them.

Several women with small children greeted Sade while the rest of us trooped through a hallway lit by only a faint, naked bulb hanging from the ceiling. She then disappeared with them as three of her male relatives led Emmanuel, Foley, and me into a room where two small boys appeared to be asleep under a piece of colored fabric on one of the two beds we sat on. The conversation lasted no more than twenty minutes. Not knowing what was said, I assumed that I'd been brought along as the adoptive mother. Everyone smiled and seemed pleased as we rose to leave, though perhaps I did not pay enough attention to Sade when she rejoined us.

Foley took off in early July. Two or three times, someone at the Gallery said he had called on the phone there but left neither a number nor a message. I spend most of the remaining weeks of my stay doing what I had done while on my sabbatical two years before. I sat on the porch of the gallery reading books on African history and the literary theory that now dominated the field of English studies, taking notes on my laptop and writing voluminously in the journal I kept there. On Sundays I went by taxi to Nike's house, a few miles from the gallery, and walked along the dirt road to the church whose service had so delighted me on my first visit. I would spend the rest of the day at her house, where the students who lived there would talk to me and make me a meal. I always brought my laptop with me, and these young people would stand behind me as I wrote, having no compunction about pointing out my typos. During the week, I walked to a roadside food stand close to town, where I bought my rice and beans. Often a student came with me, assuming, rightly, that I would buy something for him or her as well. They seemed to feel that I, an American, was simply obliged to do this. A regular question wherever I went was, "What did you bring for me?"

"I didn't bring you anything," I invariably said. Why? "Because I don't know you."

Foley and I had not talked about what arrangements would be needed to raise his brother's child together, but he assured me several times before he left that he wanted to bring a member of his family to enjoy the opportunities of life in America, and I believed him.

"You are missing your *oko*," Nike said with a wifely smile when I complained to her about these missed phone calls. "Don't worry, Kate," she added. "Your husband loves you." I must have sounded unconvinced, though, because of a remark I remember the Commissioner making that evening. "If you want to know if your husband has gone to Zimbabwe, look in his passport." This man knows something that I don't know, I thought.

A week after Foley left, I heard that Sade had been taken to the hospital, where she was kept for three days because of high blood pressure. "High blood pressure?" I asked. "She's not even twenty years old. Is that something to worry about?" Someone assured me that this was a common side effect of pregnancy, and she did leave the hospital after a few days.

Then I woke up one morning to hear that she had given birth to a boy, and I was relieved as well as thrilled. August 8, 1996, is a date on which everything else that happened that year converges. I did not visit her in the hospital, but a few days later I followed the dirt road between our houses and knocked on the frame of the door I remembered.

Emmanuel brushed the batik curtain aside to let me in and pointed to a chair. With its light green walls and colorful curtain over the door, the room was a lot cheerier than the one in which I had talked to Sade's family. Bright sunlight from outside streamed through the window, its narrow panes slatted horizontally to let air in.

A tired Sade was stretched out on the bed next to the baby, who lay on his back. Without looking at me, she gestured to me to pick him up.

"What's his name?" I asked in Yoruba, venturing one of the few sentences I knew as I held his delicate body against my chest and ran a hand over his small, downy head. I remembered holding my son when he was that age, and the same rush of love at first sight came to me as I stood in the small, hot room.

"Gbenga," Sade said. "You like?"

"It's my favorite name," I said. "You like it, Emmanuel?"

"I love it," he said, clearly thrilled. "I think he looks like me." I thought he looked rather like Foley. He would certainly have the wide smile that ran in the family and flashed out from every photograph of an African child I've ever seen. I still have photographs of him taken at his naming ceremony eight days later, and the face caught by the camera still calls up the belief that came over me when I first picked up this baby: there would be no turning back. Whatever might happen, we were in each other's lives for good.

His naming ceremony was a big occasion for Emmanuel, who distributed small invitation cards calling Gbenga "omo Emmanuel Bamidele," with no mention of Sade. The list of Gbenga's names included Arowogun, his famous carver great-grandfather that Nike and Foley had told me about, and Babatunde, which means "the father returns," connecting him to Foley's and Emmanuel's now-dead father and that father's many other children. An evangelical pastor friend of theirs presided over the decidedly Christian ritual, which took place in an open area behind the house. Sade looked gorgeous in a green-and-white striped outfit with a matching sash and head tie, but she sat to the side while a sister of Emmanuel's held the baby, making it clear whose family was welcoming him into their midst. Her young face was expressionless, and it struck me that she might be feeling marginalized by all the focus on Emmanuel and his relatives. Perhaps we two women had something in common after all.

I have little memory of the ceremony and the dancing that followed it, mainly because I felt so acutely out of place. Someone made a video of it that I eventually threw away because I looked so old, so awkward, and most of all, so white. I managed to hold the baby and to dance with him in my arms, hearing the words "*omo* Katie" chanted by the gyrating guests around me. Before I left, I assured Emmanuel that it had been a lovely party, but I've never felt so white, so much an outsider to my husband's culture, before or since, as I did on that day.

I left Nigeria a week later with two beautiful pictures of

Gbenga that I framed and put in my study back home. One month after that, I learned that I'd been cleared to become a citizen. I traveled downtown one morning and, speaking only a partial truth, put my hand to my chest and agreed, along with some hundred of my fellow "foreigners" in a pillared building in Lower Manhattan, to "renounce and abjure all allegiance and fidelity to any foreign prince, potentate, state, or sovereignty of whom or which I have heretofore been a subject or citizen." In a moment of solidarity with these strangers, I cheered at the words that gave us citizenship, with all its rights and privileges. I had lived in the States by choice, becoming a dancer, a student, a professor, a wife, and a mother. But I had never voted anywhere, and was surprised, when Election Day rolled around in November, at the pleasure I felt pulling a lever that helped to give Bill Clinton a second term. I had changed my citizenship for Foley, and I'm glad I did.

By that time Foley said he was back in Osogbo. He was pleased when I told him, over the phone, about my new nationality. "You are a good wife, Kate," he said. "I will never do anything that makes you unhappy."

My life that fall had become intensely busy, since I had joined my program at the New School. This meant that I had to ration my time carefully. On my free evenings and on the weekends, I worked on a new chapter or revised an earlier one, absorbing the criticisms written on my pages by my fellow students. I had always enjoyed going to school, and this program gave me just what I wanted: a structure with feedback and deadlines and the camaraderie of fellow writers. Perhaps the real reason I had married my husband was to write about him.

"Why don't you stay in Nigeria?" I asked Foley at the end of one of our phone conversations. "I'll come there for Christmas, and we'll see each other then."

He readily agreed, and I settled into my demanding routine. Did I miss my husband's cheer-producing presence? Yes and no, since he never showed up when he said he would. On the other hand, I knew that the Nigerian sense of time is very different from ours. It is not money there, as it is with us. You can't save it there, and you can't waste it. It is simply out of your control. So I chose to think that my husband was doing what he wanted while I did the same. I also saw my writing affirming the value of our marriage. Virginia Woolf wrote that experiences did not become whole until one had put them into words, and at moments I sensed what she meant as I started piecing together the story of how I left a privileged world I didn't want to join and took a wild ride to this complicated place in my life. And since my marriage was part of this story, it was reassuringly present for me even when Foley was, as I believed, in Nigeria doing what he had done before he met me, that is, his carving.

# 5

I could not get a plane reservation between the end of my semester and Christmas, so I arrived in Nigeria a few days into the New Year, 1997. I know now that the carved nativity scene I carried so carefully across the ocean did not make the good impression on Foley's mother that I was imagining. I'd been hoping she would see this offering as a sign of the Christian faith we presumably shared. She would have preferred the money I had paid for it, he would tell me later, and I wish I had known this when I bought her the crèche I admired from the Met Museum gift shop. But thinking of myself as a new member of her family, I saw everything through the lens of the African home I imagined I was bringing into being. I had no sense of his mother's difficult position, first as the last of his father's eight wives, and then as a widow, features of life for women in Nigeria that made her world utterly remote from mine. Sons are desired in traditional cultures because of their greater ability to help their parents, and Foley was his mother's only son.

In the plane's toilet stall I put on my African clothes, as usual, before disembarking. When I walked through the airport's scratched Plexiglas doors, I saw, for the first time in six months, my husband's smiling face among those in the line behind a wooden barrier guarded by the omnipresent military officers, and I felt a now-familiar rush of joy. Perhaps because Emmanuel was with him, it seemed to me that this long break in time had not damaged the family tie I was so happy to have with both of them. "How is Gbenga?" was my first question. "And Sade? How are things with her?"

"Everyone looks forward to seeing you," said Emmanuel, giving me a welcoming hug. "Sade and Gbenga are good."

On the ride to the rented house where I would be sleeping for the next two weeks, Foley did not ask me what I had been doing since we saw each other last, and I did not press him either. We'd spoken on the phone regularly despite the static-filled connection that always annoyed me, and he'd told me he missed me often enough to keep me from imagining possible deception.

"Nike and the Commissioner have invited you to dinner," said Foley before I gave in to exhaustion after my long trip. "I think they want to talk about your invitations."

"So let's go together," I said to Foley. "I know you don't like going to their house, but I want to stick to my guns, and I'm really going to need your support."

January is the hottest month in Nigeria, and the power is often out. It was out when we arrived at the same house where I'd stayed in on my last visit. The ceiling fans were immobile, and I could not use the boiling-ring I'd brought to make the tea that always picks me up, at home and elsewhere. So despite my apprehension about the upcoming dinner, I welcomed Nike's hospitality because she had a generator and a flock of students—unpaid servants, really—who would bring me tea, lump sugar, and tinned milk, as they had when I used to stay there.

Sipping my tea in their plant-filled living room under a skylight that opened onto the second floor, I explained to my hosts why I would not invite people I didn't know or pay their cab fare when they arrived at my door from JFK Airport.

"Of course you are right, Kate," the Commissioner said. "Nike, we should call a meeting of the students tomorrow and explain what our good friend Kate has said." Foley was silent, and I saw how uncomfortable he felt being in a place where his friends were working for nothing but room and board. I was "our good friend," while he and his mates were more like Nike's children. In fact, he and his mates called her "Mama Nike" just as they called me "Mama Kate."

"You will come to the meeting, of course," the Commissioner said as we sat down to a meal in Nike's dining room, the same place where she had presented Foley as "hot" to me on my first visit to Nigeria. The dinner, served by two of Nike's students, was delicious, which for me meant not too spicy.

But that night I found it hard to fall asleep. What kept me awake was not just jet lag or worrying about the upcoming meeting but the shouting that came from a speaker system set up at one of the tiny, evangelical churches that are scattered everywhere in the town, often in a building with a tin roof but no walls. The voice coming through the static-inflected microphone was the pastor's, urging his flock to shout, wave their arms, jump up and down and even throw themselves on the uneven dirt floor. They are called "night vigils" because they start at one or two in the morning and end at dawn. There was competition among these many small churches, and Nike's students often pressed me to come to *their* church, the only one where the real Jesus was to be found.

When I woke up, still somewhat jet-lagged the next morning, I went with Foley to a nearby market to buy tea, lump sugar, and powdered milk for my breakfast. Then, at around noon, we walked in the undulating midday heat past the gallery to the work area where the meeting would be held. He took my hand as we stepped out of the sun and into a building that was open at the sides and roofed over with thatch in imitation of old-fashioned Nigerian houses. Inside, a dozen long tables were lined up in two rows on the cement floor. On a regular day, white cloth would be spread over each of these tables, ready for the wax, melted on a small kerosene stove at the end of the table that would be dribbled over it before it was immersed in boiling dye and turned into batik.

But that morning the tables were cleared and some forty students sat in rows behind them. Foley moved to the back and stood by himself, but I was pointed to a chair between Nike and the Commissioner, the three of us facing the students. This man's position of power was very much on display, since it was he, rather than Nike, the school's founder, who did all the talking.

"The reputation of our school depends on you when you travel," he began. "Kate is our good friend, and if you abuse that friendship, you will be expelled from the school."

He turned to me as he spoke, without smiling, and I did not smile either. In fact, I have never seen him smile, this in a country where it seemed to me that people smiled much more than they did where I came from. "She will report to Nike and me," he continued, "the name of anyone who imposes on her." This threat was not lost on me, because it was delivered in English. The commissioner's native tongue was Igbo, one of the three main tribal divisions in that fractious country, and he'd never learned enough Yoruba to communicate with the people over whom, as their commissioner of police, he had the power of life and death. The students applauded when he said what a good friend I was to everyone.

The meeting ended quite quickly, with no mention of the prickly subject of my invitations, and the students who worked at Nike's house brought bean cakes for all. I felt warmly welcomed back to this community as I milled around among the tables, but from what Foley told me, I sensed that the Commissioner, who was now Nike's husband, had taken charge of her school and turned it into something like his own private military dictatorship—a cover for his own drug business on the side, if Foley was right. He was asking them, as I mentioned earlier, to provide records to prove that they had not engaged in any criminal activity, records that were either expensive or did not exist. I was to be a spy who reported to him, and I moved as far away from him as possible. Foley beckoned, so I joined him as soon as I could.

"You see," he said as we headed home under the hot sun, "how wicked that man is."

"I don't think he has grasped the fact that I'm not writing invitations for people I don't know," I said. "He's someone who likes to control everything. Being a police commissioner is the perfect job for someone like that."

"He is a bad commissioner," Foley said. "People say he's friends of Abacha." Sani Abacha was Nigeria's president then and the most corrupt leader in its thirty-some years of independence. The Commissioner could not have held the position he did if he was not part of that man's entourage. My vision of a future with Foley and his family and community had always included, not only friendship with Nike, but a second home in Nigeria. But the presence of this controlling man in her life began to make my vision of mutual confidences less likely. As for the students, would they still be my friends if they saw me as his spy?

"Let's go to the gallery," I said as Emmanuel came up to join us. "I left all our wedding presents there with Mr. Ben for safekeeping."

Mr. Ben lived in the back of the gallery and kept watch over the carvings and batik clothing on display there. I hadn't left many items: a carved bowl from the pastor of the church behind Nike's house, a set of mugs for my tea, a few African outfits that I knew I would only wear in Africa, and a beautiful *adire* quilt I had bought from one of the male students, a symbol and a stand-in for my new African home.

"I'm sorry," said Mr. Ben, "but everything has been stolen." I stared at this gray-haired man in disbelief. In the past, I had sensed that he did not like me, but I could not have imagined him acting against me. I knew he was probably lying, but I couldn't get words out of my mouth.

"He sold them," Emmanuel said. "He works for the Commissioner and Nike, you know."

"This is Nigeria," Nike said when I told her, the next day, about the supposed theft. It's a phrase that people invariably used when something happened that didn't make sense to me. "Buy a metal trunk," Nike said when I spoke to her later, "and lock your things in it." I did this, and when I had packed it, a young woman friend of Foley's and mine picked up the trunk, balanced it on her head and carried it from my room to hers, about a mile away. Then bending over, she set it at the foot of her bed and promised to take good care of it.

I don't know how the Commissioner found out about our plan to adopt Gbenga, but we came up against his opposition to it just before I left. It reached us in the form of a command for the four of us—five, if you count Gbenga on Sade's back—to return to the place where Foley and I had our first one-on-one conversation on the back porch, surrounded by hairy brown yams and woven baskets. As we squeezed into a taxi, our borrowed vehicle having developed a rattle that needed the attention of a mechanic, I had no idea why he and Nike would want to see all of us.

We were ushered into a small study, with a long couch and two easy chairs facing one another, by a young woman student who asked if we would like a "minerals," the word for a soda in that part of Nigeria. My companions were unwilling to accept this gesture of supposed hospitality, but I asked if she had a bitter lemon. Most of the small roadside stands near us carried only Coke and Fanta, but Nike knew the tastes of her Anglophile visitors like me, and a bitter lemon soon appeared.

Sade, Emmanuel, and I occupied the couch, leaving two large chairs for Nike and the Commissioner. Foley stood by the door, as if to let me know that however things turned out would be fine with him. We waited, more or less in silence, for about five minutes. Then Nike and her husband swept in and sat down facing us, both wearing the traditional African tunic, heavily embroidered around the neck, that men wear knee-length with matching pants and women wear in an ankle-length version. Nike had gained international recognition by raising batik design to the level of an art form, and she wore her art on her body as well as displaying it in museums.

Once again, the Commissioner did all the talking. Nike, who

seemed to do all the smiling for both of them, kept her gaze on her husband.

"This meeting is mainly for your benefit, Kate," he began. "As I have told you many times, we have always been your friends and want to remain your friends. But there are some things that this young man has said to us that we feel you should know about." I looked at Emmanuel, toward whom he was gesturing, and then at Nike. Neither of them met my eye.

"First of all, you need to know," he went on, "that adoption is illegal by Nigerian law." He pronounced the words "Nigerian law" with a gravity that seemed aimed at reminding me that he, as a police commissioner, had at his command a small army.

"I know about Nigerian law," I said sharply. "I'd have to show that I've been caring for Gbenga for two years while a search is done for his parents." Nike's lawyer in Lagos, a woman who handled her divorce from her second husband, had laid this out for me when I saw her on my way home after Gbenga's naming ceremony, reinforcing what Nike had said about orphans not being adopted because the extended family always takes care of them. "But the law we need to conform to is American law. Gbenga needs to be in the States legally."

"Nevertheless, it is against the law we have here," the Commissioner said sternly. "And Nike and I are unwilling to have our good name and reputation associated with an action that is against our laws." He looked at Nike as he spoke, and then back at me. "But this is not the main reason for inviting you here," he went on. "We have spoken to Emmanuel and told him that signing a document in America will mean giving up his rights as the father of his child, and he has told us in no uncertain terms that he is not willing to do that."

I took a deep breath at this point but said nothing. "My American son," Emmanuel had said in my kitchen in New York before he ever knew the sex of his child, with an emphasis on the word "my." And as far as I was concerned, Gbenga would always be his. I was simply transferring Gbenga from one part of his family to another. I had envisioned Emmanuel unproblematically involved in Gbenga's growing up, both in the States and in Nigeria.

As for Sade, I wanted her to see her son as often as we could arrange it. I'd read about open adoptions and wanted to work out a version in which everyone would be part of this very extended family. At a minimum, one of us could bring her to the States for special events in Gbenga's life. And of course he and I would spend summers and winter holidays in Nigeria. If he later decided that he wanted to stay there, I would not stop him. But to get the education Emmanuel was so keen on for his son, Gbenga would have to be legally Foley's and mine. Of course parenting is also a matter of who's around. If Foley lost interest in raising a child in whose small body his father's spirit had been reincarnated, I would be the consistent parent. If Gbenga, like me, ended up living a life in two places at once, why would he not enjoy that?

The Commissioner then turned to Sade and asked her if she would be willing to bring Gbenga to the States and leave him there. She shook her head, and I jumped up as if I had been shot. "Then it's all off," I said, keeping my voice as steady as I could. "This adoption will not happen." Nike also stood up, but her husband told her to sit down. "I'm doing this for you," he snapped. "To protect you and the reputation of your school from all these ugly rumors."

"What rumors?" I wanted to know.

"Many people are telling me that Emmanuel is twisting Sade's arm," he said. "They say he is selling his child. I don't want Nike's name and picture in all the papers, and it's just the kind of thing our newspapers love to print. I refuse to let anything happen that will damage her reputation."

Did Nike believe any of what her husband was saying? It had been her idea, after all, that I should adopt Funmi. How could she have been so intent on my taking that little girl then and turn around and be so against me now? Nigerian law had surely been in effect then, too.

I looked at Foley but he was looking down, as he usually did in the Commissioner's presence.

"All this young man wants," the Commissioner went on, "is a

free ticket from you. When he gets to the States, he'll say he's so sorry but he just couldn't get a visa for Sade and Gbenga."

"We need to talk now," I said. "But first I want to use the bathroom." I closed the door to the small bathroom next to the office and, quite unexpectedly, began to sob loudly. Once I started I couldn't stop, and after a few minutes the Commissioner opened the door as I sat on the toilet seat with my head hung over my knees and told me I should please calm down  He showed no embarrassment at having invaded my privacy.

When I came out of the bathroom, still crying, Nike came over and hugged me, and so did her husband. "We're just trying to help you," he said. "We don't want people robbing you. You don't know how this culture works, but I am an expert." I pulled away from them and walked into the adjoining parlor, my entire body shaking. Then, hearing silence in the room behind me, I turned and went back. "You're a *liar*, Emmanuel!" I screamed. "You tell me one thing, then you turn around and say the opposite to this man. Did you actually tell him what he just said?"

No one said a word, which only added to my anger. "Okay, let's just get out of here. Is one of your vans free, Nike, to drive the five of us back into town?"

"I'm sorry, they are all out doing errands," she said, making it clear whose side she was on. So I led our group out onto the porch, across the courtyard, and past the guard at the gate. I walked ahead by myself until Foley came up beside me. "I will talk to Sade when we get back," he said. "I think she was frightened by the Commissioner."

"Who wouldn't be?" I answered. "He's a terrifying man."

Just then a cab slowed up, but since it was almost full, as most of them are, we could not all fit. "Let Sade and Gbenga take it," I said, and the two of them squeezed into its back seat as I handed her twenty *naira*. As the cab pulled away, Emmanuel came up and walked next to Foley. "So what's with *you?*" I spat at him, my anger still surging inside me.

"Kate, he said that Gbenga would no longer be my son if I gave him to you in the States."

"But that's bullshit," I said. "How can Gbenga not be your son? He will always be your son. I don't understand why this man is so against what we are doing."

"He's a bad man," said Emmanuel. "He wants to hurt me, and Foley, too. And you."

I wanted to ask why again, but I knew I would get the same answer Foley always gave me. The Commissioner was a bad man. Crazy. Perhaps *dangerous* would be a better word.

"It annoys me," I said as we approached the gallery, "that he keeps saying what good friends of mine he and Nike are."

"Don't bother with that," said Foley, shaking his head. "They are foolish people."

It was a long trek in the hottest part of the day in one of the hottest parts of the world. But after my unexpected flood of tears, I felt amazingly calm. Whatever was meant to be would be. At the same time, I was convinced that Gbenga was meant to grow up in the States. Above all, in whatever battles lay ahead, I did not want Commissioner to win.

When we reached our rented home, I fell asleep for two hours. When I woke up, still feeling calm, I went in search of Foley and found him sitting on the porch in front of Nike's gallery. "Sade is okay," he told me. "She did not understand what the Commissioner said." And why would she, since the Commissioner had spoken in English? "She is saying that she wants to go back to school eventually. But she wants to wait till Gbenga is older, maybe a year."

"But the longer she waits, the harder it will be, no? For her as well as for Gbenga."

"I don't know. Why don't you go and see her?"

"But we can't talk. You need to come, too. In fact, maybe all three of us had better go," I said as Emmanuel came, toward us. "We could take some pictures of all of us." Back in the States I'd bought a camera, mainly to take pictures of Gbenga. I kept it, along with sunglasses and sun screen, my wallet and a book, in a batik tote bag that I always carried with me.

Emmanuel shook his head. "I'm very angry at that woman," he said. "People are saying bad things about me and she believes them. What kind of behavior is that for a *iyawo?*"

"What sorts of bad things?"

"Like I'm going to sell my son."

"...Who's saying that besides the Commissioner?"

"Her friends. Maybe her family. But I think it's that wicked man who started it. He wants to make trouble for us."

"He says he wants to protect Nike," Foley said, "but he's a police commissioner. I hear that he's going to be sent somewhere else. He has done bad things here."

"What sorts of things?"

"You name it," said Emmanuel, who'd had more schooling and was more fluent than Foley in English. "As an army man, he can do whatever he wants."

When we got to Emmanuel's room, with its pale green walls and boxes piled high against them, Sade was sitting on the bed next to a sleeping Gbenga. I sat down next to her. "I'm very disappointed in her," Emmanuel said as soon as he walked in the door. He began shouting at Sade in Yoruba, a language that sounds aggressive to my Canadian ears even when no one is angry. Sade said nothing, but this only made Emmanuel shout louder until Sade grabbed my arm and pleaded, "Please, Kate." Perhaps it was this fear-filled gesture that sealed my belief in a connection between us, one that would survive no matter what.

"Look, Emmanuel," I said firmly, "it's not easy when your friends say bad things to you about your *oko*. People say things about Foley to me all the time. Like he has another wife— things like that. Maybe you want to believe they're lying, but it's easy to think they know something you don't. Especially when it involves a language you don't know," I added, looking at Sade. "So lay off, okay? We're all doing our best."

Emmanuel sat down, and even mumbled an apology, to whom I don't know. Sade let go of my arm and thanked me.

"I'll always defend you, Sade," I said, "because without you there'd be no Gbenga." I turned toward the baby just then and tickled his stomach. He gave a giggle of pleasure, lying on his back. We laughed too, and the energy in the room lifted.

A few days later, Emmanuel told me that Sade's family wanted her to stay in the States for six months. "What will she do there other than look after Gbenga?" I asked Foley. "She doesn't speak enough English."

"It's what her family wants," was all he could say, and I wondered what Sade wanted. Clearly Emmanuel wanted to spend as much time as he could in the States. So for her, being in New York meant being part of that American side of his life. "E-man," as he's called, has a wonderful sense of style that Foley utterly lacks. He often wears a white dress shirt and wide jeans that ride low on the hips, and walks with an American swagger. "Whassup?" he likes to say. But did he want *his* son, this boy whose ancestry went back many generations, raised in the States by his brother and not by him? From time to time he told me he did, and if that was really true, I sensed that Sade might get behind the adoption plan out of a desire to spend time with a sweetheart who clearly wanted a life in America. But how would this work at a practical level? They couldn't all live with me permanently.

Despite these misgivings, I moved on to the next obstacle, paying for passports and visas for her and her son. This was complicated, because each person has to demonstrate a compelling reason to come back to Nigeria: a profession, a business, and above all a family at home. Foley had needed such a "family" when he first came to visit me.

To get a passport for Sade, we needed to provide the U.S. Embassy with evidence of a husband and a few children who would not be traveling with her. "How can we do this?" I asked Emmanuel. "Do we need birth certificates for them?"

"Lots of people don't have birth certificates. What we need is pictures."

I couldn't believe that this would be enough, but I asked, "How will we get them?"

"No problem," Emmanuel said, and sure enough, he found a

male friend with two young children, both older than Gbenga, all three of whom were induced to smile for the camera.

As for me, I was not entirely over my anger at Emmanuel. But I was not willing to go as far as to take the side of the Commissioner. To entertain the thought that this man was my friend and was sincerely trying to help me would set me, not only against Emmanuel, but against Foley as well. I saw him only once after our meeting at Nike's house, and when he again delivered his "inside information" that Sade had absolutely no intention of relinquishing her child to me, I assured him that I was grateful for his concern. But I was never going to agree with what he said about anything. If he found out what we were up to, he could probably have put them all in jail. But even without such extreme evidence of his power, we knew we had to be careful.

# 6

I felt a rush of solidarity, as I always do when I stand behind a barrier in the International Arrivals building at Kennedy Airport in the company of my fellow New Yorkers who have gathered with me to meet passengers arriving from various parts of West Africa. We are all holding woolen hats and gloves, scarves, and one or more winter coats for our friends and relatives who will soon come through the swinging plastic door,s pushing carts piled high with suitcases but wearing only the bright cotton fabric that serves them fine back at home.

That icy day in February I was carrying a new turquoise snowsuit for Gbenga, a winter coat of my own for Sade, and a down jacket for Emmanuel borrowed from one of my male roommates. As the three of them came through the automatic doors that separate the baggage claim from the waiting area, I was almost overcome with excitement to see Gbenga tied to Sade's back. The three of them had made it over so many hurdles since I left them six weeks before, and Sade had gone along with the complicated moves. Surely the hardest part of the struggle was behind us now.

"How was your trip?" I asked as I hugged everyone gleefully. "How did Gbenga like being on a plane?"

"A lot better than his mother did," said Emmanuel. "He slept most of the way, but Sade was really scared."

Fear of flying. I had never really felt it. I was the name of the Erica Jong novel I'd taught in my courses on women writers when I first went out to Rutgers. Women Writers was a subject I'd had to learn from scratch, since Virginia Woolf was the only woman admitted onto the syllabi of my English courses at Columbia. "Well, nothing to be scared about now," I said as we held each other. "You're here!" Sade untied Gbenga, almost seven months old, and we put him in his snowsuit. "It's just the right size," I said. "And doesn't he look great in it?"

"American boy!" said Emmanuel, tossing him into the air. But when I looked over at Sade, I could see that this expression, which I had heard him use several times, was Emmanuel's vision of Gbenga's future but not hers. Back in Nigeria I'd asked Foley to explain what his brother meant by that phrase. It came down, as relations between my country and his always seemed to do, to a matter of money. A son who had an American education would have access to resources that went beyond anything that Emmanuel and his brothers could bring to their families in Nigeria. So that was the lens through which he saw his son's American future. But having raised a son myself, I doubted that Sade was with Emmanuel on this. Nevertheless, she had brought him across the ocean. Why would she do that if she had no intention of going along with what her sweetheart wanted? In fact, I was so totally caught up in the miracle of their arrival that I did not take in the implications of this conflict playing out before my eyes. I was also concerned with the absence of my husband, the future father of the family that I was imagining, and whose smiling presence I needed to make the image real.

The four of us piled into a cab and sped toward the city. Sade huddled nervously against Emmanuel, who put his arm around her shoulders while I held Gbenga on my lap. Wrapped in my fur-collared suede coat, she looked frail, though I'm sure she was glad to feel a connection to the ground.

When the New York skyline came into view behind a jagged cemetery on our left, I turned Gbenga toward it. "Look," I whispered in his ear. "There's your new home over there."

When we reached the lobby of my building I pressed the button that summoned the wood-paneled elevator and, as we rose up six flights, I saw Sade's eyes widen with the same fear she must have felt on the plane. Gbenga was securely tied on her back by then, and she shut her eyes as Emmanuel and I held the two of them between us. She would react in the same way to the escalator in Penn Station when I took her and Gbenga to Rutgers to see what I did there. America did not seem like a place where she would feel at ease, despite the constant talk I always heard in Nigeria about what a great place America was. The image I picked up there was of a country where money flowed like water from a tap.

When we got to my floor, I ushered my guests inside with a flourish and showed them where they would be sleeping: a small room whose glass door could be closed and curtained to make a reasonably private space. I'd put a poster from *The Lion King* on one wall and covered the fold-out couch with the quilt I'd bought for Funmi. I'd given her doll away, but I'd kept the stuffed animals and bought two more. There were Pampers also, and several toys that spoke or lit up or played tunes when you pushed the right buttons, gifts from my neighbors whose children had outgrown them. Everything in the room was part of my effort to let her and Emmanuel know that Gbenga would be loved and cared for here in this apartment, in this city, in this part of the world. I'm truly ashamed now about how blind I was to her feelings, how I walked in Emmanuel's shoes, supporting his wish for an "American boy" but not hers.

Since lots of children lived in my building, I was able to borrow toys, some baby clothes, and a metal-and-canvas rocking seat. I also procured the loan of a canvas baby carrier on a metal frame. Nancy, the carrier's owner, also offered the number of her pediatrician. The head of our co-op board produced the business card of an immigration lawyer who dealt in foreign adoptions.

On every floor my neighbors were welcoming when I mentioned Gbenga's imminent arrival. My building had six- and eight-room apartments, so unlike apartments closer to midtown, or perhaps farther away from Harlem; we had plenty of children in the building. I'd lived with these people for years, but now I was seeing a side of them I'd not seen before. Or perhaps I'd simply never called it forth since my life in it did not include children and nannies pushing strollers.

Early the next morning I was off to teach my two classes at Rutgers. My students and friends there were filled with good will for a happy outcome to this new phase in my life. I had mentioned to Wilma, one of the department's secretaries, that my father and Foley's father had both died in 1995 and had the same first name, George. I'd told her about the Yoruba belief that a family member is reincarnated in the first baby born after that person's death. "And I can use some of the money my father left me to raise him."

"It sounds like those two Georges got behind this to make it happen," Wilma commented. I enjoyed talking to her more than to any of my department colleagues, since I knew, from my own experience as a graduate student with a baby, that the demands of academic life and those of motherhood do not easily fit together.

"Wherever they are," I said to her, "I hope they're both very pleased."

Foley arrived a week later, and the effortless cheer he always conveyed to me reinforced my belief that something good was in the process of happening. I had never actually asked him straight out how he felt about adopting his brother's child and becoming a father to Gbenga, but I saw how much he enjoyed throwing his future son in the air, and how Gbenga crowed with delight whenever his prospective father, as I now began to see him, came over to pick his son up. "I want this for you," I had said to him in Nigeria.

He had always answered, "It's for my family." I understood him to mean that, as an "American boy," Gbenga would join his father and uncle as a future source of needed resources back home. In their eyes, and in the eyes of everyone I was getting to know in Nigeria, my country had everything that was lacking in theirs. What I was doing in adopting one of theirs simply fell in line with that belief.

At first, Gbenga was wary of the talking, blinking toys I had borrowed, since they were obviously unfamiliar and perhaps a bit frightening. He would learn to crawl, though, up and down the long hallway that runs the full length of the apartment. Nigerian children are carried on a mother's back pretty much until they can walk, and some people say that children who enjoy such prolonged close contact with their mother's body are better adjusted because of this initial security. But crawling is said to help with coordination and even language acquisition. Gbenga certainly took to it, especially if one of us rolled a ball in front of him. Emmanuel and Foley resumed applying their carving skills to the furniture of their former employer in Philadelphia. With the two men gone during the week, Sade and I were alone with Gbenga, and I had to leave the two of them when I went to Rutgers.

Into this unpredictable space came Jemilat, the second wife of the carver who was Abike's first husband and Foley' cousin. She must have come to the States with him, leaving all the children he had taken from Abike, along with the one they'd had together, in the care of relatives back home. Foley's male friends also left family behind when they came here with the single goal of providing support for those families, and they were gone for as long as their visa would allow, perhaps as much as a year. It was a simple fact that everyone I knew in Nigeria saw my country as a land flowing with money from every tap, the diametric opposite of their own. Years of history lay behind this belief, and I was beginning to see that it literally enveloped everything I did there.

I did not really like Jemilat, and she made no effort to connect with me either. I also wondered what she was doing to make money in the States. Nevertheless, I couldn't really object to her hanging out in my living room. And talking to Sade in a language I could not understand or speak. After all, Sade needed some companionship.

Since I could not persuade either of them to go outside into temperatures they had never felt at home, I took Gbenga with me in my neighbor's carrier when I went shopping. Feeling him against my back brought back happy memories of my first marriage, when I had done the same with my son thirty years before. Gbenga soon became a something of a celebrity, not only in my lobby and elevator, but at the cleaner's, the hardware store, and especially in the supermarket where we went every few days. The cashiers there referred to him as my grandson, and I remained Gbenga's grandma in their eyes even when he wasn't with me. Most of them were African-American, and some of them probably had children being looked after by *their* mothers. But they were not crossing a racial divide, and I did not think far enough ahead to imagine parent-teacher conferences, or play dates when Gbenga got older. I certainly did not think of him as a teenager, which I now know to be a dangerous time for an African-American boy. My Toronto sister's life with her granddaughter was filled with these demanding events, but race wasn't an issue for her either.

Though I was enjoying Sade's presence in my home, I was also beginning to make plans for her departure, having impressed her, or so I hoped, with the care and affection that would surround Gbenga as he grew up. I called Stella, a friend of Foley's who owned the store in Brooklyn where he bought powdered yams, dried fish, and other staples of the diet he was used to at home. I'd met her only once, but I trusted her enough to ask her if she knew someone who would like a job doing child care for twelve hours two days a week, covering the time when I was teaching at Rutgers and taking my two classes at the New School. She gave me the phone number of Leah, who had come from Nigeria, Stella said, with two teen-age children of her own ten years earlier. Since most of the parents of small children in my building had African-American nannies, I saw Leah as part of a company of friendly fellow stroller-pushers. The fact that I was essentially raised by nannies and teachers must have provided an invisible setting for the future I was preparing to launch.

When she appeared my apartment, I brought her into the kitchen where Sade was feeding Gbenga from a jar of baby applesauce. "Here, why not let me do that," Leah said after greeting Sade in Yoruba, and Sade handed her the baby and the jar. But he must have picked up the tension that was swirling around the kitchen where we were sitting, because he squirmed and refused to eat until Sade finally took him and gave him her breast.

It concerned me that she was still breast-feeding, since I'd hoped that she would wean her seven-month-old so she could leave him with me. But I didn't actually say anything to her about it. I had nursed my son for a year, and I knew that separating a nursing mother from her baby would involve tears on both sides. But it began to dawn on me that she had no intention of handing her son over to me, in defiance not only of me but of Emmanuel as well.

"Don't believe what she says to you," Leah told me as I walked her toward the elevator an hour later, after showing her around my apartment and giving her a brief history of my marriage "She is not going to let you keep that baby. I understand Nigeria better than you do."

*I'm sure you do*, I thought, not at all sarcastically, as I summoned the elevator. When its door opened, I managed to say, "I'll call you and let you know what happens."

I know she meant it as a friendly warning, but her clear pronouncement, coming from a Nigerian woman who had raised children herself, sent me into my bedroom holding a hot cup of tea, feeling totally drained of energy yet unable to blot out with sleep the thought that, no matter what I did, this was not going to work. Being *both* the household provider who paid the bills *and* the mother who shopped and cleaned, I began to see the appeal of the traditional division of labor, not just for men, who got to be out in the world, but for women confined to the home. I very much enjoyed spending two evenings a week out of the house in the company of my fellow writers, many of whom had made major alterations in their lives to become students at the New School.

When Foley and Emmanuel returned on the weekends from

Philadelphia, home became a lot more cheerful. Their Nigerian friends who had found living arrangements in Brooklyn came by to visit, and Foley helped me with meal preparation and dishwashing, just as he had done the first time he came to New York. I never asked him directly how he felt about becoming Gbenga's legal father. I just assumed that we were on the same page, probably because he acted the part so well. But my two American housemates insisted that I was being taken for a ride financially. "What can I do?" I asked them. "If this is going to be Gbenga's new home, I want Emmanuel and his friends to feel comfortable here." In fact my roommates were as charmed by Gbenga as everyone else who saw him, throwing him up in the air the way his father did and holding his hands when he took his first guided steps down our hallway.

After Gbenga and his mother had been in New York for about three weeks, the two of us took our snow-suited charge ten blocks down Broadway to my neighbor Nancy's pediatrician to check on the status of his shots and to set up what I hoped would be an ongoing relationship. Dr. Nesselson and his nurse seemed supportive of the transfer of Gbenga to me, assuming, from our presence together, that it was voluntary on both our parts. It did make the office paperwork complicated, since the names of "mother," "patient," and "person paying the bills" were not the same. But I could tell that Sade was impressed with Dr. Nesselson's gentle manner, not just toward Gbenga but toward the two of us as well. Gbenga should eat only baby food from a health food store, he said, which would help with Gbenga's diaper rash as well. If I had no other reason to adopt Gbenga, I would have wanted to do it so that I could take him regularly to this wonderful doctor's office.

But the good feelings that united Sade and me on our walk home from this office were not the ones I began to notice as the weeks wore on. I knew that she was aware of Emmanuel's wishes on the subject, and that pleasing him on this front went against her natural desire to stay connected with the child that had emerged from her body. But I didn't know how to sound her out on this subject, and that made me tense in her presence.

One afternoon when I was feeling particularly restless, I put Gbenga in his snowsuit and baby carrier and we took the subway to the Barnes and Noble bookstore twenty blocks downtown. Once inside the store, I went up the escalator, and I put a fresh Pamper on him on the changing table in the ladies room. Then I put him on the floor in the children's section, where another boy was taking tentative steps, his two hands held by his smiling mother. Gbenga and I were now doing this in my hallway, though leaning over for any length of time hurt my back. "Your grandson?" she asked as Gbenga crawled toward her child.

"Yeah." I had become accustomed to this fiction in the supermarket, and it seemed easier to go along with it than to explain the age difference between Foley and me to this stranger half my age. "We just want to get out of the house for a break. This is a great place to do that."

"I know the feeling," the woman said. "I really like it here, and so does my son." We exchanged names and the names of our children, with me spelling Gbenga's name and telling her that I had adopted him from Africa. Then, as she turned back to her child, I began looking for some of the books I'd collected for Kevin. I found *The Runaway Bunny* and *Where the Wild Things Are*, both stories about rebellious children finally enveloped by the power of parental love. But preparing for Gbenga's arrival had not involved collecting my favorite children's books. We all watched *Sesame Street* and some other cartoons in a language Sade did not understand. But at least she watched TV in Nigeria, whereas books were too far out of her daily routine and too central to the part of mine from which she was excluded.

As we sat on the carpeted floor surrounded by shelf after shelf of tales from my childhood and Kevin's, along with many newer additions, Gbenga crawled across the carpeted floor toward the other boy. I noticed that he seemed to have no fear of strangers and was a very social child in general. I let him do what he did with such ease until the other mother apologized for having to get home before her husband did, which sent a flash of envy through my mind, given my inherited belief that married women are always happier than their single sisters. Once we were alone, I found puppet versions of several of the Sesame Street characters that he had been watching at home, laid out on a display table with other icons of an American childhood: Babar, Winnie, Kermit, and Dora the Explorer. But what Gbenga really wanted was to be carried, which I took as a signal to go home. So I zipped him back in his snowsuit, lowered him into his carrier, and heaved it over my shoulders.

Outside in the cold air, a truck honked loudly, and like babies all over the world, Gbenga let out a wail on which my soothing words had no effect. I walked for three blocks until I saw a slatted wood-and-wrought-iron bench outside an ice cream store and sat down in a patch of sun. A woman who was already sitting there asked what the matter was, and I told her I didn't know. I had a bottle of juice with me, but Gbenga shook his head when I passed it over my shoulder, and I assured the woman that he wasn't wet. *He knows what's going to happen*, I said to myself. *He misses his mother.* "There, there, Gbenga," I said as I held his snow-suited body against my chest. "It's going to be okay," I added, though I felt less than certain in that moment that I was telling him the truth.

We sat there until he cried himself to sleep, and I handed him to Sade with a sinking feeling about the future I had imagined.

Lying next to Foley in bed that night, I couldn't help wondering if anyone but me was committed to this adoption. "It's fine with me," he would say when I brought the subject up. "Whatever you want is fine." I noticed that he played with Gbenga more than his brother did. But he also complained about what he saw as my infatuation with our future child. "It's all about Gbenga, Gbenga, Gbenga. Not about me."

Perhaps I should have taken his response as a warning about the future, but I didn't.

"But you're the reason I'm adopting Gbenga," I remember saying to him more than once. "I want you to have a family here in the States. I want to be a good wife to you and a good mother to your brother's son."

"I know you try hard," Foley said. But I wasn't sure what he was referring to. Trying in my vocabulary didn't necessarily imply success. And in truth there was more to my wish to step into the maternal role again as a woman beyond the biological age of bearing children. Being a mother to my baby son and a wife to my graduate school husband was a time in my life that is filled with happy memories.

Then on March 28, 1997, three weeks after Foley arrived, Emmanuel came with us to City Hall to be the best man at the legal, civil wedding needed for Foley to get a green card. "Nigerian men don't wear rings," Foley said when I offered to buy him one to match my new silver band. I always admire men who wear wedding rings, a public announcement that they are "taken." So I was disappointed by Foley's response, but not enough to question the move we were about to make. We three lined up around the block with other engaged couples, who were there that day in larger numbers than usual—I was told by one of them, out of a fear of being deported if they didn't meet some new, impending deadline.

Finally, just as my knees were starting to rebel from standing for so long, we were summoned to hear a magistrate say the words that made us a legal couple in the eyes of the city, state, and country. Emmanuel had brought along my camera, and when he asked the judge if he would pose for a picture with the two of us, the judge said, "Okay, but make it quick. You saw how long the line is out there." He then made it quick, and our legal status changed in the blink of an eye.

A week after our City Hall wedding, I opened my phone bill and discovered that it came to close to five hundred dollars. Sade had made calls to Emmanuel in Philadelphia, Foley told me when I showed him the bill. But most of the calls were to Nigeria. I suspected that Sade's friend Jemilat was behind many of these, though Foley insisted that they were made by his friends who dropped by on weekends, and he promised to put a stop to it. "Don't you realize that I have to pay this bill or our phone service will be cut off?" I said to him later, when we were alone.

"I'm sorry," he said. You always say that, I thought, but I didn't say it. He would say it when I sneezed or coughed in bed, a response that puzzled me. Meanwhile I had learned about a system in which a person dialing long distance must punch in a code first. I had to tell Foley I was putting this in place, and that I would not let him know the code. I suspect that he did not like having to explain this to his friends, but he did not say anything to me about it and I was too angry at all of them to worry about anyone's feelings but my own. They saw me, not as a generous person, but as a target to rip off.

After this I decided, on the advice of an old boyfriend who's now a lawyer, that I needed some form of financial protection in writing. A legal pre-nuptial agreement requires full financial disclosure from both parties, which I was unwilling to do, since I didn't want Foley to know about the money I had inherited from my parents, or the value of the apartment I had bought with money from a childless aunt who had died five years earlier. I had, not only my Rutgers salary, but money from my parents that Sara, my tax accountant, managed. "Do whatever you would do if the money was yours," I always told her, and I didn't keep track of what that was. But I knew that it would sound like a huge amount to Foley, and even more so to his family. It would certainly validate their view of me as a "rich American" who could be freely hit on, and I did not intend to agree to the fifty-fifty split that was part of the law in New York. So I made up a neutral-sounding document that we both signed in front of a notary: *We the undersigned hereby agree that, in the event of the termination of our marriage by death or divorce, neither of us will make claims on the assets or property of the other.* When I asked Wilma about it at school the next day, she told me she would have done the same.

But Foley must have said something less approving about it to his friend Dayo, who was sitting with him in the living room, and planning to sleep there, when I arrived home from Rutgers, because he asked me why I felt the need for such a document. "I don't believe Foley married me for my money," I said, sitting down with both of them at my kitchen table. "But I sometimes think people from your country see me as this rich woman, their pot of gold at the end of the rainbow, and I want to draw some boundaries." I'm not sure that either of them understood what I meant by drawing boundaries, and the chill did not leave the room, though perhaps I was the only one who felt it.

If I thought that being legally married would make the adoption process run more smoothly, I could not have been more mistaken. Emmanuel liked to refer to his son as an American boy, but he worried about the signing of papers required by American law that would mean that Gbenga was no longer legally his. "I am not going to sell my son," he said firmly, still using the singular pronoun, one night after Sade had gone to bed and the three of us were sitting at the kitchen table. "I don't want to lose Sade and my son, too."

"But selling involves me giving you money in exchange for your child, and I'm not doing that," I insisted. "You know that, Emmanuel. I thought you wanted this adoption."

"I do," he said. "You know that. But people will think you give me money."

"How do you know?"

"I just know."

"Well, I don't know what to say about that. I've been told that there's a law in this country against paying the parent of a child you adopt, and I wouldn't do that. If you change your mind about me adopting Gbenga, just tell me. But if he's going to get the education you want him to have, he can't live here illegally. You know that, right?" Emmanuel nodded in silence. "And since you want to spend a lot of your time in the States, you'll probably see him more if he's here than you would if he stayed in Nigeria. You know you'll always be welcome in my house. And Sade, too." I reached across the table and squeezed his hand as I said this, and he squeezed mine. He really was conflicted about having an "American boy." Education in Nigeria does not open the door to prosperity, since there is no real middle class there. A few are spectacularly rich, but everyone else lives on about two dollars a day. Then, as Nike had explained to me, Nigerian children are often moved among members of their extended family. But legal documents are never necessary in such arrangements.

Then too, if you come from what is called the "first world," adopting a child from an impoverished country is not necessarily seen in a favorable light, since it carries with it the implicit statement: *My country is better than your country.* The history of racism makes that statement more unacceptable in Africa than in Asia, for instance, since it brings up the highly charged historical issue of the slave trade and its consequences. A comment of Felicia's on my first visit to Nigeria still sticks in my head. "I sometimes wonder if the ancestors of any of these people were the ones who put my ancestors on one of those ships."

And what were my ancestors doing back then? Were any of them involved, however indirectly, in the slave trade? Everyone benefited from it, even if they didn't own slaves. Was this what drew me to Nigeria, to rectify whatever it might be? All of Foley's family members, including Emmanuel, insisted that I was part of their family. But though Emmanuel really did want Gbenga to grow up here in New York, reservations shaped by long-held cultural beliefs held the decisive weight, along with the power of maternal attachment that I had certainly known first hand.

In the midst of this swirl of confusing messages, the loudest voice warning me that I was a making a big mistake was Marcia's. She was my first African-American friend, the one I met when we were students at the Martha Graham studio in the East Sixties, in a lovely brick building with a garden in the back that has since been demolished and replaced by a luxury apartment building. She left the dance world before I did and enrolled in a graduate program at City College two years before I signed up at the Columbia School of General Studies and went from there into its graduate program, where I met my first husband. She got a job at one of the city's community colleges, Medgar Evers in Brooklyn, and was very active in her union. It was the perfect place for her to pursue her two passions, intellectual work and political activism.

Back when we were both dance students in the early Sixties, I invited her to come with me to have dinner with my parents at the

Plaza. When the two of us entered their room, I don't recall their reaction to her as anything beyond a warm "Nice to meet you." Then I heard my father talking on the hotel phone. Room service was apparently on the other end of the line, and not long after that a large table with place settings and linen napkins for four was wheeled into the room where there were sofas and chairs. No one said anything about why this was happening, though Marcia told me afterwards that she knew she would not be allowed in the Plaza's dining rooms, so my parents obviously knew that, too. In any event, we all pulled up chairs and ate as if nothing unusual had occurred. I probably saw my parents the next day, and I'm sure they told me what a nice friend I had. But neither Marcia nor I spoke about it either. I'm not even sure what we would have said. Marcia is light skinned, and back then my awareness about race was close to non-existent. Dr. King's March on Washington had not yet happened, and when it did, Marcia went and I did not.

"I came to New York to get away from politics," I told her, by which I meant getting away from my father, who sometimes made us girls campaign with him door-to-door. Every year we posed, the perfect happy family I knew we were not, for a Christmas card that he sent to his constituents. I didn't have a TV until I got married in 1965, so back then I only heard about the sit-ins, the fire hoses, the police dogs, the murders of Goodman, Schwerner, and Chaney. But I never saw a *Whites Only* sign, so the civil rights struggle was happening in a part of the world that felt as far away as the Canadian world I had fled.

Looking back, what amazes me about this is that my parents, who were regular guests at the Plaza, must have known more about the status of segregation there than I did and did not want to subject my friend to the humiliation of the Plaza's exercise of it. I have since learned that New York State passed a law in the Fifties forbidding racial discrimination and set up a commission to which customers could report. But these regulations in the city, and in the North generally, were not really visible. Marcia and I rode the subway together, but our getting together didn't involve eating in restaurants. I'm sure I didn't look around, when I saw my parents at the Plaza, to see if there were any black people in the lobby or elevators, though I did learn about the hotel's then-conservative dress code when I went with them to the Oak Room several years later. I was wearing an elegant wool pants suit that my mother had just bought for me at Lord and Taylor as part of what she called "my trousseau," and we were turned away at the entrance. Of course that couldn't happen now, but I do remember my first pair of slacks with a zipper up the front, like men's pants, rather than up the side or the back.

Marcia gave up dance for academia a year before I was invited to join a small dance company. I should have been thrilled, and perhaps for a short time I was. But even though I'd finally achieved what I'd come to New York to do, becoming a real dancer rather than just a person who took classes, attaining this dream did not bring me the happiness I'd been hoping for. In fact, it threw me into such an acute depression that I asked the therapist I'd started seeing to find me a place where I could be taken care of while he was away. I think now that I couldn't allow myself to be happy out of a fear that my happiness would be yanked out from under me by forces I could not control or even understand. I had broken my mother's rule that connected happiness with marriage as the one goal allowed to women, a rule so deeply embedded in my psyche that I could not seem to get past it.

The hospital the therapist located for me had been founded in 1882 on fourteen acres as the Long Island Home for Nervous Invalids, but by the time I got there they were giving out both insulin and electroshock treatment left and right. Upon my release, I got back to my West Village apartment, and James Waring, the head of the dance company, took me back. But the sugar you take to bring you out of insulin shock added pounds that I had to take off quickly before showing up to start rehearsals. I don't know how I managed to do it, but I did.

"I could never have agreed to go to a place like that," Marcia told me the first time I saw her after that in a Jose Limon dance class.

"How come?" I asked as we changed into our street clothes.

"Once they had me," she said, "I'd be afraid they would never let me out."

"Really?" I said slowly, unable to relate to her fear. Why would they not let me out? I see now how naïve I was about this matter, as about so many others. Recently I went back to that place and got a copy of my records. My diagnosis of schizophrenia, and a prognosis of "guarded," came from a doctor who refused to believe that I was a dancer. How I got out, I don't really know. But it was that conversation that let me know, in a way that I've never forgotten, that Marcia's way of seeing things was rooted in the world of an inner-city America that I didn't even know about until I left home and moved to the States.

This difference showed up again when she came to my apartment and met Sade and Gbenga. "Why are you doing this, Kate?" she asked, sitting across from me at the oak table in my eat-in kitchen, a mug of tea in her hand. Sade and Gbenga had gone back to their room.

"Good question," I said. "And I can't give you a simple answer. But everyone in Nigeria talks about the opportunities here that children don't have in Nigeria. So I'd want Gbenga to go to a good school, for one thing."

"What sort of a school? A public school in the city?"

"I guess I haven't thought that far ahead. Emmanuel keeps talking about education. I'm sure he sees his son going to college, too. Gbenga could go to Rutgers for nothing as a child of a faculty member.

"...But what if that's not how it works out?"

"What do you mean?" I took my tea out of the microwave, poured a large amount of milk and honey into my mug, and sat back down across the table from her.

"Have you thought about how you would react if Gbenga doesn't take to school? I know Kevin did, and so did you. But what do you see yourself doing if he doesn't?"

"I guess I haven't really thought about it," I said.

"Well, let's think about it now. I'm like you. I loved school right from the start. But lots of kids hate it. Mainly boys, and particularly African-American boys who live in pretty risky environments. You know that from the kids you worked with in that youth at risk organization."

"Yeah, I know. Most of them can't study because there's no quiet place to do it where they live. So Gbenga won't have that issue to deal with. You know, school saved me, really," I added. "Especially when I went away to boarding school. My teachers there were interested in what I had to say. They told me I was smart. Not something my parents wanted for us girls. That's why I became a teacher."

Marcia nodded. "Okay. But look. Your folks stuck you with their expectations, and now it looks to me like you're doing the same thing when it comes to Gbenga. You're not thinking clearly, Kate, and that's going to give you big problems in the future. I know this isn't what you want to hear from me, and I'm not trying to hurt you. I'm trying to warn you, that's all. This could work out very badly for you and Gbenga both."

I got up and put the milk back in the fridge. Here was my oldest friend, the one who had always believed in me even when I didn't. "I feel like you're saying that I won't be a good enough mother to Gbenga."

Marcia set her mug of tea down on the table with a bang. "That's in *your* head, not mine. Of course you're a good mother. Kevin's a great kid, and that's really thanks to you. All I'm saying is that you have a lot more money than Sade does. So you need to look at all this with that in your mind, and ask yourself why you are doing this. Money is a form of power, you know. And white people have more of it than we folks do."

"I know that. But what good will looking at it that way do? She and I were born in different places. There's nothing I can do about that."

"I'm not *asking* you to do anything about the fact of racism and what it has produced. Just look at it, okay?"

"I *do* look at it. Just about everything in my life comes from having more money than other people. The fact that I went to Columbia, where I was so happy. I'm sure that helped me get my job at Rutgers, and I love being there."

"But it didn't help when it came to getting tenure, did it? You had to work for that. You're sounding like you think you don't deserve the good things you have. Like you feel guilty for having the privileges you've had, and you're somehow trying to compensate for them. That's how I see your whole involvement with Nigeria, if you want to know the truth."

"What makes you think I feel guilty?"

"The fact that you let people abuse you. You didn't get angry at these people who ran up huge bills on your phone." She came over and put her arm around my shoulder. "Come on. I'm just asking you to be careful. I don't want you getting ripped off even more with this adoption. You don't see the whole picture is all I'm saying."

"But Emmanuel wants his son to be an American boy, and I guess I want that, too."

"But what about Sade? Women have so little power where she comes from. And you're a feminist. That means taking the woman's side over the man's. Look—I'm talking like I have all the answers, and I sure as hell don't. So maybe you should get angry at me. But ask yourself why you're so committed to this adoption. Why are you doing it? It's not going to save your marriage, if that's what you are thinking. That's what women always think."

"I know. I think my mother thought that I would save her marriage when I was born. I'm doing it so Foley will have a family in America. That's why I want to bring Gbenga here. But I need to talk to Foley about what *he* wants, and I promise to do that."

Marcia's arguments made sense, and looking back now on that conversation in my kitchen, I'm ashamed that they did not persuade me to abandon my vision of Gbenga growing up in my apartment. Hearing him when I woke up, and greeting him when I came home from school, kept pulling me toward a future for the two of us that I simply could not, at that point, let go of. It was he, and not just Foley, who would give me the real African family that I wanted to have.

This clash of points of view came to a head when we all went to meet the lawyer I had hired, on the advice of the head of my co-op board, to take care of the complicated paperwork. Ben Fried had an office on lower Park Avenue. I'd met him on my own a week earlier, and when I mentioned the difference in age between Foley and me, his face told me he was skeptical about our marriage. I noticed several photographs of a smiling wife and two teenage daughters on his desk, a regular family unlike anything I'd had. He nevertheless agreed to handle Foley's green card and Gbenga's adoption as part of a transaction for which I did not need to pay until he had seen the parties involved.

The night before this meeting was a tempestuous one. Over the phone, Mr. Fried had asked me to bring in written statements from Emmanuel and Sade asserting their voluntary participation in the adoption. Because of her lack of English, Sade would have to copy what I or Emmanuel wrote. But she decided that she did not trust either of us enough to do this. I asked Foley to try to intervene, but he was "not happy" with his brother, and I wondered if Emmanuel had told him anything about his plans that he had not told me. "You know Emmanuel has a hot temper," Foley said. "No one can say anything to him."

"Do you know what he wants? Is he for this adoption or against it?"

"My brother is crazy," Foley said, using the word he used when someone did something he didn't like. He did not offer anything more than this unrevealing diagnosis. So we all went to bed that night with no letters written and nothing resolved. Talking about feelings, positive or negative, is not supported in the world Foley that grew up in, and perhaps not really in the world I grew up in either. Even our more inwardly focused culture within does not encourage it in men. When Nigerian men talk among themselves, I have felt excluded, not just by their Yoruba language, but because they spend much more time laughing than I and my friends do. Talking about serious subjects is a sign of intimacy among us but not, apparently, among them.

The next morning, the five of us waited impatiently for almost half an hour in a waiting room filled with magazines and plants.

We had brought several toys for Gbenga, who received many admiring glances from passing employees, and I wondered if any of them had a sense of the complicated situation they were observing. The secretary who ushered us into our meeting pulled a third leather chair in front of Fried's imposing desk so that Sade, Emmanuel, and I could sit facing him.

I carried Gbenga into Fried's office. "Did you bring the documents I asked for?" he said after shaking hands with all of us. If he drew any conclusion from my apologetic, negative answer, he did not show it at first. "I understand that this is really a matter of adopting between members of a family," he began, sitting down at his desk. Foley sat in the back of the room, just as he had stood on the sidelines during our catastrophic meeting at Nike's house.

"Yes," said Emmanuel, looking directly at Fried. "Gbenga is *my* son, and I am giving him to my brother and his wife." He put the emphasis on the word *my*, as he always did.

I understand that," said Fried. "I'm the father of two children myself. But a child belongs to the mother as well as to the father." I saw Emmanuel about to protest. "No, wait a minute," Fried continued. "I know how it is in your country, but this is not your country."

"But this is my wife and my child."

". . .Are you two legally married?" Fried asked. "I hadn't realized that."

"He never told me anything about this," I said to Fried, and I wasn't sure I believed what Emmanuel had just said. When I came for my initial consultation, I had told Fried that Gbenga had been born out of wedlock. Recently Emmanuel had referred to Sade as his wife, but the Yoruba word is the all-purpose *iyawo* whose root, *iya*, means "mother." I doubted that the two of them had actually had a formal ceremony. I was Foley's *iyawo* long before any ceremony made that an official fact. The word could mean "girlfriend" as well as official wife.

Fried turned to Sade, who was looking down at her empty lap. "Do you understand that you will lose control over your child if you sign these papers?" I had wanted to tell him what I had said to Emmanuel many times, that this was legal language only. But the way Fried said it, I knew it was truer than I'd been willing to admit, though Marcia had been clearer than me, telling me that that I was wrong in siding with Emmanuel. I wondered in that moment if my friendship with my long-time friend would survive, and I can only be grateful that it did.

Sade looked alarmed, and Foley approached her and translated. She stood up and started to cry. Emmanuel then jumped up, too. He grabbed Sade by the shoulder and began shouting at her in Yoruba. My memory tells me that he hit her, though it all happened so quickly that it took me a moment to realize that my visions of a future life with Gbenga had collapsed. There was nothing left to do but leave.

"I'm sorry, Mr. Fried," I said, avoiding his gaze out of shame about what he had seen. "I can see that this is not going to happen."

"That's right," he said. "I can't do it. I'm sure you had the best intentions."

"Thank you," I said. "And I apologize for taking up your time." He was right about my good intentions, certainly, but only up to a point. Gbenga, like all Nigerians, came from a long line of ancestors who had lived through struggles and traumas that I knew about only from reading. Raising a child, one always steps into the unknown. But with Gbenga I would be stepping into many more layers of that unknown.

Emmanuel continued to yell at Sade in Yoruba as we stood waiting for the elevator. Foley stepped in and told his brother to be quiet, and we managed to get out of the building looking, I suspect, not so different from many groups of people who find themselves in situations where lawyers have to be called in. I suddenly felt hungry, and I think it was not only the absence of breakfast that brought that feeling on.

"I'm starving," I said when we reached the street. "Let's find a coffee shop and sit down. I have to get out to Rutgers, but we can talk for a bit now. "Don't worry," I said to Sade, handing Gbenga to her. "The lawyer frightened you by saying you would lose your son. But we're all going to be part of Gbenga's life. We just need to find a lawyer who understands how children get moved around in Nigeria."

Emmanuel was still fuming as Sade placed a sleeping Gbenga on her back. I think I knew by then that bringing in a friendly lawyer would not clear up the conflicts surrounding the whole issue of adopting an African child.

When I came back from Rutgers late that evening, the guest room had been stripped of clothing and toys, of everything associated with Gbenga, and Sade and Gbenga were on their way to JFK. Emmanuel had taken them there, Foley said, so they had obviously made up. But I wondered how she had managed to get a seat on a plane a week before the date on her ticket. Whose idea had it been that she leave? Probably hers. But why did he let her go without him, and without saying a word to me? Was there any truth in anything that had gone on between any of us over the last two and a half months?

She didn't believe that she'd still be a part of Gbenga's life, I told myself as I surveyed the almost-empty room. I guess she never has. But why did she come here with Gbenga if she did not want to leave him here? Maybe she thought I would adopt her too, though I hadn't thought of that possibility until that moment.

I was upset over what had happened, but more than that I began almost immediately to miss their presence. The years when I was mothering Kevin at Gbenga's age had truly been the happiest of my life, and standing in that denuded room with only the *Lion King* poster left on the wall, it hit me how hard I had tried to bring those feelings back into my life.

I was also embarrassed because, while some of the items that Sade had taken were gifts from my neighbors, some of them were loans, including the baby carrier. Over the next weeks I had to go to each of these women, tell them what had happened, and offer to reimburse them. I was glad that Sade had left the pictures of Gbenga taken at his African naming ceremony that I had framed and put in my study. While they were here, I'd snapped many more pictures of him, by himself and with Sade, and Foley had taken a few that included me. I'd made two sets and given one to her a few days before the meeting with

Foley laid the entire blame on his brother, whom he accused of conning me out of the money I'd paid for everyone's plane tickets. But when Emmanuel returned from the airport his talk was all about the Commissioner. "That wicked man is telling everyone I wanted to sell my baby. He wants to destroy me, but he won't succeed. *Layer, laye*," he added, the Yoruba word for "never". I thought back to "that man" and his accusations the previous winter at Nike's house. He had hardly been Foley's friend when he accused him of bigamy. It seemed easier to go along with Emmanuel's version of whom to blame, letting our common enemy bind us together. What I didn't know then was that it would not be the last time we did this.

With Sade gone, Emmanuel became particularly charming to me, and I remembered how much I'd enjoyed his company the previous spring, before the news of Sade's pregnancy set in motion a drama in which larger forces pulled and tugged at us. I saw that he was trying to get back to where we were then, but he has always had an ebullience that I can't resist.

A month later, he flew back to Nigeria, promising that he would straighten things out, whatever that meant. I was still invested in a future with Gbenga that made Foley and me into the supportive family unit I had not grown up with, and not just a couple, while Marcia urged me to imagine a future in which Gbenga grew up with his biological mother and I was an occasional, and welcomed, grandmother. "People used your maternal feelings to get what they wanted," she told me the next time we saw each other. "And Emmanuel and Sade wanted different things. If I were you, I'd be grateful to her for preventing you from doing something that would have brought everyone a whole lot of problems."

"I think that's true. Thanks for being my friend in all this."

"The two of us look at the world through different sets of glasses, that's all. And nobody has more than one set of glasses."

"You are good, Kate," Foley said when I asked him what I

should do. "People want to cheat you," he went on, "but I will never do that. You are my wife, and I love you." I told him I loved him, too. I think we were both speaking the truth, in our own way.

That night I turned on the TV, and as it happened, PBS was broadcasting a production of Puccini's *Madame Butterfly*. The wife of Lieutenant Pinkerton, Butterfly's love, just happens to be named Kate. Butterfly, who has borne a son by her American love and believes that he will return to her when he sees this son, commits suicide on learning that his American wife intends to adopt her son. Hearing her sing out her pain brought me face to face with the knowledge of what my adopting her child would have done to Sade. Music reaches into places in the soul that words alone can't touch, and I fell asleep with her aria ringing in my head, newly aware of what I had been trying to do and been thankfully prevented from doing.

# 7

While Emmanuel, Sade, and Gbenga were in New York, my focus was on them rather than on Foley. "It's all Gbenga, Gbenga, Gbenga," he said more than once. But once we were alone, it wasn't attention from me that he wanted. I think now that he saw me as someone who could open a door to the "big money," as he called it, that his masculine sense of self-respect, as well as his family back home, demanded. The view of America that he brought from his home country, fueled by the American movies that they watched on DVDs, told them that America is where people get rich. Emmanuel had the same issue, I think, which was why he wanted an "American boy." That view of America has a long history, and there is some truth behind it. But in my New York City neighborhood, Africans deliver carts of groceries. Some say they even have advanced degrees from their country, but stay here doing menial work because there is even less for them at home. Foley could not have passed his GED exam without hours of studying, and even with it he could end up being paid less than minimum wage. I have to admit that this reality had not crossed my mind when I made my initial invitation. He said he'd given some carvings to galleries in Soho but they never paid him.

But if there was no way for them to move up economically, no Nigerian version of the American Dream—a phrase that annoyed me as a Canadian—what did becoming a Nigerian by marriage hold for me? All I can say is that it gave me the possibility of a new chapter, a future I could not predict, a story whose turns would not be given by what had preceded them. For a woman my age, dating had not presented the prospect of future happiness. So why not try this, and do what I needed to do to keep it going?

So it looked as though the promise I'd made to him on the ride to the airport at the end of my first visit had nothing real behind it. I had no connection to the African art world, and neither did Max and Felicia, my initial guides on this adventure. They knew the director of the National Black Theater, who used Foley and two of his fellow visitors to carve some decorations for her theater while I was staying in Nigeria with Nike. But no further work ensued from that. Foley did have one exhibition the autumn after our Nigerian wedding, a joint show in Queens with Tom, an American carver who'd studied with him at Nike's school before I arrived. But when I phoned Tom to ask about the whereabouts of Foley's pieces after the exhibit closed, he called Foley a liar. "All Nigerians are liars," he said, but he didn't go into specifics, and I didn't really want to push him.

In fact, I didn't really want to know the negative things he saw in Foley that I did not see. And that not wanting to know kept me from looking beneath the surface, just as my mother had done with my father's infidelities. *Eyes Wide Shut* is the title of a movie starring Tom Cruise and Nicole Kidman. But it's also a perfect description of me throughout most of my relationship to Foley, Nike, and the marriage into which they had drawn me.

Foley did show me a few battered clippings from Nigerian papers that included his picture, and I bought two books on Nigeria that included photographs of him carving. One shows him in Kenya, where he went with Nike before I met him. But once he was living with me away from the community at the gallery, he showed no interest in making new carvings, and the ones from Tom's show seemed to simply disappear. On my first visit, I'd watched him carve a perfect circle into a large block of wood that someone had brought "from the bush." He was sitting with several of Nike's other carvers, including two of his brothers, Emmanuel and Lawrence, each perched on a low stool. I'm attracted to men who look totally absorbed in their work: conductors of the choruses in which I have sung, for instance. But since then I had not seen Foley absorbed in this activity that defined him in my eyes, either there or here.

He also told me that, of all his father's children, he was the only male who'd had no real schooling. "I loved to carve," he said, "even when I was small, and I was good. So I carved next to my father while my brothers went to school, and he sold my work."

"Were you happy doing that?"

"For some time," he said. "But I did not want to stay in Osi all my life. Nothing is there that I want. I went away and studied carving with another teacher, and I did not tell anyone where I was. That teacher brought me to Nike."

"I didn't want to spend my life in Toronto either," I told him. "We have that in common."

I'd read about African children on whose labor a destitute family hopes to depend: boys sent to distant mines with a promise of reimbursement that never materializes, young girls married to older men whose promise of support results in pregnancy in bodies that develop fistulas and other complications. I don't know if Foley's father was a harsh parent. He didn't seem that way when I made my ceremonial bow to him at our engagement ceremony. But one night in our bedroom Foley showed me a wide, flat scar on his thigh from a cut he gave himself while carving. "My father would not take me to the hospital for some stitches," he said, and perhaps there were other incidents he did not mention.

There is a school in my neighborhood that promises to teach English to non-native speakers. On the sidewalk outside we would pass clusters of young people from many backgrounds. But when I asked him once if he was interested in going there, he shook his head adamantly. Perhaps this was because, having never been to school, he could not have known what went on there. Then there was another school that I used to pass on my way to the New School from Penn Station. Posters in its ground-floor windows promised training and licenses for skills that command good wages: plumbing, automobile, and electrical repairs. But when I told him he could make good money if he went there, he was equally firm in not wanting to go to a school.

What he did want, he told me, was "a driving license." He needed it to work as a security guard, a job that requires no skills other than showing up. Foley loves to drive, and car ownership in Nigeria confers status but requires vigilance. I saw this when we bought our 1978 Datsun right before our engagement ceremony. This car had a number etched onto the surface of every removable part, so it could supposedly be traced if stolen. But there are no money-back guarantees in Nigeria, so you can't just drop your car off and get the repair you were promised unless you watch it being done. Once, we briefly abandoned the Datsun at a mechanic's near the gallery where it spent a good deal of time, because it ran out of gas fifty yards out onto the road. Someone had siphoned off the contents of our tank rather than waiting in a long line for fuel.

That summer I saw his pride in car ownership, and by any standards Foley is an excellent driver. Navigating Nigerian roads is a kamikaze activity at which he excelled. His quick reflexes and nerves of steel serve him well where no one turns on their headlights until it's pitch dark, where there are no speed limits or rules of the road, no seat belts, no dividing lines, and no laws for keeping vehicles spewing billows of black exhaust off the road. On the road home from Lagos, our Datsun's steering column once lost most of its traction. Sitting in the passenger seat, I was tense as he kept the car in the right lane, carefully negotiating curves and potholes. But when I offered to massage his shoulders while we waited for the mechanic in Osogbo, they had no knots in them. It was I who needed a back rub, I who had an American license and several accidents as part of my driving history, whereas he had never hit, or been hit by, another car.

An American road test rewards none of these abilities. Yet it had never occurred to me that a license like mine was a requirement for the most minimal kinds of employment. Foley failed the road test the first time, making a U-turn "Nigerian style," in one swift motion. But the real stumbling block was the written test, which is really a literacy test. He finally passed it after failing half a dozen times, at which point I realized that he could barely read and did not want me to know it. But he never blamed himself, as I would certainly have done, for failing so often. His cheerful persistence reminded me why I wanted him to be a part of my life in a permanent way.

This is how I learned that literacy had not been needed in the life he led before coming to America. Nike is fluent in English, but she can't read. "I don't enjoy it," she told me once. "It's too much work." Foley wasn't interested in improving his English beyond what he had brought with him from Nigeria, where everyone speaks at least a little. At first I didn't see this as a serious limitation, and by the time I did it was too late.

Two months after our City Hall ceremony, we had our first interview with the INS. I had become a citizen in a building not far from the taller one where, for some two hours, we waited anxiously in a packed room on plastic chairs to hear our number called out. Our interviewer was an African-American woman, and I wondered how she felt about white women marrying black men. We'd brought along an album of photographs from our Nigerian wedding that showed us standing next to Nike, her husband, and Foley's two oldest brothers, each of us holding the bowls that were part of that ceremony. "What religion is your husband?" she asked me.

"I'm Christian," Foley chimed in, "but Yoruba, too." She looked puzzled but didn't pursue her questioning. We produced statements from our new joint checking account and were ready to answer the kinds of questions whose answers would prove that we were not marrying to avoid immigration laws. But she didn't ask about the color of our toothbrushes, who slept on what side of the bed, or any of the other trick questions my friends had told me about.

"Do you think that's it?" Foley asked as we headed back along Chambers Street toward the uptown subway.

"It seemed awfully easy," I told him. "It looks like she thought we were a lovely couple. "And she's right, no?" Foley smiled and put his arm around my shoulder.

Shortly after this interview he applied, license in hand, to an agency in Manhattan that places security guards. Perhaps because he let the agency know that he intended to go back and forth to Nigeria, he never got a permanent job or a raise. Over the summer he worked at the National Academy of Design, an elegant building on Fifth Avenue that housed works from the Hudson River School. I've been to many museums and seen security guards standing in silence, presumably for a whole day. I can't imagine earning a living in that way, but Foley did not complain, since the job only involved donning a uniform and taking a crosstown bus from my house. I hesitated to think of it as *our* house since I had lived there for so long without him. And as it turned out, he didn't think of it as his home base either. But standing alone on duty, surrounded by the paintings of some of my favorite artists who meant nothing to him, must have felt like a horrible fate for a man who'd been part of a laughing, soccer-playing community of men. Then in the fall, he was moved to a new job, working the night shift at a Bronx warehouse where he was required to stand outside.

"I can't do this," he said. "I want to go back to Nigeria."

"Permanently?"

"Of course not," he said, flashing his disarming smile. "I want to set up my gallery. Better than Nike's." This was his new mantra. She was not his boss now but his rival.

To return to Nigeria while his green card application was pending, he had to apply for a document called an "advance parole." One gets this by producing a letter saying that a member of one's immediate family has died, so one of his brothers obliged, though the father they referred to had died in 1995 and their mother was still alive. Lying and forgery are often needed to move things forward in Nigeria, but I was surprised when he got the required document so quickly and took off, his plane ticket paid for I don't know how. I had begun to worry about where his money came from, but like my mother, whose behavior I had vowed never to adopt, I didn't ask him about his finances just as he didn't ask me about mine.

His need to reconnect to his homeland might have alerted me to the disappointment that life with me in America had brought him, but in fact I was beginning to feel disappointed in him as well. His sense of time was so different from mine that it was almost impossible to make plans to do things together. In Nigeria before the arrival of cell phones, you could not arrange to meet someone at a specific place and time. Too much could intervene: power outages, pot-holed roads made impassable by neglect and rain, fuel shortages that required long lines. Even with cell phones, patience is still very much needed, and people who grew up there have a lot more of it than I do.

Foley always apologized for being late, and I'm sure he meant it when he said it. But he missed a performance of the Cirque de Soleil that he certainly would have loved, because he hadn't shown up by the time I left home and I was too annoyed with him to leave his expensive ticket at the box office. When he was in Nigeria, at least I did not have to deal with his failure to live up to my expectations. To tell the truth, we were happier in the company of members of his community than we were being alone with each other. Being with his friends drew attention away from the limitations of our shared vocabulary and our ineptitude in communicating one-on-one. Very different histories led us to this deficiency, but it was one we shared.

When Foley called me from Osogbo in November, he announced that he had found a lawyer who promised to persuade Sade to sign papers allowing him to bring Gbenga back to the States as his son. But there was a catch: The lawyer wanted five hundred dollars up front. I had pretty much given up on Gbenga when he left these shores, but when I heard Foley's voice and then looked over at Gbenga's baby pictures, my hope returned full blown. Of course I should have told him I would give the lawyer the money myself. Instead, I went to Western Union the next day with cash in my hand, then called Foley with the code he needed to collect the amount he asked for. Why would I do such a thing? The simple answer would be that it looked like my only hope for securing Gbenga's future as an "American boy" and creating a family in which my husband would play a major role. Could a Nigerian lawyer show us a way around the many obstacles that Nike's divorce lawyer had pointed out to me?

But another part of that answer was simply that I could. While I was at my boarding school in Canada, I often heard the phrase from the Bible, *Unto whom much is given, much shall be required.* It could have been the motto of the school. We, the ones to whom much had been given, were in training to be the ones for whom much would be required. So we couldn't splurge on ourselves, and I don't let myself do that. The gulf between Foley's income and mine was huge, and I took great pains not to let anyone in Nigeria know how wide it was.

But Foley's family also supplied something that mattered to me coming out of my family of origin: a sense of belonging: "the we of me." It's something we all want, or so I believe, and it's supposed to come initially from our families, then later from a spouse and children. Unwilling as I was to go back, for visits on holidays, to an unwelcoming family in Toronto, I'd felt homeless, especially on holidays, even though I had a place to live. My parents didn't seem to miss my presence. Going back for visits simply reminded me that no one there was on my side or knew who I was. Even after acquiring friends, a husband, a son, and a lovely apartment, I could never quite fill the space left by that first absent "we," or shake the dread of falling back into homelessness. Remembering this, I couldn't give my new away-from-home "we of me" a reason to reject me, a rich American in their eyes, for not being willing to share my abundance with them. So I did what I could.

"I'm spending Christmas with my son," I told Foley when I gave him the code over the phone. "I'll see you right after that."

I then headed for my neighborhood toy store, where I bought Gbenga a Fisher Price tricycle before taking the train down to Washington with gifts for Kevin, his wife, Mitzi, and my new grandson.

A week later I carried the tricycle in its large cardboard box out to JFK. To my relief, it arrived in Lagos on the same plane that I did, several hours late but intact, along with my unviolated suitcase. It was close to midnight, and the customs officers showed surprisingly little interest in what I had brought. Perhaps this was because I was now coming as the wife of a Nigerian. These small successes gave substance to my belief that a second home in Nigeria was coming into being, bit by bit.

I moved quickly toward the door and looked out at the lineup of waiting people. I didn't recognize any faces, but a guard urged patience. Ten minutes later, Foley and his friend Lateef came toward me. Preparing for this trip, I had imagined sweeping little Gbenga into my open arms. But by the time I'd stepped out into the heavy night air and the noisy crowd that filled the parking lot even at that late hour, I saw that bringing a child to the place would have been unwise.

With Foley's hand in mine, my backpack slung over Lateef's shoulder and my suitcase balanced on his head, we made our way past the sharp voices of money-changers that always frightened me. In the parking lot sat a white Mercedes that Foley had rented, certainly a step up from our rather short-lived Datsun. "You like?" he asked.

"Absolutely." Opening the back door, I prepared to stretch out along the smooth red leather seat resting on strong shock absorbers and decided that there was a reason why people will pay more for those cars. It was on the return trip to the airport three weeks later that I learned that the renter, not the rental company, is responsible for repairing a vehicle when it breaks down.

Nigeria had no official curfew, but highway driving after ten at night is assumed to be unsafe. "I guess we will have to sleep here in Lagos," I said. "Where should we do that? And what about food? Have the two of you eaten?"

"Whatever you like," said Foley, a passive stance that annoyed me often.

"What do you mean, whatever I like? This is your part of the world, isn't it?"

"We've been here for many hours," said Lateef. "Your plane was very late."

"Yeah, I'm sorry." No one spoke, so I asked, "What about Nike's new house in Lagos? Do you think someone would feed us if we went there at this hour?"

"Do you remember Florence?" Foley asked. "She's there now, and I'm sure she would make us something." Florence had been a cook at Nike's home in Osogbo during my first two visits. She had been fired, I was told, for gossiping about her boss and the Commissioner. It seemed a good sign that Florence was back at her old job, yet Foley said nothing about Nike. Were they still friends? He did not seem eager to see her, but he'd made no real plans. Had my plane arrived three hours earlier, we could have made it back to Osogbo. But after such a long plane ride, I found myself annoyed, rather than charmed, by his mode of "living in the present," which in this case involved a failure to foresee a problem and make a contingency plan.

Nike's home in Lagos is in an area called Lekki Beach, a short distance from the Atlantic Ocean but a long, slow drive from the airport. Lagos is a teeming city, its population density per square mile five times that of New York. But its traffic lights do not work, and at night the streets are, if anything, even more crowded than during the day. Markets lit by candles or kerosene lamps line the paved roads filled with cars whose drivers lean on their horns. Children are up past what we think of as their bedtime, hawking newspapers, sunglasses, and plastic packets of "pure water, pure water!" New York may call itself the city that never sleeps, but in Lagos, darkness is the backdrop for intense, noisy activity lit by headlights, candles, and kerosene lamps.

As we began to smell the ocean, the paved road became a dirt track on which two cars could pass only with difficulty. We finally pulled up to a locked wrought iron gate, honked, and waited in silence for about ten minutes. By then, I was ready to spread my winter coat on the ground and sleep right there, but at last the gate creaked open and we pulled into Nike's courtyard. The generator was off, Florence told us, so there would be no food till morning. Lekki Beach is where many of Nigeria's immensely rich were building houses with crystal chandeliers, pointed Gothic windows, spiral staircases, and other emblems of European elegance. I got to see all of these up close the next day in Nike's marble-floored palace. But there is no public electricity, just as there are no paved roads. So each home has its own generator that turns on noisily at dawn.

Nike's kitchen was all stainless steel and clean Formica surfaces. I sat at the counter, and Florence made me a cup of cold Bournvita, the ubiquitous malted chocolate drink that's a remnant of British rule. Before I stretched out on the bed under a length of printed cotton, I asked Foley if his lawyer had given him the papers I'd paid for, with Sade's signature on them. "You will meet him when you get to Osogbo," Foley said evasively.

"What does that mean? Do you have the document?"

"I don't have it. But he said he'd had a good conversation with Sade. He will give it to you when he sees you."

Lying next to him without touching, I was too upset to fall asleep quickly despite having left New York more than twenty-four hours earlier. Nevertheless, I must have dozed off because the shuddering generator woke me just as light began to come in the window. I heard Foley's voice and caught sight of him talking by the gate to the young man who'd let us in. I noticed his wallet lying on the bed, so I looked through it, thinking it might contain some information about this lawyer. What I found instead was a small plastic card with the words *Komolafe Infant* on it—Kehinde's last name. There was no other information on it, no date, just Kehinde's last name. I put it back, though I have since wished that I had kept it rather than putting it out of my sight, if not entirely out of my mind. I asked him about it after we had settled into our living quarters in Osogbo, but he said only that Kehinde's brother had given it to him, and the next time I looked in his wallet it was gone.

I think now that I had inherited, from my mother and a whole train of women going back I don't know how far, a wish not to know what my husband did when I was not around. My mother learned what my father did with other women partly because he did it with the female half of couples who were their friends. He also did it with "a German spy," which made newspaper headlines. But what could that knowledge do but cause her and her predecessors pain, since so few of them were able to act on it? Having a lot of women has been, and still is, a sign of status in some cultures. It's called polygamy.

As soon as I entered Nike's Western-style kitchen, Florence offered me eggs and toast for breakfast. I was numb rather than hungry at that point, but an empty stomach was certainly contributing to my jitters, so I eagerly said yes. "And some tea too, please."

"*E ku ojo meta*," Florence said with a smile. "Long time."

"Yes," I said, repeating her Yoruba words to remind her of the few lessons she had given me when I lived at Nike's, greetings that begin every interaction among Yoruba people. "*Bawo ni?*" I said. How are you?

"*Dada ni*," she replied. "You remember your Yoruba."

"I haven't gone much beyond our lessons," I confessed.

Florence brought my breakfast into a large room off the kitchen furnished with upholstered sofas and a cabinet with empty glass-enclosed shelves on either side of a TV set. Then my hosts swept in and gave me warm hugs. "You're looking very young," the Commissioner began.

"I guess married life suits me."

Still standing, he said to Nike, "You need to have your carver here." When he appeared, we all sat down, the two of us facing the two of them. "For what I'm going to say to you," the Commissioner continued, "your husband needs to be present. What I want to tell you, I am telling you as your friend. I assure you that Nike and I are your best friends in Nigeria." I looked over at Foley as I registered this dubious disclaimer. His eyes were fixed on the floor.

"What I would like to tell you now," he began, taking off his horn-rimmed glasses and looking directly at me, "is that your husband is a bigamist." I looked at Foley again, but he didn't look up or speak. "By the time he married you," the Commissioner went on, "Foley already had two wives and four children." He handed me a piece of paper with two names on it.

It was not the first time this subject had been hinted at. I had heard that it was common for African men to use American women as sources of income for a family in Africa. "Foley is not like that," I said many times, though I know that women like to see their man as exceptional. Once when I was at Nike's house, one of her American guests asked me how I dealt with it.

"What do you mean by *it*?"

"I mean, all his wives. It must be so difficult."

"Who told you about them?" I asked, though I knew the answer.

The first name was Yetunde, whose husband, the father of her three children, had supposedly been killed. She had been his "Embassy wife," he had told me, the one whose photograph and other documents he needed to get a visa just as Sade had needed documentation giving her a Nigerian family. I'd seen the two of them together, and though I'm not good at reading Nigerian nonverbal communication, I saw no signs of an intimate attachment.

The Commissioner then started in on the second wife. "This woman is the mother of the little girl you were going to adopt. What's her name?"

"Funmi," I said, remembering what Foley had told me about her biological father taking her from Kehinde. I was shaken but unwilling to let the Commissioner see the effect of his words.

"Not only that," he continued. "This woman is now in the United States living in Buffalo Rockaway. You know where that is?" I decided at that moment he did not really know what he was talking about, though I didn't point out that Buffalo and Far Rockaway are rather far apart. "And your husband had another child by her just this past May. In the States. I have a phone number for her. You can check for yourself."

When did this happen? Foley and I lived rather separate lives even when we were both in New York, I going with a friend to movies I knew he would not enjoy, he going to Nigerian parties in Brooklyn. I counted nine months from May: Foley was in Nigeria, back from Zimbabwe. Gbenga had just been born, and I was in New York beginning my program at the New School. When I next saw Foley and he told me that Kehinde and Funmi were "not around," Perhaps I should not have believed him, but I did. The card in his wallet clearly came from the States, but how did he get it? And what did it mean?

"Both of you were involved in my wedding here," I finally broke in. "You stood in for my father. How could you have done that if you knew Foley was married?"

"We didn't know," they both said at once.

"That's impossible," I said. There was no way they could not know. I called up my earlier conversations with Nike, first at her dining room table and later on her porch, where she had assured me that Foley was single and childless. "I came here to Nigeria in 1993, Nike," I said firmly. "And he'd been with you for three years. You can't tell me he could have had a wife and children and you didn't know about them. Gossip here travels like brush fire. You know that as well as I do. If Foley was married with a family, how could he hide it from you? And why would he want to? He went to Kenya with you, right?"

"You don't understand Nigeria," the Commissioner said. "I'm in a position to know what I'm talking about, and I assure you that you have no better friends in Nigeria than Nike and me."

"I think I need to have a conversation with my husband," I said as I stood up, eager to get away from these oppressively elegant surroundings. But the Commissioner was not quite done.

"Do you know that your husband is also an armed robber?" To this I just smiled and nodded, remembering the incident he was probably referring to. When a robbery happens in Nigeria, the police round up anyone who has been seen in the neighborhood. Foley had spent a night in jail a few days before our wedding because he drove past the house of a man who was robbed.

As I looked around Nike's elegant second home, I wondered if these accusations could deny Foley a green card. The Commissioner was certainly smart. He could never have risen to his position in the corrupt, militarized world of Nigerian politics if he had not known how to maneuver and intimidate. He knew where to find the pockets of fear in my brain. I didn't know then why he was so determined to upset me. I think now that it was because he saw Foley as Nike's valuable possession and me as a thief, guilty of stealing his wife's prize carver, He was a police commissioner and looked at the world through that lens. And she had adopted his view, as good wives were expected to do.

By this time we were all standing up, and the Commissioner assured me that I was welcome to visit him and Nike any time I wanted. "You are part of our family, you know," he said, and I winced as I followed Foley through the kitchen and into the courtyard. I knew that his "you" did not include Foley, who clearly knew it, too. They had treated him as though he were not present, and he had responded in kind.

In that moment I stood by my man with no hesitation, since the only alternative would have been to side with an individual who took such relish in hurting us both. Yet Nike's silence must have been as painful to him as the Commissioner's accusations were to me. After all, she had taken him into her school and made him one of its stars. The silent man I stood next to was the one she had promoted to me on our walks along the road behind her house. I don't think he could have anticipated the tirade that had just taken place, or he would not have brought me to this ostentatious home.

As we walked toward the car, Nike came outside and offered me a blouse with a batik design, making me more confused than ever about her role in what had just happened. She was under the control of her husband now, but what did that mean for Foley and me? As I held it against myself and thanked her, I remembered that Olabayo, her oldest son, had just had a baby in the States. "How do you like being a grandmother? I have a grandson too, you know," I added as I reached into my wallet to show her a photograph. That was all there was left to our woman-to-woman connection, but as we drove away from her castle-like house surrounded by others just like it, I was not yet ready to let it go. In fact, I would say now that I was not yet ready to sever my tie to the Africa to which I had connected by marrying Foley. Without him in my life I would lose all that. At least this is what I told Marcia when I got back to the States. "You're crazy," she said. "But that's what I like about you. You never do what's reasonable."

We climbed into the Mercedes, Foley's friend Lateef reappearing and sitting in the front seat next to Foley. None of us spoke until we reached the main highway and turned north toward Osogbo. "That man want to destroy me," Foley said, and I saw Lateef nodding.

"Why?" I asked.my fellow passengers. "What did you ever do to him?"

"It's because I have success," said Foley. "From you."

"And Nike can't go against him," Lateef added. "He rules the gallery now."

"So he wants to hurt me too,"

"He can't control me," said Foley. "He want to do that. Because of you."

"Well, he can't destroy our marriage, so if that's what he wants he's not going to get it." I couldn't see the faces of my fellow passengers, but I needed to let them know that we were in this together, united against a common enemy. No, I would not let him win.

The car held up all the way to Osogbo, with my husband the expert driver at the wheel. As he steered it off the four-lane highway onto what had been a dirt road between Ibadan and Osogbo, I noticed that some of it was now paved. As we got closer to Osogbo, unfinished cinder-block houses were scattered alongside more road-building, especially in the neighborhood near Nike's house. But the "we didn't know" that I had just heard kept ringing in my head. When we passed the gallery, I crumpled up the piece of paper the Commissioner had given me and tossed it out the window.

In happier days, Foley and I had stayed in a dormitory where Nike's most impoverished students lived for nothing. But we could not expect a welcome there now that the school was under the Commissioner's control. A number of our old friends had been accused of crimes and expelled. One of these, nicknamed Pelego, which means "woodpecker," had recently inherited from his father a multiple-dwelling compound built around a cement courtyard. Foley's brother Lawrence was renting a room there, and Foley had arranged for us to stay in another. I'd always been fond of Pelego and was grateful for his offer of such warm, communal accommodations. Later I wondered if I should have offered to pay him, but I didn't think to do so at the time.

After settling in, Foley and I walked along a dirt road lined with cinder block houses to the flat where Yetunde, the "first wife" of the Commissioner's malicious narrative, lived with her three children. Emmanuel and Gbenga were there, and Gbenga's first reaction to me was to burst into tears. "Don't worry about that," Foley said. "He did it to me, too." I then produced a teddy bear whose t-shirt read *Someone At Rutgers Loves Me.* Sade had not taken it when they left, and when I handed it to Gbenga, he immediately stopped crying.

Foley had asked Yetunde to cook for me, since I had no stove or pots of my own. Each Nigerian family has its own kerosene stove in the communal kitchen that occupies one end of a typical apartment building. People store their food and dishes in their rooms and bring their own toilet paper to the bathroom. Husbands and wives rarely eat together, a fact I unhappily learned when Foley returned from New York the summer before our wedding. It might have been a warning that the marriage I saw myself embarking on had very little grounding in the world as it actually was. But I didn't see it that way, or at least I didn't take it as an indicator of my limited powers.

That summer I had no stove, so I'd shopped, cooked and eaten with the women students who lived in the dorm with us. We ate when the rice, beans, and tomato-based sauce was ready rather than wait for the men, who arrived later, expecting to be fed after playing soccer and perhaps enjoying a Star beer, a popular brand in Nigeria. I'd pictured Foley and me eating dinner across from each other at my kitchen table, but that was never going to happen. The distance between our worlds could not be bridged from one side only.

This time I ate my meals with Yetunde's children while Foley ate with his friends in a roadside canteen whose food has more hot pepper than I can tolerate. While I read a book connected to my academic life back home, on one of the upholstered chairs in her living room, her children played and fought.

The issue of hitting children came up again one day when Emmanuel came by with Gbenga. Soji, Yetunde's youngest, was fighting with Gbenga, and Yetunde appeared brandishing a stick. Jumping up, I grabbed it with the intention of giving her a taste of her own medicine. "Don't *do* that!" I shouted. But the two children separated, and my outburst was met with laughter from the other adults in the room, who saw me raising a ridiculous objection to Yetunde's perfectly appropriate behavior. Whatever might come from the adoption, I saw myself raising Gbenga in a part of the world where hitting a child was frowned on—though not everywhere in my country, as I would come to learn.

Back at Pelego's compound, we opened up the tricycle, and Emmanuel and Foley got to work with the packets of hardware that were included. It was too big for Gbenga to push the pedals on his own. So Femi, Yetunde's older son, pushed him around Pelego's courtyard; then he and his sister Foluke took turns. They were as much too big for it as Gbenga was too small, but this did not stop them. Then Soji, who was the same age as Gbenga, demanded his turn and got it. I had also brought for everyone a large inflatable plastic ball. Before I left it was punctured and lay at the edge of the courtyard, with no one willing to acknowledge its demise and dispose of it.

Spending my time in Yetunde's living room, I sometimes thought about my son, who had now given me a grandson. I thought about Nigerian children sharing a bed and sleeping in the same room as their parents, and about little Henry's bedroom in Arlington with its wind-up mobile, its large Winnie the Pooh wall hanging, its array of stuffed animals, several of them wearing t-shirts that also read *Someone From Rutgers Loves Me*. I had a photograph of Henry in my wallet that Gbenga took out every time he saw me, and I wondered if perhaps he knew that the person in the photo had a special relationship to him.

Other people liked the photograph also. They called Henry "*omo* Katie," Katie's child, as if there were nothing strange about my being the mother of a child nine months younger than Gbenga. But possessives don't mean in their culture what they do in mine. In Nigeria, Henry was simply a member of my family. Motherhood is so central in this deeply patriarchal world that mothers are often called the *iya* of their child rather than by their own names. As for me, everyone called me "Mama Kate," just as they called Nike "Mama Nike," meaning that I was not just my grandson's mother and possibly Gbenga's as well, but the *iya* of everyone I was willing to help.

# 8

Meanwhile, I had not seen Sade. Emmanuel said she was "in the area," but I never did learn more than that. Then, on New Year's Eve day, she and Emmanuel showed up at Pelego's compound without Gbenga. Foley was working under the hood of the Mercedes in preparation for a two-hour drive to the family compound in Osi that we would be taking as soon as he was done. Yetunde and her children would come with us. Lawrence, his girlfriend, and two cousins would follow us in a second car. "We will come by public transport," Emmanuel told me. "Gbenga was sick," he explained. "But he's fine now." Catching sight of her for the first time since leaving her in my apartment, I walked toward her and gave her a hug.

"I thought you were angry," she said hesitantly.

`"I was, but I'm not anymore. It's in the past now." Holding her against my chest, I felt delighted at the prospect of reviving a connection I was sorry to have lost. I couldn't help thinking that this might be the beginning of a whole new chapter in the story of

Gbenga's adoption. "I'm a Capricorn," I have told my friends when they remarked on my persistence. "It's what we Capricorns do. We climb up the side of a cliff."

Night had fallen quickly, as it always does in Nigeria, before we reached our destination time to join about eight hundred of the townspeople at an Anglican service that would end by ringing in the New Year. Osi is a tiny town compared to Osogbo, but on a festive occasion such as this, everyone would be at a church of some sort. New Year's Eve in Nigeria is not the obsessively couple-oriented event I knew from back home. Even when I had *been* part of a couple, its noisy celebration always got on my nerves. Now it felt good to be sitting in a pew with six members of Foley's family between us, listening to a sermon delivered dramatically in a language I did not understand and trying my Yoruba on hymns whose tunes I knew from home. At midnight a bell rang and everyone shouted "Hallelujah! Praise the Lord!" Then Yetunde and I filed up to the communion rail for a small piece of bread and a sip of grape juice.

That night, and for the next two, we all slept on thin straw mats on the upper floor of the house belonging to Emmanuel's mother. All, that is, except Foley, who told me later that he refused to sleep there because he was still fighting with Emmanuel. "Because of you," he added. "Because he cheated you."

I assumed that he was referring to the plane tickets I'd bought for the three of them. But I'd talked to Marcia about this, and she had said, "In the long run, I think it's good that she did that. Raising Gbenga here would create huge problems for you. I have two brothers, and I know something about what it's like to grow up as a black male."

"I wish I had your first-hand knowledge," I told her at the time. What would she say about Foley's mysterious behavior in general, and this instance of it in particular?

"Where do you think he is?" I asked Emmanuel. "Would he be seeing—"

"You mean a girlfriend up here? No way. Foley doesn't like Osi, so he's never here. I don't come here much myself," he added.

"Nothing to do." I did my best after that to put my fears away, though I was not happy to see so little of him. I did see a lot of his mother because she, along with Yetunde, Sade, and Emmanuel's mother, prepared the meals the rest of us ate. I was the only one who could not help with the cooking or speak their language.

I had brought along a book, as I always did, this one background reading for my course in eighteenth-century English literature. Reading it, I felt myself in two similar worlds, one of which had ceased to exist two centuries earlier. There was no electricity back then, no flush toilets, and no police force until Henry Fielding established the Bow Street Runners in 1749 to protect Londoners from the desperate people who flocked to London as large landowners threw their tenants off land once claimed in exchange for working on the landlord's property. Back then the highways and city streets were scenes of frequent robberies, and public hangings were the standard punishment for even the smallest theft. Wasn't Nigeria pretty much like this now, where highway checkpoints are places where a bribe is demanded at gunpoint, where people have fled towns like Osi for the slums of Lagos, where crowds gather in a stadium to watch armed robbers killed by a firing squad? As I read, I kept asking a question: How could it get better here?

On our last day in Osi, a small, unplanned gesture made the bond I felt with Sade more tangible, for me at least. I had brought with me a heavily beaded, rose-colored chiffon dress that Foley admired and wanted me to wear on New Year's Day, which I did. I'd bought it in a thrift shop, and back at home I had not worn it often, since it was shorter than I like and exposed too much of my legs. As I was folding it to pack, it struck me that Sade and I were the same size, but she was shorter than me by five or six inches.

"I have something for you," I said, and handed it to her. "Try it on. I want to see how it looks on you." When she put it on, I said, "You look fabulous. It's just the right length for you. Now go show it to Emmanuel." Of course it looked stunning on a pretty woman less than half my age, and of course he loved it. Sade was clearly pleased, though I'm sure her life afforded even fewer occasions to wear such a dress than mine did. Still, it felt like a good omen served up by chance, a way to let her know that I valued a connection with her that I saw as unbroken.

As we were about to leave, I learned that Lawrence, his girlfriend, and the cousins had taken the car they had come up in back to Osogbo two days earlier. Perhaps I wasn't the only one for whom time in Osi moved much too slowly. "Bo-ring," said Lawrence when I saw him again in Osogbo. "Nothing to do." Osi is a town of mostly elderly people and the grandchildren they are taking care of, and has little interest for anyone who can get out. This drain from the country to the city is a problem in Nigeria, as it is wherever it occurs. "Boring" is the usual excuse.

The remaining six of us squeezed once again into the Mercedes, and thanks to Foley's skill behind the wheel we made it back to Osogbo miraculously intact. I'd slept a lot, eaten many pounded yams, finished my book, and gone for several walks with Sade and Gbenga. But I was definitely glad to be back where I could sit on a real toilet. I'd grown up with more than a little squeamishness about bodily functions, so life without running water, which included peeing into a pot in the middle of the night, was difficult for me. The flush toilet was invented in the modern world in 1785, my book told me, though not put into general use till much later. Before that pretty much everyone lived the way I and everyone around me had been living for four long days.

Two days before I was scheduled to leave, the elusive lawyer finally showed up at Pelego's compound after having missed two appointments. He promised to set up, and then attend, a meeting at the American Embassy for Sade, Emmanuel, and Foley, to take place a week after I left. These were the conditions under which Sade could sign the necessary legal statement of consent allowing Foley to bring Gbenga back to the States.

I did not like this lawyer, who mainly wanted to discuss the possibility of my helping him get into an American law school. "Why would you do that?" I asked. "You have a law degree here, don't you?"

"I wish to study international law," he said, giving the phrase a vague aura that convinced me that he was making things up as he went along. It struck me as unlikely that studying law was what he wanted to do in the States, and I suspected that he wasn't a lawyer at all.

"I'm not connected to that world," I told him. It was all I could think of by way of a reply.

Sade, Gbenga, Emmanuel, Foley, and I set out for Lagos the day before my plane took off. We planned to spend the night in Lagos because Emmanuel had made an appointment for that afternoon with Suzanne, a woman from the American Embassy who was handling his visa application. Emmanuel claimed that the Commissioner was spreading rumors at the Embassy that my Rutgers letters were forgeries. I, too, wanted to regain my good name there, or at least to understand why Emmanuel was having so much trouble getting a visa.

An hour into the drive, steam began to pour out from under the elegant hood of the Mercedes. We managed to inch along until we reached a taxi stand outside Ibadan. With no time to spare, Emmanuel and I soon found ourselves speeding along the highway toward the Embassy in a taxi, leaving Foley, Sade, and Gbenga to throw themselves on the mercy of the area's resident mechanic. After giving Foley half of my remaining American money, fifty dollars, I was relieved to be in the back seat of a vehicle where time was money for the driver. I was also terrified by our speed even as I was conscious of the minutes ticking away.

We got to the Embassy only fifteen minutes late, though its formidable checkpoint ate up more precious time. Luck was with us, however. The guard at the gate called up to Suzanne's office and was about to turn us away when Emmanuel spotted her heading toward her car in the parking lot. She was pleasant and assured me that the getting a visa had little to do with my invitations from Rutgers. "The letter is just a formality, after all," she said.

"I guess I know that," I answered with a smile.

"Where are you going now?" she asked, and when Emmanuel mentioned the district where a friend of his had offered to put us up for the night, she said she would be happy to drive us part way through a city where there are no working traffic lights.

After an hour of "go slow," the Nigerian phrase for bumper-to-bumper traffic, she let us off on a wide, divided avenue with tall palms down its center. It took us another hour by cab to reach our destination, a small room in the servants' quarters of a compound owned by a Nigerian academic and his American wife. The owners were "not around," the young man at the gate told us. But he let us in when we gave him the name of our host for the night, a fellow employee who was also a batik artist and a one-time student of Nike's.

To my amazement, Foley and his crew had arrived ahead of us. "How's the car? Is it really repaired?"

Of course his answer was "for now." I knew that only the rich, including senior government officials like the Commissioner, could afford real repairs to their chauffeur-driven vehicles. Everyone else relies on the roadside mechanics who supply brake fluid, a fan belt, water for the radiator, or a bolt that will get the car to a mechanic in the next town who will do more patching up with second-hand parts. But here was Foley, my husband the great driver, displaying his usual cheerfulness and patience as he introduced me to his friend, our host. His strengths amazed me once again, reminding me of that scary moment on the highway when our van had a blowout and he took charge so gracefully. As I hugged him in the cramped surroundings where he'd arranged for us all to spend the night, I loved him for possessing those strengths in such large measure, and under even the most daunting conditions.

"Our meeting with Suzanne was great," Emmanuel announced to everyone. "She really liked Kate."

"How do you know that?" I asked.

"I've met her before," said Emmanuel breezily. "I won't have any trouble with the Embassy now. She's my friend, and now she is your friend, too." I was about to protest that she would not call either of us her friend. But this was, after all, the result I'd been hoping for.

"Is anybody hungry?" I asked our assembled group, aware that my metabolism demands food more often than the one heavy meal a day that can sustain a native Nigerian. We piled into our revived car and drove to a section of Lagos where narrow alleys are lined with small cafes and shops. The cafes had two or three wooden tables with benches on either side and a metal pitcher of water next to a basin for washing the hand you used to eat, both before and after the meal. We all ordered balls of pounded yam, wrapped in saran wrap, to dip in a peppery "soup" and, for the Nigerians who are used to the meat there, a piece of some sort of meat.

"You like our yam?" our waiter asked, and I nodded to him, glad that I really did like it since enjoying the food of a culture is an entry into it.

When we had finished our meal we made our way back to our room, which was hot and airless because, as part of the servants' quarters, it lacked electricity and thus a fan. But the room's owner had made it beautiful, covering the single small window with a tie-dyed curtain that matched a longer one that served as a door. It might have been cooler to sleep outside, but Foley's friend offered his bed to Sade, Gbenga, and me, and I spent the night making sure I didn't kick anyone while the guys slept on mats on the cement floor outside, separated from us by a curtain hanging motionless in the heat of the night.

My plane would not leave till midnight the next day, so we had a long time to do very little before heading to the airport at around eight. We went for a walk in the neighborhood, its streets lined with high walls crowned with iron spikes like those behind which we had just spent the night. Peering through the wrought iron gates, we could see well-kept cars and bustling servants. Where Nike and her husband lived, even more ostentatious houses were being built, but they would have fitted nicely into this neighborhood. Perhaps this was the life to which our elusive lawyer aspired. Perhaps he envisioned, as a small down payment on it, the five hundred dollars for which he had done, and would do, absolutely nothing.

The question I've asked myself since then is why I persisted for so long in my efforts to adopt Gbenga. Obviously I thought it would save the marriage, and behind that was wanting to be seen as a generous person wanting to help, not just by Foley but by everyone in my Nigerian world.

But perhaps all the money I had spent trying to bring these adoptions about—the air fare and passports for Sade and Gbenga, and the money for the lawyer Foley must have known would be useless—only validated their perception of me as a wealthy, white American woman who could be hit on indefinitely because she had so much more than they did. I never told anyone how much I paid every month to live in my New York apartment. But no amount of evasion could conceal the financial distance between my life and theirs. How naïve I was to think I could escape being seen by them in their way.

Only lately have I come to understand that, in all my efforts to become the mother of a Nigerian child, I was very much my mother's daughter. Being raised by nannies and sent to boarding school was a family tradition that my mother passed on to me. When my grandmother died, I did not see my mother cry, as I did not cry when she died. She had always dismissed Mother's Day as a commercial ploy and was annoyed rather than pleased if I called her on that day. What point was there, then, in sending a card or a gift in an attempt to rouse real affection between us? We children called her "Mummy," the way English children do, but the cozy affection that name might have called up never really materialized. We saw too little of her for that. She joined many charitable committees and boards out of a wish, she would tell us, to have a life of her own, one that took her out of the house. I think now that living through one's children was for her a lower-class way of being.

Then there was the expert advice of John D. Watson, the predecessor of Dr. Spock. Never kiss your children. Never hold them in your lap. I remember my grandmother as a rather cold person. But both she and her daughter were told that, if mothers did not ignore their babies when they cried, their children would fail as adults. What mother would want to inflict that fate on a child? So my mother grew up in a world in which maternal affection was the kiss of death. No wonder I assumed that Gbenga would be fine in the States surrounded by multiple caregivers, attending good schools with other children and bonding with his father's brother while seeing his father often and his biological mother a few times a year. I had survived my mother's absence—the coldness she inherited from her own mother and the alcoholism that later engulfed her—by finding people more affectionate and supportive than she was: teachers mostly, but also my first husband, who praised me for being smart, a negative for a girl in my mother's world back then. That man's support had sent me into the academic world, leaving him behind and disconnecting me from my unhappy mother. Yet this disconnection kept me from putting myself in the shoes of a child who would suffer if his mother were around only intermittently. The apple had not fallen far from the tree after all.

Had I known this back then, I might have decided that it was time to end this arrangement that was a marriage in name only. But it took years for me to discover how strongly my mother's message was still sending its inaudible signals through my brain, signals that told me, *Don't give up. Stay married no matter what.* My mother must have seen this resolve as a sign of strength.

When I got back to New York just in time to start my new semester, a registered letter from the INS, dated a week into the new year, 1998, informed me that, because we'd missed a second interview, our green card application had been denied. I had taken off for Nigeria with no idea that we would be asked for another interview. But I could send a check for $200.00, and the process would begin all over again. We had clearly been much too confident about our first interview, assuming that this was it. Sending the check would put the application back on track, but it might be as much as two years, my lawyer friend told me, before we could expect to hear from the INS again, a sharp reminder that getting a green card was no longer the sure thing it had been when

I had applied in the Sixties.

Perhaps I should have seen the writing on the wall and given up on my African adventure then and there, but it never occurred to me to do so. Obviously my vision of creating a small Nigerian family in New York was completely delusional. That lying lawyer was simply the last straw, and I was coming to accept the fact that the happiness I associated with motherhood was not in my future.

When I got together with Marcia, I told her that I now understood what she said about African-American boys, and how I could not turn Gbenga into an African version of Kevin. For different reasons, we had both been in and out of twelve-step programs. "I hate accepting the things we cannot change," she said. "But you gotta do it."

"But I went to the New School to write about my marriage, and if I end it now, there won't be much of a story. I want to get to the bottom of it. I think that's what I'm here to do."

"Well, there's one weird reason for staying married," she said, and we both laughed.

Waiting for Foley to come back to the States, I also started thinking about the meaning of money in my life and how secretive I am about it, not just with him. If inheritance were only about money, it might be easier to deal with rationally. But it is as much a family's history as it is a sum of assets. I'm part of a long line of ancestors that begins in this country with one Johannes Hees, born in Holland in 1752. He came to the town of Palatine Bridge in upstate New York, arriving, like so many immigrants, with barely a penny in his pocket. He married at the age of twenty, and four years later became a foot soldier who survived the Revolution to produce a line of offspring in the new nation its leaders had created. Several members of his family are buried in that town's churchyard. But what did he leave behind in Holland, and why did he do it, enduring such hardship on the way over and in his new country?

One of my cousins had researched our family's history on my father's side. She found that his great-great-grandfather, Charles, born in 1843 according to my cousin's records, moved his entire family to Canada after the Civil War and set up a factory that made "plain and ornamental window shades, comforters, and pillows" right in the heart of the burgeoning city of Toronto. It kept on doing this through the Depression, and no one in my father's family lost their job. When I was growing up, this red-brick building still stood within walking distance of a pillared stone house that his son built, with a carriage house behind it. At some point the family must have joined the Anglican Church three blocks away, and I was christened there as a baby in a long white dress handed down through the family. But my parents went only on Christmas and Easter, though they sent us to Sunday school with a nanny.

The man who built our house, my father's grandfather, traveled to New York, where he met and married Mabel Good, a New Yorker who brought into our family a source of wealth derived from a patent medicine that was famous in its day: Carter's Little Liver Pills. These pills were a part of the post-Civil War boom in patent medicines whose unidentified ingredients were said to bring "bloom to the cheeks" and "sparkle to the eyes" of both sexes. Mabel's brother had bought out a pharmacist named Mr. Carter and made his name a household word. In 1880 the company established its headquarters at 57 Park Place, from which it would soon be able to see the newly opened Brooklyn Bridge. The Carter firm suffered a blow in the 1950s, when the Federal Trade Commission insisted that the pills had no effect on the liver. But my most enduring impressions of New York as a magical place came from my father's accounts of visits to his widowed maternal grandmother. She lived in the Apthorp Apartments on Broadway and Seventy-ninth, complete with an interior courtyard behind wrought iron gates, a still-surviving monument to the New York of one of my favorite novelists, Edith Wharton.

In fact, my building dates from the turn of the last century, and my apartment has high ceilings and a dumbwaiter like the one that brought trays of food to the third-floor nursery of our pillared house in Toronto. When my parents moved to the assisted living facility where they died, I was much more eager to claim their furniture than were my sisters, neither of whom left home feeling that they did not belong in the world where they were born. When I wake up, my mother's Queen Anne dresser is one of the first things I see. It is as if these things, acquired only after her death, are my one connection to her, and I want to pass them on to Kevin's children, along with my apartment and what remains of the money that let me buy it and fix it up. Perhaps one of them will live in it, fall in love with the city just as I did, even go to Columbia. If Foley's ancestors have shaped his life and the way he sees America, mine are still present in my life, too. They may be why I believed for so long that I, a potential member of the DAR, could be happily married to someone from a part of the world where people lived on a dollar or two a day, and assumed that he would be happy married to me.

For years after leaving Toronto, I went to great lengths to distance myself from this history, and from the very white world in which it unfolded, to become someone not at all like the women I'd left behind. But everything in it has me the product of ancestors whose way of living I can't help but admire. I read about them in the Edith Wharton novels that I teach and love. I see them in its artifacts preserved in museums, in its now totally unaffordable apartment buildings like the Apthorp, in the "old New York" calendars that hang in my study. It's thanks to these ancestors that I graduated from an elite university and still live in a building in its neighborhood, a place from which I was able to imagine a life on two continents. When I walk now along the streets where I pushed a stroller in the first hope-filled years of my graduate school marriage, I'm grateful for gifts that came to me by sheer accident of birth.

But Foley knows nothing about this history. My lying about money, so central to my family's secretive way of dealing with the subject, fit with his like two adjoining puzzle pieces. I bought an eighty-dollar electric toothbrush and told him it only cost twenty. If a package came in the mail for me, I would not open it in front of him, and I'd cut off the price tag. I've heard that people with high incomes do this all the time. Then there was the fake prenuptial agreement I wrote so he wouldn't know the net worth I've kept even from myself. Of course I'm aware of the monthly cost of my apartment, which includes a monthly maintenance as well as a mortgage. I needed to rent two of its rooms to cover the combined sum, which would surely convince him that I was incredibly rich since he had no idea that the cost of everything in New York is ten times what it is in Nigeria.

I remember him telling me once that the house where I was staying with him and two of his brothers had cost him $300.00 for the whole year. Perhaps he even thought that, for me, those huge phone bills were "no problem." I thought back to my first visit to Nigeria by myself, when a young woman asked me to leave her the shoes I was wearing when I went back to the States. "No," I said. "I've had these for a long time, and I like them."

"You can get others," she said, "when you go back to your country." I'm sure she thought I was selfish for not giving them to her, but were she and her impoverished friends entitled to anything I owned that they wanted just because I made my home in the States? So, as much as possible, I kept my net worth a secret from Foley and his friends. Like my parents, I assumed that my husband would want more, not just for himself but for his family, if he knew how much I had. But behind that is a much older belief, one that I think my parents were ruled by even though they never said it out loud: People won't like you if they know that you have more than they have. Or worse, they will like you *only* because you have more than they have. Trying to navigate the culture of lies, secrets, and silence in Foley's Nigerian world, I found myself dealing with some of the same built-in beliefs as the one in which I'd grown up.

I remember him looking puzzled when I showed him a Palestrina motet that I was working on, and telling him that the notes on its pages were written down four hundred years ago. I live in a world shaped by print, and he does not. So even the Christianity that I saw drawing us together was made out of different materials. I had been christened at a private ceremony in that long white baby dress. His father had been friends with a Catholic priest who had baptized his many children in spite of its official repudiation of polygamy. When he came to New York for the first time, I took him and two of the friends to the Cloisters, paying their bus fare and entrance fees. But the intricately carved medieval altarpieces that I thought he would love did not call forth from him the enthusiastic reaction I'd anticipated. In fact, none of the Nigerians enjoyed the visit the way I did.

On the way back to the subway, the two friends turned their backs to me and peed on the lawn of Fort Tryon Park. "That's illegal here," I shouted at them, hoping that no one had seen what is accepted male behavior in Nigeria. But they shrugged, and we sat in a not especially friendly silence on the long ride home. Foley wasn't really into museums, not even the Museum for African Art, where we found two carvings by his grandfather, whose work had been discovered by a Western art collector. So there was no way for him to enter any of the places where my history invites me in.

Coming to Nigeria, I also know first-hand how a few billionaire dictators and their cronies destroy, for the many, all hope of a better future. Hence the intense desire of people like Foley to come to the States. But economic inequality has produced so much of what I love about the city where I fled to escape from my life in Toronto: the Met Museum, the Cloisters, Carnegie Hall, Frederic Law Olmstead's parks, Tiffany's windows, and buildings like the Apthorp and the Forty-second Street library. So I live with opposing attitudes toward money and try to accept the things I cannot change. The hard part, of course, is figuring out what those are.

*Green Card, 1998–2003*

# 9

Back in my apartment, waiting for Foley to arrive, I began to question whether he could ever find remunerative work in New York. When I first envisioned our life together, I saw him working as a carver. But if he wanted to pursue it, he would have to rent a small studio in Harlem, put out flyers and business cards—in short, think of it as a business. "If you have photographs of some of your work," I told him when he arrived in New York a few weeks after I did, "I have a friend who could make you a website." Perhaps he didn't understand what a website was. I'd seen a few photographs in an album, but after I told him this I did not see them again. He seemed to lack the entrepreneurial spirit he would need if he wanted his woodcarving skills to be a source of income. His "Mama Nike" had this in abundance, and it looked as if he'd relied on her to supply that for him in Nigeria. Now it was apparently up to me to do so, and I didn't have much entrepreneurial spirit either. As an academic, I was glad that I didn't need it.

There were practical problems with this scenario, too. Shipping heavy items that rich African-Americans might want to buy, like the carved doors, headboards, screens, and chairs I'd seen in Nike's house and in the gallery, would be expensive. Even if Foley made them here, what kind of wood would he want to use? I called a few schools where people I knew had connections as teachers, to see to see if they had art programs where he could demonstrate what he did. But nothing materialized. I'd promised to help him, but I could not do everything for him as Nike had done and, presumably, his father before her.

Once back in the States, he was not happy about the delay over his green card application. He spent two months at Saint Helena Island in South Carolina, at an art studio owned by Arianne, a woman who knew Nike and had met Foley in Osogbo. She'd commissioned Foley to carve some doors for her studio. I had seen doors like the ones she wanted in the gallery and in Nike's house: three or four horizontal panels that depicted scenes of drumming, dancing, and pounding yams. But Foley ran up her phone bill, she told me, as he had mine. I'm not sure he even made the doors, and the two of them certainly did not part friends.

That spring I was busy finishing my program at the New School. Foley went back to the security guard agency and put in an application to work at the Metropolitan Museum. He came to my graduation and posed, all smiles, for snapshots of the two of us taken by one of my fellow students with the camera I'd bought to take pictures of Gbenga. As for our sex life, it did improve somewhat, mainly because I found ways to assist him in giving me the pleasure I was hoping for when we first got together. Our language barrier prevented me from being explicit about what I liked, but I was glad nevertheless when he drew me close to him at night.

But as the relentless heat of another New York summer set in, we stopped talking about the future. Not that either of us had ever put into words the visions we had of our life together. I didn't ask him about his, and my own were located mostly in the community created by Nike that was slipping farther and farther away each time I went to Nigeria. I had not given up on my vision of a second home, but each time I got on a plane destined for the Lagos airport, that vision met with new obstacles. I was frustrated, but it never occurred to me to give up. That was not the way I reacted when things did not go my way. Perhaps I even chose that difficult country and those difficult people because they forced me to reach below the surface of my well-ordered life. If I dug down far enough, I would finally reach the whole truth that I wanted to find.

Someone in Foley's family, worried about losing contact with him, called in the middle of that summer to tell him that his mother had died. Later he would discover that his mother was alive and had not even been sick, but at the time the news sent him into a state of silent, guilt-ridden grief.

He must have forgiven the person who told him this lie, though, because he made good use of it. He applied for a second "advance parole," and much to my surprise, that document appeared in the mail a month later. "What if we have to be interviewed again?" I asked him when he opened the envelope and showed it to me.

"Phone me," he said, "and I'll come back to New York." How he paid for his plane ticket I don't know, but he took off for Nigeria in early November. After he left, we did talk fairly regularly on the phone, and I wished him a Merry Christmas from my son's home in Virginia. If Kevin and Mitzi suspected that all was not well with my long-distance marriage, they did not bring up the subject, and I'm not sure what I would have told them if they had.

Then, a few weeks into my new semester, I picked up the phone to hear Foley's sister Julie over a static-filled line. "My brother is in jail," she said.

". . .How come?"

"It's that Commissioner." I later got the story in bits and pieces, some from his brothers who now lived in New Jersey, and more when Foley finally made it back to New York two months later. He spoke of being one of a hundred people crammed into a small room with little air, of everyone sleeping packed together on the bare floor. When I asked for more details, he didn't want to talk about it. He did have plenty to say, however, about the Commissioner's reason for jailing him. "This wicked man bribed one of my brothers to tell a judge that you and I had a business selling invitations to the States."

"How did you get out?"

"My brother came to the jail," Foley said gleefully. "You know that little Walkman you gave me? Well, I had it with me, and I got what my brother said about being bribed and played it for the judge. Then I showed him photographs of our wedding, with the Commissioner and Nike there, because that man was saying he did not know me. I have a lawyer now, and I'm going to sue them."

The Commissioner must have been hoping to deprive Foley of a green card by giving him a criminal record in his home country. What he could do, and did, was to send some of his officers to the airport to prevent Foley from boarding his flight to the States. Foley escaped by car to Ghana, he said, and took a plane from Accra to New York. From what I have seen and read about Nigerian police officers and Nigerian jails, he was lucky to get out alive.

I understood why Foley did not blame his brother for accepting the Commissioner's bribe. From the smallest request for a *dash*, another word for a bribe, to a multi-million-dollar deal, an exchange of money is simply required. And when people live on so little, an offer from someone like the Commissioner must have been hard to resist. Then there was growing resentment among members of Foley's extended family, because he had gone to the States to make "big money" and brought too little back. He avoided going to Osi because his mother and his father's other wives always needed money for medicine and fuel and school fees for the children they were looking after. No matter how much he might bring, it could never be enough.

Sitting in my kitchen eating spaghetti, his favorite American food, he sounded gleeful when he told me how Nike had pleaded with him not to go public with his accusations. "But my lawyer is good," he declared proudly. He then produced a wrinkled photocopy of an article, in one of Nigeria's gossipy newspapers, in which Nike laid out her reasons for turning against her former star carver while standing by "her man," the Commissioner. The two of them had done everything for Foley, she insisted. He was "an ungrateful somebody" who had "a bad character."

"But why are they doing this?"

"They're crazy," Foley said, and I never heard him give any other explanation.

"Well, they're not going to win," I told him, almost as passionate about this as he was. "Whatever they try to do is not going to hurt us."

"You are good, Kate," he said, and I could sense that he meant it. It was in these moments, facing a common enemy, that I felt closest to him even as I remembered the Commissioner's words about him being a criminal. That man was willing to stop at nothing, it seemed, to put truth behind those words.

A few days later, I was at school photocopying a handout for a class when Cheryl, my African-American department chair, poked her neatly corn-rowed head into the Xerox room and asked me to come to her office when I was free. I assumed that one of my students had complained, and I mentally reviewed my current classes for signs of discontent. Was someone unhappy with a grade? Offended by something I'd said? Africa was the last thing on my mind.

"I want to show you this," Cheryl said from behind her desk. She handed me an opened air mail letter with a hand-written address on the back and two Xeroxed sheets stapled to it. "Dean Ridgeway got one of these too, and my guess is President Lawrence did as well."

I took the letter from her, stamped on the back to indicate that it had been received on March 19, 1999. This must have been about the time that a judge had released Foley from jail. It had a Nigerian stamp, and was signed with a name I'd never heard of.

> *We like to inform you of the dangerous and shameful conduct of one of your staff KATE ELLIS. It has become necessary because this has*

*been going on for more than six years now. Kate Ellis as you may know is married to a young man from Osogbo who happens to have gotten married to two women before her. He is not divorced from these women and so, Kate is the third wife. Kate Ellis and Funsho Owolabi have been using the name of your University and in particular, your Faculty/Department to invite dubious people from Osogbo, Nigeria for Art Programmes and Exhibitions. She is not a staff of the Arts Department, which is alarming. She was here in Nigeria last December and left in January with the intention of going to write again, a letter to Funsho inviting many people who have paid the sum of N250,000 (two hundred and fifty thousand naira only) to Kate Ellis and Funsho Owolabi for an Exhibition/Art Programme on YOUR DEPARTMENT'S LETTER HEADED PAPER. Using the University and cheating the government, Kate Ellis has helped two people to give birth over there without any expense. This is bad for the integrity of your person and the image of your Faculty/University. Since this has been going on for the past six years, we deem it fit to inform you for your immediate attention and action. Please, act fast.*

I noticed the address in Ibadan on the back of the sheet before looking back up at Cheryl. Did I know the writer? she wanted to know.

"No, but I know where it came from." A copy of my old Canadian passport and a copy of one of my first invitations had given the game away. I remembered that Nike had asked me for a copy of it at some point, and I'd handed it over to her, never suspecting that she was planning to use against me. It was clear now that she was not passive at all, as I'd thought when she was silent during the Commissioner's rants about Gbenga and Foley. She had supplied the documentation for the crime of which she and her husband now had the nerve to accuse me: using my school's letterhead dishonestly. And of course she now knew how old I was.

"I did use English Department letterhead to invite my husband and some of his friends here," I said. "I thought I was simply helping a few people out."

"Have you done this recently?"

"Not recently. In fact, it's because I've stopped that the writer of this letter wants to get me into trouble. It sounds like they want to get me fired. Could they do that?"

"Of course not," said Cheryl. "The university doesn't act based on anonymous letters."

Sitting in her office,e surrounded by her academic journals and books and posters from the Harlem Renaissance, her scholarly field, I felt distant, if not exactly safe, from the world that had given rise to the strange document with its upsetting accusations and inept English. But more than that, I was bewildered and scared by the level to which the hostility it expressed had risen.

"You'd better write to Dean Ridgeway," Cheryl said, handing me the letter and Xeroxes.

"Do you think he'll do anything to me?"

"No," said Cheryl. "Don't worry about that. You have tenure, after all. But he will want you to give him your word that you will not use university's letterhead any more to do this."

"Of course I will. I have absolutely no wish to write more letters."

Not long after this exchange, I learned that Olusegun Obasanjo, Nigeria's newly elected president, had fired the Commissioner shortly after he came into office in 1998, calling him one of the ninety most corrupt members of his country's military and police. Without the bribes that his old job gave him, the man needed a new source of income and so was forced into increased reliance on the Nigerian drug world, much of it controlled by the infamous 419, the cartel that operates lucrative scams by fax and email but also takes the form of violent gangs. I read about it on the internet and learned that Nigeria is a major distribution point for drugs to different parts of the world. It's called 419 because that's the section of the Nigerian criminal code that deals with fraud. So when Foley, looking at the lists of names for me to invite to America, said, "It's drugs," I believed him. It certainly seemed likely that, with Nike's husband now out of the lucrative job as Police Commissioner, my refusal to write unlimited numbers of invitations threatened his economic bottom line—and Nike's as well. They had two very large houses to maintain, just for starters.

His escape from the Commissioner's power made Foley more determined than ever to make the kind of money that would allow him to return to Nigeria in triumph. He told me that Bodunde, who now lived with his wife in Brooklyn and owned a car, was making "big money, a hundred dollars a week at least" as a gypsy cab driver there. All that stood between him and this source of income was a set of wheels. The license that Foley had acquired after so many tries was his only concrete accomplishment thus far in the area of getting a job. If Bodunde could teach him this rewarding trade, the problem of work in the city, and thus living with me on a regular basis, might be solved. Would I help him to buy a van? I liked the idea. Now he would never be able to say that I was not a supportive wife.

In Nigeria, Foley was always happy behind a set of wheels. For my part, I believed that, if he became his own boss, he would not be able to complain about "those people" who paid him too little, as he had done when he worked for the security agency.

He was so confident about the money he would make that he insisted it would be no problem for him to take over the car's monthly payments. We went to a used car dealer in Harlem, where I produced a $300.00 down payment and signed up to pay $200.00 a month for two years. We drove home in a new-looking beige van that seated seven.

But he and Bodunde soon found out that the city has expensive regulations for gypsy cabs, or "dollar vans," as these vehicles were called in Nigeria. At first, I hoped that they might find some other use for a van: providing delivery services or some other form of bargain transportation. Bodunde seemed to know more about that side of life in America than either Foley or I did.

But a month after becoming its owner, Foley left the car with a friend in Brooklyn. This was after it got towed and I had to get it out of hock because Foley could not deal with Manhattan's alternate-side-of-the-street parking system and the two hours of double parking that allows the other side of the street to be cleaned. Finding a space is only the first step, to be followed by a careful reading of street signs and showing up at the right time to move your double-parked car. Foley did not possess these skills, and neither did I.

Sometime after that, when he complained to me that the van's transmission was having problems, I finally started to lose my patience with him. "That's not my fault," I said. "You picked it out. A used car usually has problems. That's why the owner is selling it. I haven't seen the damn thing for ages, so don't go blaming me if it's stopped running."

"I don't want to leave it here," Foley said. "A friend in Brooklyn will take care of it for me."

The whole farcical venture had been my last hope of finding a way for him to be a success in my part of the world, and it had failed. In truth, I was losing interest in making it happen. I had left my first husband when he refused to help himself, and history seemed to be repeating itself, though both times my enjoyment of wearing a wedding ring had me resist letting go of the sense of status I felt when referring to "my husband." These feelings were not the ones I was proud to own as a professor of Women's Studies, but they had not gone away. Nevertheless, if Foley was not willing to learn a trade or pursue some plan related to his carving, I could not see myself supporting a man who took money out and put none in. My way of coping with ungratifying situations, starting when I was a small child, was to detach, living in my head as someone else. Who was the real me, the woman who would stay married no matter what, or the feminist professor I was with my friends and colleagues?

Meanwhile, the part of my life that took place apart from

Foley was expanding. I give him credit for giving me the story that sent me to the New School. But before that, I had taken the step of joining my church choir, even though I was barely able to read music. At first I was the worst sight-reader in the group. I needed help and got it from one of the choir's paid sopranos who gave lessons. Slowly and painfully I improved enough to audition, after a year, and get into a group whose home base was a church in the Village, St. Luke's in the Fields. But I was always on the low end of the totem pole in terms of musical training and experience, very different from being a professor, where you are supposed to be, and actually need to be, the smartest person in the room. I had to practice at home, and Foley would sometimes show his approval by imitating what I was doing. We were both Christians, though we praised God from whom all blessing flow in very different ways.

I have no way of knowing whether sacred music would have become such a large part of my life had Foley not been supportive of it. But my singing, and my return to the church of my Anglican childhood to do that, reinforced each other as I became more involved with both, and Foley's presence in my life helped solidify those commitments. He found the Episcopal services I attended too chilly, so he did not come with me on Sunday mornings to hear me sing. But he came from a part of the world where churchgoing needed no apology, and his pride in telling his friends about my singing in a choir contrasted with what I told mine, which is to say, nothing. I had taken my first steps on this journey before I met him, but with him at my back, I was willing to step out into an area that required a level of confidence I did not yet have. He was delighted when I auditioned for my chorus that rehearsed and performed in the Village, and he and his brothers who were now here, Lawrence and Emmanuel, came to our first concert.

So marriage emboldened me, and I'm grateful to both my husbands for sending me to new places, even though they could not follow me. My first husband gave me enough confidence in what he called my "interesting mind" to allow me to move out into academia without him, and as Foley was less and less present in my life, the music that he gave me the courage to pursue filled in some of the spaces. I know that Marcia and many of my other friends thought that Foley was just using me to get a green card, but I saw him as taking me on an interesting journey, one that began when I got shot and that then took me to Africa. Whatever obstacles arose were there for me to overcome, and I was determined to do it.

While all this was happening, the INS was slowly reviving Foley's green card application. Finally, in February 2000, we went back downtown to the INS building for another interview. The steel-and-plate-glass building takes up an entire city block and dominates an area full of restored nineteenth-century factories with fluted columns, high windows, and intricate fire escapes. We followed the crowd up the elevator, took a number, and, after the usual long wait, were summoned to talk to an African-American man who was younger than Foley. I was glad I had the van records, since it was not our wedding album but these pieces of paper that carried weight with the young man behind the desk. It was not how we felt about each other but what we did as a financial unit that he saw with approval. Yet Foley also charmed him. He had not lost his gift for that since coming to America.

For a year or so after this interview, I saw less and less of Foley. His escape from the Commissioner's clutches made him wary of returning to Nigeria, but he needed to go where he could find work that could give him some kind of dignity, and being a security guard, which involved standing silently and alone in one place for long hours, did not do that. So I did not question him when he traveled on buses to parts of this country where Nigerian friends for whom I'd written invitations apparently enjoyed the employment that eluded him. A few of these friends were then living in Santa Fe. When Foley told me he wanted to join them, I assumed it was because of its reputation as a good place for artists to sell their work. "If you'd like to set up a studio out there," I told him, "we could have two homes. A colleague of mine at Rutgers spends his summers there, and he loves it."

"You can come and visit," he said without saying yes to my proposal. "Those people would love to see you. They are here because of you, you know."

I had a week's spring break in 2001 and decided to buy a plane ticket and visit him. Did I do that because I still loved him? Why did I consider him an essential part of my life when our connection was mainly over the phone? You might say that I had, not one life, but two. I was a professor who loved her job and the demands it made on her. But I was also the woman who had married a Nigerian artist who could not read, who spent summers and winter holidays in his country, who wore clothes that I bought there, and who had extensions put into her hair.

But underneath all that, I think that the suffering I saw in my mother told me that intimacy was not a place of safety. That kind of love was bound up with disappointment and loss. Marcia once told me that she thought I kept men at arm's length, and I think she is right. I saw my first husband as someone who would not leave me, so I felt safe from that disappointment. He brought me real happiness by being the enabling presence in a larger picture that included being a Columbia student, a married woman, and a mother. As long as he was in my life I was not alone even when we were apart, and I loved the freedom that he gave me to be the smart student he assured me that I was, to find a place where I belonged.

Foley gave me a different world in which to belong, and I hung onto it with both hands. So my second venture into marriage turned out to be much like my first one, though externally so different.

Foley was living in a one-bedroom apartment on the outskirts of Santa Fe with three of his Nigerian male friends. They let us have the bedroom and kept telling me how nice it was to see the person who had brought them to this country. But I was not as glad as I had hoped I would be when he pulled me close, and I went along mainly out of relief that *something* was still happening on his side. Two young African-American women dropped by on the night I arrived, and I picked up the possibility that they had their eyes on him and were disappointed to see me there, if they even knew we were married.

One day while everyone was out, I took a taxi into town and spent several hours at Ten Thousand Waves, a well-known spa on the side of a mountain overlooking Santa Fe, My Rutgers colleague had raved to me about its relaxing treatments and spectacular views, and a deep stone massage and a sojourn in a sauna with several other naked people of both sexes served as a pleasant distraction from my disappointment that he was working not as a carver but as a landscaper, one of the jobs for which "illegals" are hired because Americans supposedly don't want those jobs. If I could not do anything for Foley, I could at least do something for myself.

The next day I walked into town and wandered past craft stores selling masks and carvings and jewelry from all over the world. I bought a wide-brimmed straw hat and a two-piece black dress with a long skirt that I wore that night without mentioning its cost. Nor did I tell anyone about the spa, which was even more expensive than I had anticipated. I was simply continuing the secretiveness about money that I'd learned to practice in front of people who have less than I do. I'd done this with Foley right from the start, and it would create difficulties in our marriage that only grew with the passage of time.

Before falling asleep, we prayed together silently, as we did at home, but that was as close as we came to a joining together. We really had nothing to talk about, and neither of us was willing, or able, to say so. I don't know about his reservations, but my own hovered around the prospect of a second failed marriage. What was wrong with me that I could not make a go of this institution so celebrated, in songs, novels, and, as movies? Even if I was, by this point, only going through the motions, it felt less painful to keep doing that than to acknowledge failure.

Before I left, several of the Nigerians I had brought here showed me what they were doing to support themselves. I visited Akeem's drumming school and watched him teach a class. He'd figured out how to break down the moves passed down through generations in his family in a way that let Americans imitate what is second nature to Nigerians. I had watched Foley drum for us visitors when we were first taken to Nike's gallery, and the combination of concentration and rapid, fluid motion had struck me as extremely sexy. Akeem was now a graduate of a local community college.

Gasali, the maker of the *adire* quilt supposedly stolen from the gallery, had married an African-American woman and set up a small studio behind his house, making the kinds of clothes I had bought in Nigeria. Rafiu pounded out African scenes on sheets of aluminum and sold them in a crafts store. All three were making money from the skills they had brought with them, truly engaging with this country financially in a way that Foley was not.

They told me about a major source of their income: a five-day International Folk Art Festival, held every summer in Santa Fe, for which Gasali had the previous year's catalogue. "I made ten thousand dollars last year," he said. "But I do have to work all year to make enough goods to sell. It's really huge. People come to sell from all over the world, and some of them make even more money than me. Foley could do it if he wanted to, but he'd have to bring a lot of carvings."

What I saw in Santa Fe left me bewildered about Foley's agenda for himself. He seemed unable to stay in one place for very long, driven, I suspect, by a dream of the "big money" that did not come with slow, patient study and work, and by pressure from his family back home. Nevertheless, there were practical things we had to do if we were going to remain legally married, mainly to file our taxes together since the green card Foley would soon receive was a provisional one that would be reviewed after two years. Making money was always the stated goal of his travels, but he began refusing to provide the documents that would show how much he had made or what he had been doing. Before leaving for Santa Fe I had simply filed a joint return showing that he had made no income the previous year.

When his temporary green card finally arrived and he left once more for the world of his family, I was relieved that he would be in a place where I knew where he was. "But you need to be back," I said, "to sign our tax return. We will need it to get your permanent green card."

"I'll be back in a month," he promised as he gave me a number where I could reach him in Osogbo. "Two at the most."

That year I spent Christmas with my family of origin in Banff, Alberta, where my sister Ellen's daughter lived with her husband and children but where Foley would never have wanted to be because its winters go down to forty degrees below zero. He and I spoke on the phone, but as April and tax time approached, it was obvious that he was not coming home, as he'd promised, to sign our joint return. I forged his signature and believed him when he said he was making "big money" doing carving in Abuja, the new capital of Nigeria. It certainly sounded like he was happier there than he'd been in New York.

Perhaps this was the moment when I should have stopped calling our one-sided situation a marriage. What held me back was the thought that I would then be returning to the life I'd had before I met him, one that was successful to the outside world but was missing a piece that I had learned was essential to happiness. So it wasn't love that kept me hanging on. Falling in love meant that you lost control of your feelings, and my memories of doing that in my first marriage were followed by enormous pain when the relationship ended a year before I got tenure based on my hard work in Women's Studies and a book-length feminist analysis of the eighteenth-century Gothic novel.

I simply wanted to continue to be a wife and to spend part of my life every year in Nigeria. I've heard about women who have stayed in relationships more obviously abusive than mine, and the question that comes up is always the same: Who would I be without him in my life? *Alone. Unappreciated by a man.* And perhaps an even more debilitating question sometimes keeps us silent and in denial: *What's the matter with me that I picked such a person?*

What came up was the memory of how I'd felt off and on for the first few years after I left Toronto and came to New York. One of my favorite Bob Dylan's songs, with the famous lines about being like a rolling stone, reminded me that I was not the only one who felt this way.

My first husband took me out of that place, and motherhood had given me a steady someone to come home to after he moved out. But the sense of homelessness always hovered just beyond the present. Foley's family might be riven by rivalries among its members, but it was a group that wanted me in it. At home in Canada I came to feel like an outsider. But in Nigeria, where I really was an outsider, I was regularly told that I was one of the family. I knew that their reasons for claiming me as a relative had less to do with me than with them. But unlike my family in Toronto, they appeared to appreciate the person I'd become: a professor, a published writer, the mother of a son. Maybe all these achievements merely signified to them that I could help them. Still, there is something seductive about being able to help people in ways that make a real difference.

So despite the problems that were obvious to others, the plan that we had agreed on before he left—that I would join him in Osogbo once I finished teaching summer school—remained in place. After all, spending summers with Foley and his community of artists was one of the benefits that came with marrying him. Perhaps even the main one. Whatever happened, I did not want to lose that option. So I looked forward once again to spending the second half of my summer in my "home-away-from-home" on the other side of the Atlantic.

I planned to be in Osogbo in August for the annual festival honoring Osun, the town's patron goddess. Foley and I had gone to the festival many times, and our wedding seven years earlier had taken place one day before it began. If I had picked up the hint that he might be having misgivings about returning to the States, I did what I always did and put them aside as I acquired a plane ticket and a visa, perhaps because, while his green card let him come to the States on his own, I still needed his invitations and protection to enter and navigate Nigeria.

Landing at the Lagos airport without an adult male waiting to meet you is too dangerous. Foley promised that we would talk once we were both in his country, and at the end of each static-filled call he would shout the words that always quieted my misgivings: "I miss you."

"I miss you, too," I'd answer, relieved that my delight in hearing his voice could still be lit up. But that didn't mean I was not caught up with my life apart from him, and I assumed he was with his as well. I still saw Nigeria as part of my extended world even as the Nike gallery, its one-time center, no longer contained a circle of welcoming friends. Most of them, the ones who had once chanted, "Katie, Katie, *iyawo* Foley," were now in the States thanks to my invitations. Nigerian life is communal in ways that American life is not, and I wanted to be part of it even if my membership in it happened mainly in my imagination. I think Foley's relatives really were glad to see me when I arrived, a reaction I never got from my family in Toronto.

When Foley told me he couldn't meet me at the airport, I had been disappointed. "My job in Abuja is still going on," he'd said, but I had persuaded myself that he saw me as a wife who would be more forgiving than an employer. "I'll be in Osogbo soon," he had promised. "But I can't get away until my job is done. You know Lateef and Laray. They will pick you up."

And there they were, waving at me from the front of the line of waiting faces on the far side of the airport's plastic door. "How are you? How was your trip? May I carry your bag?" They stumbled over each other's sentences. One of the pleasures of coming to Nigeria has always been the vocal welcome I receive.

"Fine. Good to see you both," I said as their exuberant presence blotted out, at least for the moment, whatever apprehension Foley's absence had created in my mind over the previous months. "This was my first time on Nigeria Airways. It's really great not having a stopover."

My good mood diminished somewhat, though, when Lateef asked me for ninety dollars to drive me to Osogbo. I'd expected to pay for their fuel and to throw in something for their time and effort. Fuel is cheap in Nigeria, and I had counted on the three-hour trip costing about half that amount. "We had a blowout on the way here, so we bought an extra tire," explained Laray, the car's owner, "because of you." I gathered that they had not had a spare and was annoyed at the veneer of concern covering over a move to get money out of me.

So ninety dollars felt excessive. I could see that they had bought used tires, so their life expectancy was uncertain. But given our unequal resources, how could I know what would be fair? I handed Lateef the requested American hundred, though not without some concern about how much I had brought. There are no ATM machines in Nigeria, and credit card numbers are too easy to steal. What you have brought is all you will have, and I'd never figured out how much I should carry strapped to my body under my printed African clothes.

I settled in the back seat and looked out the window as we pulled out onto the highway while my companions chatted in front. Piles of cinder blocks, lead pipes, and heavy wiring were strewn along both sides of the four-lane highway to Ibadan. Though a few buildings might be under construction, the materials surrounding them looked abandoned.

Whenever I asked Nigerians how things are going on the political front, they invariably said they were getting better. Since my first trip, five presidents had promised improvement, but Obasanjo, the first Yoruba man to be elected, was now in office. Nigeria since independence has been wracked with deadly conflicts between the Muslim Hausa in the north, the Christian Igbo where the oil was, and the Yoruba, who had been brought along by the British. Would anything change now, and how would I know if it had?

Eventually we turned onto the two-lane road that required Laray's considerable skills in avoiding potholes. Wanting to supplement the small gifts I'd brought with me, I bought a pineapple and two yams from a roadside stand where an elderly woman sat under a thatched roof supported by bamboo poles, waiting for travelers like us. Sellers like her would always be there by the side of the road no matter who was in power.

Finally we arrived at a house that Foley had rented, a pale yellow two-story building with a corrugated tin roof and a small courtyard crisscrossed with clotheslines. Foley had talked about building a house for his mother in Osi, as well as a living space and gallery for himself, and presumably me, in Osogbo. But for this he needed the "big money" that he must have hoped to find in America. He also needed someone he trusted in Nigeria to supervise the construction.

The house was bigger than those that Foley had rented in the past. Garbage dumped over the wall around the courtyard was visible from the road, but putting it in a can would have been pointless since Nigeria's almost nonexistent government provides no systematic garbage collection. The house's most surprising feature was an image of Jesus painted on the wall beside the front door. His face was paler than the wall behind it. His shoulder-length brown hair matched a delicate Van Dyck beard, and one long finger pointed to his red heart. I would later find the original on a kitchen shelf, on a pamphlet put out by a nearby evangelical church. I never found out who had transferred it to our wall.

The family I had come to see was assembled in front of this portrait, welcoming me by shouting my name. Idowu, the one adult male, was related to Foley, though I never figured out how. He knew that Americans expect a hug, and he gave me an awkward one. At the other extreme was Foley's mother, who did not join the shouting. She bent her knees and lowered her head as she took my hand, a gesture of deference to a senior person that always annoys me, though I'm sure she doesn't know my feelings any more than I know hers. My relationship with her has never been easy since, unlike the other Nigerians I knew, she speaks no English. She had been a widow since 1995 and she must be close to my age, but her life has been unimaginably different from mine.

Between these two stood Yetunde, who would cook for everyone. She was said to be a widow, but I've never seen a photograph of her husband. This is odd only because Nigerians will always show you their family albums. I had first met her when Gbenga was born and she was nursing Soji, her youngest son. Where had she been before that? Foley once complained that she often disappeared, presumably to be with a man, a complaint that put to rest what the Commissioner had said about her in his living room. She was a large woman who darkened her brows with a heavy brown pencil. Like Foley's mother, she never smiled in my presence, though her children were all over me the moment I stepped out of the car.

As *de facto* head of this loosely connected family, Idowu picked up my suitcase, and I followed him to my room, leaving my shoes by the door and walking barefoot across the cool cement of the living room floor, past a sofa and matching chairs and a standing full-length mirror, all grouped around a TV set. At night the sofa often served as a bed, and this time it was claimed by Foley's mother, who had come from Osi and was waiting with the rest of us for her son to appear. A small kitchen with a sink and a kerosene stove adjoined the courtyard beyond rows of sheets hanging from a clothesline. The house had two bedrooms in addition to mine, one for Idowu and a cousin named Kunle, and one for Yetunde and her children.

These children would be in and out of my room the entire time I was there, since its door was kept shut with only a bent nail and could be pushed open with a loud bang. Privacy does not carry the importance in their world that it does in mine. The children wanted to check out the contents of my suitcase, and they admired the mosquito net that Idowu hung from the ceiling above my bed.

But most of all, they wanted to use my laptop. I had brought a converter and quickly spotted an outlet that would feed it whenever there was power. That night I made each of them a file, but I knew I'd have to be forceful in asserting my right to use the computer, too.

Kunle and Idowu were married, though their wives and children lived elsewhere. In their family albums everyone looked happy. But I had no idea how either of them spent his days, or why they lived in Osogbo rather than in with their wives. The men went home periodically, but daily companionship with one's spouse was apparently not an expected part of those women's lives.

Foley obviously shared this perspective, and I, who'd always said I did not want to be joined at the hip to anyone, did, too.

As for Emmanuel, he was now living in New Jersey, while Sade and Gbenga were in the same pale green room I'd visited as Gbenga's prospective *iya* six years before. I went there, two days after I arrived, and found a shy, handsome little boy who gave me the family smile I knew he would have. He shook my hand when Sade introduced me to him as his "Mama Kate." I did not see her again until I was about to leave. But wanting to let her know that I harbored no hard feelings about our time together in the States, I promised to send her, via Western Union, a hundred dollars "for Gbenga."

# 10

The weekend passed with no news from Foley, and I was happy to discover that I was not the only one who was annoyed. Men in that part of the world have a lot of leeway to come and go as they please, and Idowu kept assuring me that Foley would arrive "today for sure." But he also told me that Foley's mother was "up half the night worrying," perhaps fearing for his safety after the informal ten o'clock curfew had passed and he had not arrived. I was glad to know that Foley's failure to appear was seen as thoughtless behavior even as it was also dismissed as "no problem."

I kept myself busy as the next week began, rereading *The Mill on the Floss*, a novel I would be teaching in the fall, and looking forward to the Osun festival, which would happen on Friday. Its once neglected site has been restored, and the walls that line the dirt road that runs through a lush grove to the bank of the Osun River now feature sculpted figures made by a famous German artist named Suzanne Wenger. Tall wooden carvings of traditional deities rise up behind these walls above the low, dense foliage. Several days of preparation lead up to a final procession along this road, where an offering to Osun, held aloft in a calabash by a young woman said to be a virgin, is poured into the water. On this day the road is always packed with people moving toward and away from the river. Most are on foot, but a few drive cars of every age and degree of elegance, their drivers honking until the pedestrians let them pass. The whole town, it seems, turns out.

On the day of the festival, the traditional hereditary ruler of the area occupies an open space near the river. He is surrounded by his many wives, all dressed in the same bright-colored cloth with much gold thread running through it. Groups of drummers and dancers come forward to entertain him.

I was there this time with Idowu and Yetunde, and as we moved with the crowd, I noticed another white woman, who quickly made her way over to me.

"I'm living in Lagos," she told me, "doing West African programming for National Public Radio." What brought me here? she wanted to know, and as the crowd moved past us, I gave her a brief history of my marriage. "I'd love to interview you," she said, "to get your thoughts on this festival and the situation of Osogbo artists today. My name's Sylvia, by the way."

I was happy to be consulted as an expert on Nigerian culture. "I don't think they are doing well," I said over the rising and falling sound of drums behind us. What did she know, I was eager to ask, about the current state of the Nike Centre?

"I'll be in Osogbo for another week," Sylvia said. "I'm staying at Nike Davies' house. Do you know where it is?"

"I certainly do. That's where I met my husband."

"Great. Why don't you come out tomorrow morning, and we can talk some more?"

"I'd love to," I said, and we shook hands before parting. I was at that moment glad that Foley had not yet appeared, since I knew he would not want me to be going to Nike's house, the place where things had started so well between us. I shared his disenchantment with his former friend and boss, whose vicious husband had put him in jail on trumped-up charges. Perhaps that fact alone should have been reason for me to cut off communication with her, as Foley had done.

And then there was that letter to Cheryl and the president of Rutgers. Nike had to have known about it, even though someone else had obviously written it. But a Rutgers colleague who grew up in Ghana and knew Nike as a sought-after batik artist told me she thought that the Commissioner had ruined her friend's life, and I agreed with her.

So my eagerness to talk to another American about this part of the world trumped knowing that Foley would be angry when he learned where I'd been. Asking Sylvia to meet me somewhere else would have been a smart move, but I didn't think to make it. I also can't deny that, in spite of her efforts to sabotage my job, my marriage, and my plans for adoption, I was still fascinated by Nike. She had made a huge impression on me on my first visit, and I wanted to find out anything I could about the current status of her relationship with the Commissioner, who'd recently given her a baby girl. As Idowu, Yetunde, and I made our way out to the main road and into a taxi, I asked Idowu about the "PC," as everyone called the Commissioner.

"He never comes to Osogbo now," he said, which was fine with me since I certainly did not want to see him. I'd heard from Foley and his brothers that he had seduced several of Nike's young students, and rumor had it that he had forced some to have abortions and all of them to remain silent. All this only made me more eager to check out my former friend for myself.

As I should have expected, getting away without telling anyone was impossible. Going anywhere alone in Nigeria always invites questions. Nike's students used to ask me where I was going when they saw me on the road. *Where's there to go around here?* I wanted to shout. I knew that their questions were only part of the drawn-out greetings that begin every Nigerian conversation, but they still annoyed me. Sometimes the speaker would ask to come with me, hoping that I would buy him or her something.

On this trip I'd tried a few times to take a walk just to lower my level of irritation at Foley's continued absence, and someone in the house always offered to join me, not just because I'm a white woman needing protection but because the wish to be alone is incomprehensible in such a crowded part of the world. So I gave up and mostly stayed in my room, taking notes on my reading and writing long entries in the journal I kept on my computer.

The next day I headed toward our gate as someone shouted the usual question. "I'm going to be interviewed by a woman from America," I shouted back. "She's staying with Nike, so I'll take a taxi." Of course Idowu and Kunle told me that my husband would be angry when he found out, and I wondered if my action might be seen by his friends as exposing his precarious position as an African man married to an American wife whose money surely helped to support his family. I thought about Sara giving cash to her husband before they enter a restaurant, so he could be the one paying their bill. Nigeria is a fiercely patriarchal culture, and men are not *supposed* to be dependent on their women. But stronger than this concern was my desire to let Nike know that nothing that she had done, or would do, could harm me in any way. My marriage might be running into troubled waters, but I suspected that hers was also.

"I just don't think that keeping your distance is the best way to treat your enemies," I said to my hosts when they caught up to me as I opened the wrought iron gate. "They want you to be afraid of them, and keeping away tells them that you are." My irritation with Foley's absence was part of what propelled me to go back to a place where a more hopeful future had first shown up. Nevertheless, I did not feel fearful and was unwilling to act as if I did.

Getting to Nike's house that morning required two taxis, not just because of the distance but because in Nigeria you never ride in one alone. You stand on the side of the road and call out your destination to drivers in battered blue vehicles filled with passengers. With luck, a driver who is going your way will stop and add you to his load. My first taxi took me to a roundabout at one end of Osogbo's market area, where narrow streets wind between two-and-three-story buildings painted cream-colored below rusted tin roofs. Some display carved wooden balconies, the appealing style left over from colonial times. It was in one of these that I had hoped to create my second home with Foley.

A policeman stood in a small kiosk at the center of the traffic circle where my first taxi let me off. A sign declaring "God First Petroleum" rose up behind this kiosk, and bumper-to-bumper traffic filled the air with exhaust fumes. Beyond the traffic circle was a bus depot where aging vehicles, plastered with bumper stickers calling on the name of Jesus, waited to collect their low-fare customers. Everywhere I could see signs announcing *God's Glory Dental Services, Divine Stitches, Full Gospel Business Fellowship*: a mixture of the sacred and the commercial unimaginable in my country. My favorite of these signs, one that I used to see on the road near Nike's house, proclaims Nigeria's ever-present optimism: *No Sorrow Photography*.

To get a second taxi, I had to make my way past the bus depot to the beginning of the road that branches off to Nike's house. Standing next to a blind beggar seated on the curb, I only needed to shout, "Nike Davies," since she is so well known in the town. *This Vehicle Is Insured With The Blood Of Jesus* declared a sticker pasted to the window of the taxi that stopped for me, against which I was pressed for the duration of most of my second ride. Perhaps this was a reassuring thought, since insurance is not available from anyone else. But the owners of these cabs, as well as their passengers, had all gone to the Osun festival the day before. So I was curious, and still am, about what it was like to embrace two religions at the same time. Did they believe both of them in the same way? Back in the States, Foley had given me a very Nigerian answer: *no problem*. "There's only one God," he said.

As my fellow passengers piled out at their various destinations, I could sit back and survey the small stores and hotels I used to pass when I lived at Nike's house or in the dormitory not far from the gallery. The road took me past the gallery and the work area beyond it, where our traditional wedding had been held. That day the gates to the gallery were open, but the place was deserted.

Sylvia would want to talk about how global economics played a role in its slow death, but I thought there was a personal dimension to this diminution of Nike's once-powerful project to teach Nigerian women to support themselves. She was asking me what I thought about this complicated place, and she apparently wanted to hear what I had to say.

That was my frame of mind as I stepped out of the taxi and greeted the guard at Nike's front gate. As I made my way toward the porch, where I had spent many hours with my computer on my lap, I noticed some changes that displayed, not a decline, but rather a rise in her already spectacular prosperity. The deep pink bougainvillea was as lush as I remembered it, and the walls of the house had a fresh coat of white paint. But the cement path connecting the main house with the now-enlarged guest building where my group and I had spent three weeks was now inlaid with bits of colored glass that glittered in the midday sun.

The uniformed gatekeeper directed me to the back patio outside the kitchen door where Foley and I had held the hesitant *tête-à-tête* that set up our first and only date, when we silently watched a soccer game on TV. Next to it a flight of outdoor steps led to the open second floor, which served as a sleeping quarters for the students, who could be summoned by a shout at any time, day or night. A tall hedge ran along one side of the house, broken by a wooden gate. Behind it, a mown lawn was encircled by more tall, clipped hedges. Trees had been planted here and there, and peacocks wandered slowly among them. I felt as if I'd stepped into a Merchant–Ivory film set, not in colonial Africa, but in late Victorian England.

In the center of all this, two long tables were covered with Nigeria's traditional blue-and-white *adire*. One was laden with pitchers and platters, and several of the students, dressed in *adire*, recognized me. I kissed them on both cheeks before joining my fellow guests. Some of these were academics from America or visiting journalists like Sylvia, who was still asleep, her husband, a reporter from the *Financial Times*, told me. The rest were American Embassy employees fleeing a densely crowded Lagos for the

Osun Festival. It was now clear to me that Nike was making her money running an expensive bed-and-breakfast.

Before I could take a seat, Nike appeared, also wearing printed *adire*, and presented me as the wife of "one of our carvers." I thought it best to go along with her use of the possessive pronoun, so I told her guests about meeting my husband "right over there." I gestured fondly and quite sincerely toward the back porch, piled with hairy yams and cooking pots, as I accepted a glass of freshly squeezed orange juice.

The woman sitting next to me, an African-American historian from Dartmouth College who knew people that I knew in the Rutgers history department, was doing research on the cloth that surrounded us. I soon picked up a shared take on the issue I cared about most—the rumors of a coming war against Iraq—that was closer to mine than the insistence of Idowu, and the other Nigerians I knew, that America was great. All this made me glad that I'd taken the risk and come to this memory-laded place.

Finally, Sylvia appeared, bringing her tape recorder. By the end of our interview, I found myself wishing that I had a few friends like her in Nigeria, people with whom I could have a conversation based on shared assumptions. Her English husband was nice too, and it was mainly out of a wish to see them again that I accepted Nike's invitation to come back the following Saturday for dinner. Back at home, I told Idowu that Nike looked thin and not too happy. Plumpness is highly valued in Nigeria, and the Commissioner himself had told me, in happier times, that I was too scrawny for his taste.

"You know you're asking for trouble if you go back to her house," Idowu said, looking away for a moment from the video he was watching.

"I don't agree. It can't hurt to be friendly. I love being here with you," I added, "but I like meeting new people too."

Ten days after my arrival in his country, Foley finally walked through the front door of the house where everyone was waiting to see him. His anticipated presence lit up the room, as it always did. I felt glad to see him, but I noticed that my feeling was not as strong as it had once been. Perhaps it was only the effect of his unexplained absence, which he'd kept extending for reasons he never shared. But I also saw that he, too, had changed, that even as he smiled and greeted everyone, he wasn't fully with any of us. I'm not a fan of public displays of affection, but Foley's coldness was obvious to me, and presumably to the others as well. Everyone except his taciturn mother made a big fuss over him, but I sensed that he was holding back a part of himself, and perhaps not only from me. I now know what it was, but at the time I was more concerned with my impending visit to Nike.

I waited until the following day to tell him about my interview with Sylvia and was relieved that no one had mentioned it before I did. "Nike will poison you," he concluded when I asked how he felt about my plans.

"How could she? She's having a big party. There'll be too many other people." I wasn't really asking for his permission to go, but I knew it needed to look like I was. The man I married had never seen himself as a patriarch wanting to be obeyed by his woman. He was different, Nike had said, and his friends agreed. But did that mean that they would not judge him negatively in the light of those traditional standards? I'd heard these same friends make comments about bossy American women even when, a moment later, they assured me they weren't talking about me.

"I want her to know," I said, "that she can't hurt me. Or you either. If I avoid her, she will have won."

"She's dangerous," he insisted.

"How so? What can she do?"

"You don't know her," he said. "She's a wicked woman."

"He's right, Kate," Idowu chimed in. What made them so sure? I wondered. What did they know that I did not?

"But I really want to go." In fact, now that I'd told Nike I would come, I was determined not to go back on my word. I knew that by doing so I was really making a larger statement about Foley's avoidant way of dealing with her. If I went along with him I'd be endorsing what struck me as his increasing paranoia with no understanding of what had brought it on. Nike had been his *iya* in the days when everyone at the Centre called her "Mama Nike," and he and the other men did a full traditional bow, a kind of push-up, before addressing her. She had been my *alarina,* and I still had the batik blouse she had given me when Foley and I went to her house at Lekki Beach and I had the feeling that her police commissioner husband, the guy she had married to protect her as a single woman in patriarchal Nigeria, had taken over, not only her school, but her life. I wanted to see for myself if that had been an accurate hunch.

"All right," he said. "But make sure you tell your son it's not because of me that you died."

"I'll make you a bet," I said, not sure if he was really serious, and if he was, what that said about his state of mind. "If I die, you have won. But if I don't die, I've won. How's that?"

Foley just shrugged, and for the next two days we didn't really speak. His mother remained in Osogbo until the end of the week, and her presence may have given him an incentive to behave as though nothing had changed. But after she left he slept in the living room to be next to the phone, which rang at all hours. "I don't want to disturb you," he said when I mentioned this, though my concern was mainly for what others would think. The door to my room, held shut by its thin bent nail, could be opened from the outside only with a sharp bang. But who could be calling him so often? I thought of my friend who's in the FBI, who told me that they have a special section dealing with Nigerian white-collar crime. But mostly I was bewildered and embarrassed by this new degree of public withdrawal, and numbly aware that we were not really happy in each other's company. I assumed that the others noticed where my husband slept, and wondered what they thought was his reason for doing so.

The day of Nike's dinner finally arrived, and Foley was out, as he often was. Since his return, I'd grown more and more convinced that a show of fear on my part would give Nike just what she wanted. And behind her, at what close range I was now not sure, lurked our real enemy, the full force of whose power over anyone he disliked had been brought home to me by Foley's arrest. I felt uneasy when I pictured my *oko*'s reaction on my return, but I also felt relieved, as I got ready to flag down a taxi, that he wasn't around.

I put on my most elegant traditional outfit, made from a pale blue *asoke*, a striped fabric with a silver thread running through it. Perhaps this outfit was why the cab driver charged me twice what I had paid the week before, leaving me with not enough cash for a taxi ride home. Nike might invite me to stay in her guest house, though my fear of Foley's disapproval would not let me accept her offer. Or she might let one of her drivers take me home. Or loan me the fifty *naira*—about thirty-five cents—that I would need to get home.

I counted some fifty guests assembled on the open upper floor when I arrived. Strings of Christmas lights edged the waist-high outer railings, and the dinner was set out buffet style: rows of entrees, silverware, cloth napkins, and china plates. Nike was standing at the top of the stairs when I came in, and I asked her how she was: *"Bawo ni?"* She was obviously prospering to a degree I had never seen before and clearly enjoyed being surrounded by people she considered important. But she looked even more drawn than she had in the heat of the day a week earlier.

"I've had a hard year," she said simply, and I concluded that her marriage had come apart even if it maintained a smooth surface. I was familiar with this way of handling disappointment. My mother had done the same until her mind left her well before her body gave out.

"Me, too," I said as one of the students handed me a bitter lemon soda. Nike had always boasted that her husband had eyes only for her, and I wondered how long it had taken her to learn about the Commissioner's behavior, just as I'd wondered how old my mother had been when she learned of the first of my father's affairs. "It's just gossip," Nike used to say. That was my mother's public front as well, and perhaps mine also, more than I was willing to admit.

I sat at one of the long tables near Sylvia, but she was giving all her attention to a fellow American journalist sitting next to her and was clearly not as interested in my company as I was in hers. The man sitting next to me was Swiss, and I learned from a story he told me how other observers, both Africans and outsiders, see Nigeria as a corrupt and dangerous place, putting it in a category all by itself. He was visiting Lagos, he told me, but lived in Kinshasa with his wife and two children. I asked how Kinshasa was different from Lagos. "People are much more aggressive about money here," he said, and he told me about being robbed in a bar in Lagos. "I know you should never leave a drink," he said, "but I must have been a little drunk because I did just that and went to the men's room. The next thing I knew I was waking up in a hospital. My wallet was gone, and my hotel room had been stripped. I still have no idea what they put in my drink, but I was told that they'd left me in a ditch, so I'm lucky to be alive."

"Do you know how you got to the hospital?"

"Not really. The thieves had my cell phone, and I think the police got them when I told them my number." We then turned to the subject of American politics. In that group of people who knew the Third World first hand, the consensus, seven months before the Iraq war, was that George Bush was a disaster, and that the death of Saddam Hussein would usher in more real damage and instability to the Middle East than anything he, Saddam, had inflicted or could inflict.

This unanimity of view around me was not surprising, since many of Nike's guests were Europeans. Even the American Embassy people to whom I spoke insisted that you can't impose a democratic system on a country where conflict is controlled only by ruthlessness. Nigeria had given them a perspective that we shared, one we could talk about over a delicious meal, which included groundnut soup and fried plantains, two of my favorite African foods, as well as several varieties of meat, including some kind of snake that I passed up.

After dinner, the students carried our chairs and we followed them down the stairs and into the courtyard for the entertainment. On my previous visits, some of Nike's students had danced for her visitors, accompanied by drummers. For this occasion, in what I took to be one more sign that her school was in decline even as her guest house flourished, the dancers had been brought in from Lagos. They were sloppy and unskilled, and there was too much slapstick for my taste. I could hardly wait to tell Foley about his enemy's deterioration and to give him the details of the dinner and dancing as well as her drawn face. Her husband had destroyed her school and alienated many of her former students, not just Foley and his brothers. Now he, to use a favorite Nigerian expression, was "not around."

Yet the food and the wine were real treats after a week of Yetunde's starch-based meals. Nike's house guests must have paid a lot more than I could have afforded, given how long I'd stayed with her on my sabbatical, for the taste of "the real Nigeria" that she provided, complete with soft bed, abundant food served by her students, and transportation in one of her yellow vans, to the Osun groves or the King's palace. Her facilities were less elegant then, but my first impressions of Nigeria had come to me through the same filter. Perhaps my belief that I could make a home in this part of the world, even if I couldn't imagine moving to it permanently, was buttressed by amenities that disappeared when I left her guarded premises.

By eleven I was beginning to worry about getting home. I was too offended by the climactic moment in the dancing, in which a very heavy girl was carried by a bunch of staggering men and dropped on the floor, and by the laughter that this produced all around me, to approach Nike. But being a lone white woman standing on the roadside waiting for a taxi late at night in an unpopulated area was not a good idea, even if the problem of the fare could be surmounted by a quick trip to my suitcase under my bed at the end of the ride. I'm usually cautious on the subject of divine intervention, but I can only ascribe to some such force the appearance just at that moment of Baba Sunday—Foley's friend, who had stayed with us for three months.

"I went by your house to greet Foley and heard you were here," he said when I rushed over to him, trying not to draw attention to myself as I pushed through the applauding crowd whose opinion of the performance was so different from mine. "I don't trust Nike, so I thought I'd better come and get you."

"Thank God you did, Baba Sunday," I said, hugging him breathlessly. "Let me say goodbye to Nike, and I'll be right with you." I had to endure another dance number before I could thank my hostess for a delightful evening.

"Is Foley angry?" I asked my rescuer as I settled into the front seat of his Peugeot, parked outside the gate.

"Yes. You were very foolish to come here." Baba Sunday spoke English better than anyone else I knew except Nike, though it was not the language he usually spoke.

"Is that what he thinks or what you think?"

"It doesn't matter what I think," Baba Sunday said. "In Nigeria, wives do not defy their husbands like you did. It makes him look bad, so you look bad, too."

"Do I look bad to you?"

"No, because I know you. But in Nigeria, what the husband says is the way it is. You know that."

"Yes, I know," I said as we approached the now empty kiosk near the market.

"Did you enjoy yourself at least?"

"The performers were awful compared to what Nike's dancers used to do. It looks like everything connected with the Nike Centre for Arts and Culture has fallen apart."

"It has. Nike makes all her money from visitors now."

"Well, they seemed to like the entertainment, but I certainly didn't."

"So why did you go?"

"She invited me. Why should I not have gone? Foley said I would be poisoned, but it was a buffet dinner for fifty people. She could not have gotten at my food only."

"Was the food good?"

"Yes. There was lots of it, too."

"She's still a very wicked woman."

"She's a very rich woman. Maybe the school has fallen apart, but I'm sure she's charging her guests a bundle. She may be suffering, but not financially."

"That doesn't make what I said not true."

"But I'm curious about her. I don't see why she would want to do any of us harm." We drove the rest of the way home in silence, each of us deep in our own incommunicable thoughts. Baba Sunday was older than Foley, and I trusted him to give me an assessment of my behavior in Nigeria from a Nigerian observer's perspective. And that night it was particularly important to me that he do so.

When I walked into the living room, Foley and Idowu were sitting on the sofa, watching a Yoruba video. "I don't want to talk to you," Foley said without turning in my direction.

"Well, I guess I should get back to Lagos, then, and take the first plane out of here."

"Okay, if that's what you choose."

"It's not my choice.... Look, this is crazy." I walked in front of one of the stuffed chairs and the sofa so I was standing between him and the TV. Idowu moved over so I could sit down between them, but I shook my head and turned toward Foley. "I'm married to you," I said. "And I want to stay married to you. It makes no sense that things should fall apart over something like this. I understand why you are mad about what I did tonight. But there's a lot of things that you do that I don't like. Or understand. The people I had dinner with come from where I come from. And I can talk with them about things I can't talk about with you. What's wrong with that?"

"Good night, both of you," said Idowu. "I'll see you in the morning."

Foley turned off the TV as I sat down on the couch.

"I think something has been bothering you for quite a while," I began. "What is it?"

He paused for several minutes. "I just don't feel good living in New York with you," he began. "That's why I came to Nigeria. I decided to live my life like I'm not married."

"I think I've been doing the same thing," I said. "I think neither of us is all that good at being married, when you get right down to it. We certainly aren't connected the way married people I know are connected. But what did I do to make you feel that way? What do you want that I haven't given you? I wrote the invitations that got you here, and I could have gotten into serious trouble about that. And I changed my citizenship to get you a green card." I was too taken up with my own anger at him to mention that Nike was behind this serious trouble.

"You give me what I ask, but you don't do it like this." He extended his arm with his palm open. "It's like this." He closed his fist tightly.

"Give me an example, something I did."

"I don't know one. I feel like a small boy is all."

"That's because you act like a small boy. You do things behind my back. You wrote checks without telling me. I had to close our joint account after that. Don't you remember going to the bank with me and trying to open it again?"

"I wrote only two," he said. "And they were small small."

"Three. And you didn't tell me. Then there was the phone bill. I'm sure you didn't feel good asking me to punch in the code whenever you wanted to call long distance, but you didn't give me any choice. I have to pay my bill, or my phone will get cut off. We could have talked about how many calls you needed to make, but you just did everything behind my back." Of course there was more to it than that. The fact that he was living in my apartment, surrounded by all of my things and none of his, was like living in the home of your parents growing up.

"I'm sorry about that," he said simply.

"You're always sorry. But what should we do now?"

Foley looked down. "You know, if I don't take care of my family, no one here will respect me. When you are a man my age in Nigeria, there are things they expect you to do."

I did understand that this was true. I also knew that his family saw me as the main source of the support they wanted him to provide for them. They would not be happy if we split up. One thing a man his age was supposed to do was to build a house for his family, and he'd shown me blueprints for one in Osi, not just for me but for his mother and probably some others as well. But it didn't seem to be getting built. When he lived with me in New York, it was on my premises, and this absence of a home he could call his own, along with the fact that I was giving him money, probably contributed to his feeling like a small boy.

We sat in silence for a while, listening to the throb of insects outside punctuated by an occasional car horn. Finally I said, "Maybe we'd better just go to sleep. Maybe in the morning we'll be able to think more clearly." We both stood up and put our hands on each other's shoulders, not an embrace of people who share warm feelings but an acknowledgment of shared weariness. Then he followed me into the room where I'd been sleeping alone.

As he usually did, Foley fell asleep immediately. Lying far enough away from him that our bodies would not touch, I kept going back to what he had said about feeling like a small boy. As long as he needed my help, I believed that we would stay married. But money was the form that such help usually took, and an American man would also have felt like a child in his position. Perhaps even Sara's husband felt that way.

Twice the phone rang from the living room just as I was sinking into sleep, and Foley got up each time and spoke loudly to the caller in Yoruba. "Who was that?" I asked as he lay back down under my hanging mosquito net. "And what did they want from you at this time of night?"

"It's the man who got me my job in Abuja," Foley said as if that would resolve, not just the late hour of the calls, but the unspoken mystery between us.

"Is he calling from here or from the States?"

"From U. S. I'll explain tomorrow."

"Okay." I'm a verbal person in a verbal profession, and I've had to be good at learning things to get there. But I had no idea how to talk about his criticism of my generosity, not just to him but to anyone. Perhaps its very existence was what made him feel like a small boy. That and the fact that he lived in my space in

New York. Perhaps we just did not have enough things that we *could* talk about. Listening to the insects pulsing beyond the slatted window, an occasional blast of music from a car radio, and intermittent cries from a distant night vigil, I lay motionless on my back next to my sleeping husband, alternately upset with him and with the man calling from the States, but no more answers came.

# 11

The next morning I woke up to the sound of Foley's voice talking to his cousin Kunle outside. "I'm making tea," I called out. "Do either of you want some?"

Foley shook his head without looking in my direction. But Kunle, apparently unaware of what had gone on, turned to me with a smile and said, "You know, Kate, we don't drink tea in Nigeria." He came inside, and Foley followed him while I remembered the reaction of Foley and his friends to the brownies I thought they would love because I love them. "Too sweet," they had said, smiling and showing their beautiful teeth.

"Well, let me get some for me then," I said, looking at Foley. "We need to talk about last night. Do you have any more thoughts about what we said?" He walked over to the couch and sat down without answering my question. "Well, I have some things to say, but I can't do it on an empty stomach."

Foley shrugged, an ambiguous signal that nevertheless sent me into the kitchen, ducking under lines of drying laundry strung across the courtyard. As I plugged in the electric kettle and took a tea bag from the small Lipton's box I had bought when I arrived, I thought about the shaky status of my marriage. I knew that my presence in his life did little to cushion his troubles in America, most of which revolved around his difficulty earning money. But I didn't think he saw ending the marriage as a way to fix that.

I retrieved the powdered milk and lump sugar that went with the tea from a shelf above the sink filled with dirty dishes. Foley was alone when I carried my mug over to one of the stuffed chairs and sat down facing him. "Okay, let me start," I said, assuming that he wanted to have this conversation as much as I did. "I think we are both going to have to talk more about our feelings. If you had told me a long time ago about feeling like a small boy, we could maybe have done something about it. I mean, other than pull away from each other. Can I tell you what I've been feeling?"

Foley was silent so I went on. "I feel like I'm surrounded by secrets. Maybe it's because I don't speak Yoruba, but it always seems like there are things going on that I don't know anything about. Do you know what I mean?"

Foley thought a minute before he spoke. "I do have a secret that I've been keeping from you. It's something Nike told me never to tell you, but I want to tell it now." I looked at him and he paused again. "Femi is my son."

I could hear Femi's voice coming from the courtyard in front of the house, where Yetunde's children were playing noisily. *Only Femi?* was my first thought. *What about the other two?* "Who's his mother?" I asked. Yetunde was the obvious answer, but I had never been able to see her paired with Foley. Then again, even established couples in Nigeria don't employ the kinds of gestures that signal a tight bond in my world.

"She's someone I knew in Osi," he said. "Long time. My mother never liked her, and I didn't want to marry and stay in Osi, so my mother took care of Femi until Yetunde married."

"Was this when you disappeared from Osi and didn't tell anyone where you were?"

"Yes," he said after a moment's hesitation.

"Okay, but why didn't you tell me all this before now?"

"Nike said you would never marry me if you knew."

"Knew what? That you *were* married? Or *are* married?"

"No. I just didn't want to marry and live in Osi."

"I'm getting the feeling that you don't want to marry and live anywhere. How come you wanted to marry me?"

"Because you were going to help me be great, like my grandfather. He traveled, you know, and he married white. If I stayed in Osi, I would never be great. I went away from Osi because I wanted to be great."

"How many wives did your grandfather have?"

"I don't know," said Foley. "But many."

I had always seen his ambition, the flight from home that had brought him under Nike's roof, as a sign that we had something in common. But for him, being "great" apparently involved more than having an international reputation as an artist. Having "something in common" shows up between people who have a shared history. It doesn't have to be exact. Marcia and I were dancers together, dancers who turned away from that world and became academics. We started in very different places, but our paths converged. We see many things very differently, but we like talking about them. We wouldn't be friends if that weren't so.

"So you want many wives, too?"

"No," said Foley sharply. "I tell you that many times. I wanted you to help me is all."

"And I did help you, didn't I? You've had more help than anyone else that I invited to the States."

"No," he said. "You didn't help me be great." How could I have done that? I wondered. It's not something a person can do for somebody else.

"But I did more for you than I did for any of the others that I invited to the States. Like buying you a van. You lived for free in my house, and you came and went. I let you have the freedom to do what you needed to do. What more could I have done?"

"You helped people who cheated you," he said. "Like Emmanuel. I never cheated you."

"I know." Neither of us spoke for a while. I didn't know what else to say, and perhaps he didn't either. I had never said anything like this to him in all our time together. In fact, the two of us always prided ourselves on the fact that we never fought. But why did we not? This was not really a marriage as my culture defines it: a coming together of two people because they deeply love each other. But growing up at home, I had not seen marriage as a desirable state. Had it not crippled my mother? So I would be a dancer, a star, a writer: someone who elicited admiration for what she created. I didn't need a husband for that, and a husband might even get in the way of my dreams for myself.

"I'm sorry," he said finally, looking down at his shoeless feet.

"Okay," I said. "But what about Femi? Does he know you're his father?"

"I told him, but I said I couldn't tell you, and he shouldn't tell you either."

"Well, I love Femi. Let's call him now."

When Femi appeared at the door, Foley spoke to him in Yoruba. He came toward me and I put my arm around his thin shoulder. "How're you doing?" I asked him. "*Bawo ni?*"

"*Dada ni.*" The look on his face as he turned toward the two of us told me that Foley was speaking the truth. It occurred to me that having a real small boy in his life in America might lessen his feelings of being one himself.

"Are you sure there isn't anything more where this came from?" I asked. "Any other women or children in your life?"

"No, that's the only one. And you are my only wife. I keep telling you that, but you never believe me."

"You know that hiding things does a lot more harm than telling me. As you can see, I'm perfectly happy to have Femi as a stepson. Why in the world would you believe Nike?"

"Some people said I should tell you, but she said you would go against me. She knows people from America more than me."

"Well, just don't keep any more secrets."

"I won't do that."

Foley's description of Nike as "wicked" now seemed more accurate to me than it had the night before. It looked as if she was just using him to get me to write invitations for her students. I noticed right away that Femi became more demonstrative toward Foley after his parenthood was acknowledged, and that Yetunde's other two children did not. Yet even as we three hugged each other, I couldn't help thinking that they were his children, too. Had they had all been told how to act in front of me?

"It seems to me that Femi and Foluke look a lot alike," I said to Yetunde the next time I saw her. I was hoping she might confirm my suspicion with an unguarded gesture, though I had no idea what I was looking for.

"Really?" she said. "I think Foluke looks like me."

I couldn't agree with this, but I let it go, knowing that Foley's stories about his past would always be shrouded in the thirty-some years that he had lived before we met. I could choose to believe them or not. Before his most recent departure for Nigeria, I'd taken the Commissioner's advice and looked at his passport, with its invented birth year, to see if he had really gone to Zimbabwe. "They don't stamp it when you go to somewhere else in Africa," Foley said when I confronted him. By then I had traveled to South Africa, and my passport was stamped when we entered Zimbabwe to visit Victoria Falls. And I've learned since then that the eight members of the Economic Community of West African States have a common passport, but of course Zimbabwe is not one of them. The truth is that I still wanted to believe in Foley's honesty and was not willing to side with the Commissioner against him. That powerful man was still my enemy, not, as he always claimed about himself along with his wife, my best friend in Nigeria.

"Tomorrow is August 19th," I said to my husband a few days after our discussion about Femi. "Do you remember something special that happened on that date?" When he looked at me blankly, I said, "We had our Nigerian wedding ceremony seven years ago. You remember?"

"Of course I remember," he said with his usual captivating smile. "Long time."

Back in New York, I had often found him watching the video of the wedding or looking through our album of photographs. It may have been an expression of his homesickness rather than of his connection to me. Still, it was something he did much more than I did. Neither I nor my friends could watch the part of the video in which a dog was held by his front and back legs and cut in half by a machete, a sacrifice to Ogun, the god of carvers. But they were impressed by the procession with drums along the road from the house where we slept to the space where the ceremony was held. Most of all, they loved my favorite part of the ceremony, the dance troupe that was in Osogbo to perform at the Osun festival the following day, a wonderful addition to the ceremony that happened only because of Nike's friendship with the group's director.

"Well, how about we do something special?" I said now.

"What do you want to do?"

"Like go out to dinner," I said, "to celebrate our new agreement about having no secrets." Foley always agreed to my proposals, and I counted on him to understand the importance of this one to me, given what we had just been through.

On the morning of the 19th, he mentioned that his money was still in Abuja. "If you bring three thousand *naira*," he said, "I will pay you back tomorrow." I was less concerned about being paid back than I was about the amount. Three thousand *naira* was about twenty-five dollars. A meal at a restaurant costs only a few dollars a person, so why did we need so much?

But I didn't ask. Perhaps I should have pressed him then about his finances and this mysterious job in Abuja. Instead, I took half the amount he'd asked for from my locked suitcase and put on my elegant *asoke* wrapper, head-tie, and top in preparation for a big night out. Julie, one of Foley's sisters who had come to visit with her children, tied my head-tie, and we both admired the effect in the long mirror in the living room.

When I went outside, I saw an unfamiliar car with a strange man in the driver's seat and Foley in the back. I got in next to him, assuming that the man in the front seat was simply going to drive us to the restaurant. Then two other men I didn't know climbed into the car as well.

"Who are these people?"

"This is my teacher," he said, pointing to the man in the driver's seat. He taught me carving when I left Osi. These are my friends from Osi. They want to celebrate with us."

"...Why didn't you tell me?"

"I wanted to surprise you."

"Well, you sure did that. But you never ask *me*, and I really wish you would." I leaned back in the seat sat beside him, silently fuming since it was impossible to continue this conversation in the presence of strangers.

"I only have fifteen hundred naira," I announced, handing him the money as we passed the roundabout where I had flagged down my second taxi to Nike's. "I figured that would be enough to feed the two of us."

"That's all right," said Foley. "I'll go to borrow from my friend after we drop you. But he is coming to eat with us, too."

"Why so many people?"

"They are my friends," said Foley.

Great, I thought. I am spending my wedding anniversary with five men, only one of whom speaks my language. When we reached the restaurant, everyone got out, and while Foley disappeared, the four of us trooped inside and arranged ourselves at a table with a white cloth on it. Fortunately, from my point of view, the small black-and-white TV set perched on the bar allowed me to turn my back on my fellow diners. It showed a panel discussing the fate of a young woman, Amina Lawal, who'd been condemned, under the Muslim sharia law to be stoned to death for adultery. Back in the States I'd signed petitions to oppose her death, so I focused on the TV set. Twenty minutes later, Foley and this other friend arrived, so I joined the group and we ordered a rather ordinary meal: pounded yam with fish or meat.

I can't say that I felt very celebratory, even though it was his marriage to me that we were celebrating. But what he said about inviting his friends to celebrate reminded me of a dinner party we had made in the States. Both were examples of how Nigerian culture is much more oriented toward community than mine is. Nigerian meals don't include dessert, but we'd served ice cream, and that night we had run out of it by the time two latecomers arrived. I mentioned the twenty-four-hour supermarket two blocks away, and all the men decided to go with Foley in search of more ice cream. Buying food in Nigeria is not a solitary task. You talk to the people selling what you came to buy, with bargaining an essential part of the ritual. So for a Yoruba man, a special occasion involves, not two people dining by candlelight, but a party for friends who will go to the store with you if need be. That is how you show that you "have success," and nothing I might feel or wish was going to change that.

For the rest of my time in Nigeria, Foley was often out, and I spent my time reading or going for walks. When we left Nigeria at the end of August, we promised that we'd see everyone again at Christmas.

Back in New York, summer hung on into early October, and wanting to give substance to my hope for our new "no secrets" agreement, I began collecting Christmas presents for my far-away family. Twenty-dollar dresses still hung in racks along the sidewalks of my neighborhood, and knowing that they would be gone closer to Christmas, I bought one for Foley's sister Julie and one for Yetunde. I thought the two boys would like battery-powered cars, so I added two of those to a pile in one corner of the bedroom. I saw all these items as visible signs of the new beginning that I imagined, one that include a twelve-year-old African child. For me that meant that things would now become more the way I wanted them, though I must have known that Femi was the only new element in this beginning.

We also began gathering documents to support an application for Foley's permanent green card, since a temporary one he had was only valid for two years. This second application did not require an interview, only paperwork. Mr. Fried, the lawyer who witnessed my humiliation five years earlier, had left me a message telling me that he would be willing to handle Foley's green card, but I was too embarrassed to call him back. "We don't need a lawyer," I told Foley. "What we have to do is slow and tedious, but it's not that complicated." I don't know if he believed me, but he didn't object.

I had closed our joint checking account, at around the time I bought Foley's van, because of the checks he wrote. They did not total more than two hundred dollars, and he promised not to do it again. I suspect we both knew that he could have really wiped me out, but I did not want to have to hide my checkbook from him. At the same time, I knew from our two interviews with the INS that financial unity was the one thing they wanted to see, so I was willing to reopen it. But when we went to Citibank to add Foley's name, a woman in a cubicle shook her head. "My computer shows many unpaid debts," she told us.

I had no idea what amount she was talking about, and she wouldn't tell us. "These things are confidential," she added, her eyes fixed on her computer, and I later realized that she must have had access to his credit score. It was a red flag waving in my direction, but a part of me was glad that we could not use my bank account to demonstrate to the INS the authenticity of our marriage.

"We can go to another bank," Foley said as we left.

"No, we can't. The same rules apply everywhere."

An application for a permanent green card requires two letters stating that the marriage has not been undertaken to avoid immigration laws. We asked Sean, the elder of my two roommates, and Donovan, the doorman with whom Foley had become friends, to write these. Donovan is Jamaican and was having immigration problems of his own, so he had no problem writing a short letter at my dictation. But Sean was not so amenable. He kept putting it off, and when Foley finally pressed him, one night when I was out at a singing rehearsal, Sean must have told him that he wanted to speak to me before doing anything.

"I don't know if I'd be perjuring myself," Sean said as I fixed myself a bowl of what Nigerians call "leaves," adding some tomatoes, raisins, and avocado. "Is there any way I could be called into court? I think Foley is an okay guy, but I don't think he's telling us everything that's going on, and I'm not willing to cover his ass."

"What do you suspect?"

"Nothing specific. I just have a feeling we're not getting the whole picture."

"I know what you mean. And believe me, I have a lot more at stake in getting the whole picture than you do. But right now, I don't know if Foley is a liar and, if he is, how long he has been that way. But there's no chance of you going to court," I said to him. "I have a lawyer friend who tells me that the INS is completely overwhelmed right now rounding up people suspected of being terrorists, and since 9/11 everything has been running a year and a half behind schedule. But once a person makes it through the first round, a permanent green card is pretty much automatic." I was hopeful about Foley getting his green card, imagining that it would eliminate some of his "small boy" feelings.

"It's only a couple of sentences," I told Sean. "You don't have to go into detail."

"Okay, you write it out on your computer, and I'll sign."

Foley woke up when I got into bed. When I told him that Sean had agreed to sign, he said he'd already sent the other documents to their destination in Vermont, the processing center for the eastern region. ". . .How could you do that?" I asked. "They want two letters. With only one, they will simply throw your application out."

"Well, let them," said Foley, his voice shaking. "I thought Sean was my friend." I had never seen him that upset. He seemed so close to tears that my first impulse was to hug him. But I also wanted to know what had brought him to a state that seemed so irrational to me. Was he trying to get deported as a way of ending his time in America?

"Sean *is* your friend," I said. "But you haven't been here much, and he's concerned about what that means, that's all."

I could have reminded him of our "new beginning," but I was

thrown into confusion by what he had just done. If Marcia and my other friends were suspicious of him, as I knew they were, then why was he suddenly acting as if he didn't care whether the application succeeded, as it surely would not with a missing letter? Was he trying to tell me he was fed up with his life here? Despite these questions, I printed out a letter that Sean signed, and sent it Express Mail the next day so that it would reach the Vermont office on the same day as the rest of our documents. I couldn't be sure if that would work, but to satisfy my conscience I had to be a good girl and keep trying.

The issue of how Foley would make money had not come up when we were in Nigeria. But since nothing about his situation had changed, I was almost relieved when Foley announced that the man who'd gotten him his job in Abuja was now in Washington, D.C. "I need to join him," he said. "I will go there on a bus." He now had a cell phone that worked, and we stayed somewhat in touch. In the small *a capella* chorus I had just joined, one that sings Renaissance sacred music only, I was discovering how much I needed to practice in order to pass for the competent sight reader its director expected me to be. With these new demands on my time, I did not mind being left to myself, as long as Foley and I spoke on a regular basis. I still saw these built-in absences in my marriage as a way to give myself the time alone that has always been so important to me.

But I also wanted him to see himself as part of my family. So when I told him that we'd been invited for Thanksgiving to Arlington, Virginia, where my son, his wife, and their son and baby daughter were living, I was happy when he promised to come. Children light up when they see Foley, and the pictures I took of him with Henry, my first grandchild, on our visit there as a couple two years before, are visible evidence of this power of his. In fact, it was little Henry's delight when Foley played with him that melted at least some of my son's reservations about this man who was only five years older than he.

I was expecting to hear from Foley the week before Thanksgiving to set up a time and a place where we would meet. But the service on his cell phone was cut off, and by the time I left for Penn Station on Thanksgiving morning, headed for a crowded Amtrak train to Washington, no call had come. I knew that Kevin and Mitzi had a device on their phone that filtered out calls from telemarketers, which meant that anyone calling from a number the device did not recognize would not be able to get through. Also, Kevin's dial-up internet service tied up his phone a lot now that Henry had discovered computer games. Once I left my apartment, in other words, the chances of connecting with Foley were close to zero.

Knowing this, I was furious that he had not called, but I made excuses for him on the grounds that calling ahead was not done in his world, especially not in Osi, where no one in his family had a phone. These excuses notwithstanding, I was feeling bereft by the time I arrived at Washington's Union Station, and I acted out this feeling as I walked through the subway turnstile. I was bringing Christmas presents for everyone, since they would be spending the holiday with my daughter-in-law's family. I had a purse, a suitcase, and a shopping bag to manage as I bought a Metro card and moved toward the turnstile. But my wallet must have dropped from under my arm, and I didn't notice it until I reached the platform at the bottom of the escalator. By the time I made it back up the escalator, no one had seen it.

I found a quarter lying on the subway platform and used it to buy a transfer, issued inside the metro station, which let me take a bus that let me off near my son's red brick house. Had I not found this quarter, I could have called collect and asked to be picked up. But since I was feeling so thoroughly shaken, it felt good to be able to walk on my own steam through their front door with its fan light, and into a warm, aromatic kitchen.

"Where's Foley?" Henry asked immediately as his father carried my bags into the living room.

"He's made place cards for everyone," explained Mitzi. "Including one for Foley." The dining room table was set, and Henry had drawn outlines of his hand, adding legs and a head to make a turkey above each of our carefully printed names.

"I don't remember what he looks like," Henry said as I picked up Foley's card, intending to show it to him the next time I saw him.

"I don't get to see him that much myself," I said, a stab at humor that didn't draw a smile from anyone. I told the story of my lost wallet and then, after calling to put a stop to my credit cards, I made a concerted effort to immerse myself in a holiday dominated by the voices of small children. Henry had a new Rescue Heroes toy to show me, and baby Olivia insisted on being carried. "I left my wallet in a shopping cart in Toys 'R' Us," Mitzi told me. "Thank God some nice person returned it. We can get you a new one, though, in the mall tomorrow." She and Kevin had to have sensed that I was upset about more than the lost wallet, but they didn't say anything and neither did I.

That night, after settling into the fold-out couch, I pulled out a book I'd bought from Barnes and Noble the week before: *Anger,* by the Vietnamese Buddhist monk Thich Nhat Hanh. It was as if my hand had acted on its own before my brain gave the command, and I'd read the first chapter by the time I walked up to the cashier. The book uses similes that transform anger from a poison into nourishment. You do this by telling the person with whom you are angry that you understand that he is suffering too, and by doing this you heal the relationship. I was not sure I believed this, but I picked up the book whenever an angry conversation with Foley exploded in my head. And whenever I asked why this was happening to me, I answered: so that you can learn how to be at peace under any circumstances. Thich Nhat Hanh could do it. Buddha and Jesus had certainly done it. Even Foley was more adept at it than I was. I never found out whether he actually intended to show up, but by the time I got on the train back to New York, Thich Nhat Hanh's Buddhism had inserted itself into my life like a seed that would continue to grow. I also had a nice new wallet as well, an "early Christmas present." Though I was not happy to be going home to a missing person, I was grateful for being able to feel calm. I saw it as the next phase of the journey I was on, one where I was learning to live in the present. The calm I was feeling would probably disappear, but I knew I could get it back.

# 12

When I got back to New York, a message from Foley told me that he had tried to call Kevin's house from a pay phone in a subway station but couldn't get through. Perhaps if I'd checked my home messages using Kevin's phone I could have forgiven him. The person who has made you angry is suffering too, Thich Nhat Hanh reminded me, and I wondered if perhaps Foley, too, might have felt abandoned when no familiar voice came on the other end of Kevin's line. But while I was there, I had been too angry at not hearing from him to do that. I've always focused on his cheerfulness, so I've tended to assume, especially when I'm angry with him, that he does not suffer and therefore doesn't care, or even know, that I do.

This anger did not disappear, even after this message and my reading of Thich Nhat Hanh. Why couldn't he plan ahead? "My phone doesn't always work," he said when he finally called, and he was his evasive self when I asked what he'd been doing before and since. Perhaps I might have made more of an effort to tell him how his absences made me feel, and what I did to handle those feelings, the way I had done in Nigeria. But I come from a world where talking about things is seen as a way to change them for the better, and he does not. Even if he had wanted to improve his English, it might not have been enough to bridge this gap between us. He did, however, promise to spend Christmas with me in New York, and after that we'd go to Nigeria together as we'd promised his family we would do.

In the intervening month I began to incorporate Thich Nhat Hanh's mindful breathing into my daily routine and marveled at how such a simple act could be so calming. Yet even with all my efforts, by mid-December a cloud of depression had returned, set in motion by the upcoming holidays. *Have no expectations*, the Buddhists say, but there I was, counting on Foley to spend this expectation-laden holiday with me. But because I had to wait for his calls and had no way of knowing when, or even if, they would come, I succumbed to panic. I had never imagined myself as the starring female in a romantic scenario. I suppose this was a reaction to what I've been calling my mother's spell. But I see no other explanation for the ten years I spent married to a man whose happy smile made him the picture of what I wanted. Finding the perfect picture of a husband was my mother's proudest achievement.

But feeling unloved was a state I'd battled against for as long as I could remember, and because of this I clung to the belief—supported by less and less evidence—that Foley loved me. I had family and friends, a job I loved, and a nice place to live, but I was stuck in an emotional place I objected to when I saw it in someone else, a place where singleness makes you feel unlovable. I know that Marcia does not feel this way, and I'm sure that her supportive mother had a lot to do with that. But spinsterhood, with all the negativity implied in that word, has been looked down on for centuries and is still a difficult, lonely place for women to be in many parts of the world, including Africa. My intellectual work as a feminist had rejected this premise, but our emotions live, not in our heads, but in our bodies. Kevin and his family were spending the holiday with Mitzi's parents, as they did every second year. So each time I thought I might spend it alone, my body reacted as if this was an irrefutable truth. I focused instead on presents for my family in Nigeria, and imagining their smiling faces calmed me. I found a set of paints and colored pencils that I knew Femi would love and added it to the two summer dresses and the two battery-run racing cars piled up in my room. But I also needed a visa, and the Nigerian Consulate required a copy of the first five pages of my husband's passport to get one as the spouse of a Nigerian citizen.

"My passport is not with me," he said when I asked for it the next time we spoke. "It's with my friend in Brooklyn. You know, the son of Sunny Ade." I owned a CD of King Sunny Ade and His African Beats, and enjoyed listening to it, but I'd never seen or met his son.

"Okay, but why are you keeping it there?" Was this nothing if not another red flag?

"I'll tell my friend to send you a fax of it tomorrow," Foley said, and the next day I had the pages I needed. But why had he not left his passport with me? It certainly looked like a sign that he had transferred his American home base from the Upper West Side to somewhere in Brooklyn. When I called 411 to find out the name of the person whose 718 number was written across the top of the fax, it turned out to be a business in Far Rockaway under an unfamiliar Nigerian name. Swallowing my doubts, I went ahead and got the round-trip plane ticket that you need to show to the Consulate if you want a visa.

Then, going on faith, I filled my suitcase with my gifts. What would I do with them, after all, if I did not take them to Africa? I imagined the shrieks of joy that the kids would utter as their electric cars zoomed around the room, and the appreciative smiles I would get from the women as they donned their dresses.

So I continued to hope, as I finished my semester, that time together in Nigeria would set our life on a more united course. I was counting on Foley's family to bring him around, which was probably why I focused on the presents. I was sure that this family wanted us to stay together. Perhaps they could get through to him in ways that I could not, say something to him that would change the game. I went ahead and decorated a small tree, and called Lawrence and Emmanuel, his two brothers now living in New Jersey, to invite them to join us for another half-African, half-American dinner. Foley did show up on Christmas Eve, but I needed more than Thich Nhat Hanh's words to damp down my disappointment when he told me that his employer would not let him go to Nigeria because the job he'd been hired to do was not finished.

"Why do you let him control you like this?"

"He gave me a contract," Foley said. "I won't get money if I don't finish." That made no sense to me. Finish what? But I was so confused that I didn't know what to say.

He was pleased with the gifts I'd bought him: a pair of olive drab hip-hop pants and a VCR tape of *Sarafina,* the musical about the Soweto uprising we'd seen on cable. This was one of the few places where our tastes in movies coincided, along with anything with Denzel Washington in it. I could not watch the horror films that resonated with his culture, where spirit possession and curses are believed to cause real damage. He also adored wrestling, finding it immensely funny. I could not watch this either, though I tried to joke about our different tastes.

He had no present for me, however. I deflected my disappointment by remembering that Nigerians don't do Christmas the way we do, with decorated trees and a Santa in every mall. Nor do the ones I know have money to stage the kind of scene that Norman Rockwell would see as an example of freedom from want, a freedom most Nigerians do not have. When Kevin and Mitzi ask me what to get me for Christmas or my birthday, I never know what to tell them. Foley probably asked me this question on our first Christmas together, and maybe I said I didn't want anything. But I also have a hard time identifying, let alone voicing, what I *do* want. He undoubtedly never learned that women like flowers. Or chocolate.

When I imagine Foley's resentments of me, what always comes

up is my closet full of nice clothes, my ability to buy a book or a CD whenever I want one, and a bank account into which a paycheck arrives every two weeks. I have more than I need, and feeding his sense of being "a small boy" around me must have been the belief that he does not. He was nevertheless pleased when I told him I would go to Nigeria "for the two of us." and was impressed by the pile of presents. We watched *Sarafina* together on New Year's Eve. Then he saw the VCR of *Training Day* I'd bought for Idowu. His friend would never notice that it had been opened, he said. I remember showing him, earlier that day, my itinerary and ticket from our Nigerian travel agent, and I'll never know for sure if that's when he saw the four hundred-dollar bills I had tucked in behind it. I had asked the teller at my bank for them because they are the denomination that converts into *naira* at the highest rate of exchange.

My flight left at a quarter of six in the morning, which meant being at the airport by four. I'd called a car service the previous day, and Foley, who can wake up at will, got me up and came with me to Newark Airport. As we stood in the line to check in, I took out the envelope holding my itinerary and cash. "I had four of these yesterday," I said to him, though I wasn't exactly sure when I had last counted the bills. "Look here—I have only three now."

"Look in your other bag," said Foley. "I'm sure you'll find it there." Nothing in his face told me he was lying, but I knew without looking that the money was nowhere in my suitcase.

"I don't think so. Why would I have put it there and not with the others?"

At that hour, the ticket line was short, and we moved ahead quickly. Because of heightened security, I was not allowed to lock my checked suitcase with all my presents in it. This seemed dangerous given Nigeria's reputation for theft at the Lagos airport, but there was nothing I could do but surrender it and then give Foley a desultory wave before heading on into the waiting area alone, just as there was nothing I could do about my missing hundred-dollar bill. I had a long wait once I had checked in, so before boarding I found a pay phone and called Foley on his cell. "I've looked everywhere," I told him. "And I didn't find my missing money."

"I don't know anything about that," he said, and repeated his certainty that I would find it. I did not ask him where he was when I called.

But sitting in the boarding area, I had to ask myself, Who could have taken the money if not Foley? If he needed it to get back to his job, he could have asked me for it, though I'm sure I would have voiced my suspicions about his employer. As far as I knew, he had never stolen cash from me before, though I didn't always keep track of how much was in my wallet. When he had access to our joint checking account, he always made a point of not knowing my PIN number.

Waiting for my flight to be called, I told myself that I would probably have spent the missing money in Nigeria, giving the economy a boost by buying another African outfit I didn't need. I didn't need the money, in other words, and that knowledge reminded me of times when I had gone home, a struggling dancer trying to make it on her own without much ability to do so. Several times I had taken a twenty-dollar bill from my father's unguarded wallet, knowing that he would not notice because his assets made him pretty much invulnerable, at least in relation to me. I'd also known he would have given me the money. It had just been too humiliating to ask.

Perhaps Foley saw me the way I saw my father. Nothing he could do would really harm me, just as nothing I could do could harm my father. Maybe someone who is seen as financially invulnerable attracts thieves. Maybe the only way to avoid all this would have been not to go to Nigeria at all, or at least not to go back after my first visit. As Billy Joel pointed out, your chances of getting burned go up when you're close to the fire.

But seeing the fire up close was what I'd come to do. I'd set out to see up close what made Nigeria the way it was: so overtly religious, so filled with mistrust and corruption from top to bottom. I couldn't put the fire out, but I wanted to live like the hero in Joseph Campbell's *Hero with a Thousand Faces*, who descends into the depths and comes up again with something invaluable.

I was traveling British Airways with books and a blue-and-white *adire* outfit in my backpack, knowing that I had more Nigerian clothes in the metal trunk at the foot of Nike's student's bed. As usual, the Nigerians waiting in London to board the flight to Lagos were curious about why I was going, unaccompanied, to their country. "You think of Nigeria as your home now?" asked a corpulent father traveling with a wife and four boisterous children under the age of ten, and I found myself answering him, almost automatically, "Yes, I do." An oversimplification perhaps, but not a lie.

At around six the next morning we landed, moved with greater dispatch than I'd seen in the past through the rituals of getting our passports stamped by the curt but efficient military officers, and collected our bags. My unlocked suitcase appeared intact. Perhaps the new administration of President Obasanjo had actually brought some improvements.

I caught sight of Idowu on the other side of the barrier between the airport and the crowd of people waiting to meet arriving passengers. "Everyone will be happy to see you," he said with the smile I find so winning in all the men related to Foley. When I handed him two of my remaining hundreds to change into *naira*, he told me immediately that we needed one of them for a taxi to Osogbo. "Ninety dollars," he said, the same amount Lateef and Laray had charged me on my previous trip.

"Why so much? Why don't we take public transport?"

"We'd have to go outside the airport to do that," Idowu said. "Inside they have a special area for taxis, and this is the rate they charge." Knowing I would be away from home for nine days only, it had not occurred to me, setting out from my house less than twenty-four hours earlier, that I would not have enough money for such a short visit. I was due back at Rutgers right after the Martin Luther King holiday, and there was a major demonstration in Washington that weekend opposing the American plan to invade Iraq that I was determined to join. I would spend the weekend with Kevin and Mitzi, as I usually did, and might even connect with Marcia.

"But how will I get back?" I immediately asked. "I didn't bring enough money to pay this much both ways."

"Oh, someone from Osogbo will drive you back," Idowu said as he disappeared into the crowd standing around the edges of the parking lot, in search of someone to change my money. While he was gone, I put my third hundred-dollar bill in the secret pocket of my waist bag. When he returned, he counted out twelve thousand *naira*, which he handed to the waiting driver, and did the same with the rest of the bills before handing them to me.

"There's no problem," he said as he put my suitcase in the trunk, reminding me that, in Nigeria, I saw what the people around me saw, but with very different eyes. I did not tell him about what Foley had done. Instead I lay down on the back seat, as I usually do after my long flight—less out of tiredness this time than out of a wish to avoid conversation.

We made the three-hour trip without a mishap, which rarely happened when the driver was someone I knew. "Taxi drivers keep their vehicles in good repair," Idowu said. "They need them to make money." Money is the driving force everywhere, but particularly so in Nigeria. The world has come to see it in the stream of e-mails that promise a share in some huge stash hidden by a former dictator come from there. I remember one that announced the inauguration of a power company to rival the Nigerian Electric Power Authority, to be run, the fax said in the usual awkward English, by "a former head man of the Enron" who apparently saw in Nigeria the kind of unregulated business climate he had been counting on in the States.

We reached the same yellow house with Jesus on the wall I'd left six months earlier, and the children rushed out to hug me. But a trip to the toilet showed me immediately that improvements under the democratically elected Obasanjo had reached only so far. In August the house had intermittent water, just as there had been intermittent power. The water tower would empty and then slowly fill up again automatically. But this mechanism had broken down, and someone had to bring water in buckets from a distant tap and store it in tall, black plastic vats. One of these stood outside the small cell with mold on the walls where a rusty shower head extended above a pail and bowl on the cement floor. In August this shower had worked. But now I was sorry to see a smelly, unflushed toilet next to it, telling me that the progress visible at the airport, whose newly clean bathrooms now supplied toilet paper, were not in place here. I could have poured a pail of water in it, as someone must have done from time to time. But I didn't. "Culture shock," I would call it: moving too quickly from one world to another.

"Is somebody going to fix the water tower?" I asked, and Idowu shrugged.

Back in the room where I had slept before, I began unpacking my suitcase. First there were the dresses I'd bought for Yetunde and Julie in the optimistic frame of mind I had left the country with on my previous visit. For Foluke, Yetunde's daughter, I'd found a two-piece outfit that fitted her perfectly. Yetunde put on her dress and Idowu immediately took the video of *Training Day* out of its box, saying not a word about its lack of a cellophane wrapping.

I was right to have anticipated the hit that the two battery-operated cars would make. But it took more than the four hours stated in the directions to charge their batteries, since the supply of electricity was erratic and went down to "half-mast" for much of the time that it was on.

"This is worse than it used to be, isn't it?" I asked Idowu.

"Yes. We don't have power sometime every day now. More people use it," he added. "And the NEPA doesn't make more."

"How come?"

"Sabotage," said Idowu. "People stealing copper wire and other things." Something else about which nothing could be done.

But once their batteries were fully charged, these cars gave as much pleasure to the adults as they gave Femi and Soji, whose presents they nominally were, demonstrating the Nigerian capacity

I so admire for having a good time. Still, the exuberance did not lift my spirits as much as I'd hoped, and after a couple of hours, I fell asleep under the ceiling fan in my room, which stopped or started or moved very slowly depending on the power that fed it.

After two days of getting accustomed to the heat and the slow pace of life in Osogbo, I mentioned to my hosts that I wanted to go back to the woman who had done such a beautiful job braiding my hair on my past visits. After my first disastrous experience with getting my hair braided, in preparation for my wedding some ten years earlier, I had become quite proficient at asking for, and getting, the look I wanted, both in the States and in Nigeria. Yetunde offered to buy me some extensions, and I gave her two thousand *naira* to do that. I always got my hair braided at least once during every visit to Nigeria, and I'd had it done in Harlem as well. It was the outward and visible sign of my status as one of the family. Foley always loved my braids, so even though the process of putting them in and removing them was time-consuming and not pain-free, I still wanted to enjoy that way of announcing my connection to his country.

The visit to the hairdresser the following day was the high point of my stay. Some of the stalls in Osogbo's market area line the curbs in front of two- and three-story concrete houses. Others, invisible from the main road, face one another along narrow alleyways. This hair salon would be impossible to find if you did not already know where it was, as Yetunde and plenty of other women obviously did. In Nigeria, women and men spend more time with members of their own sex than in mixed company, and that small shop was a gathering place for Nigeria's woman-to-woman culture. Some of its patrons brought their children with them, and some were pregnant, but they were all there for several hours of banter with not a man in sight.

"Of course I remember you," the owner said with a big smile directed to us both.

"Well, I want you to do exactly what you did the last time. Everyone in the States loved my hair then, and I did, too. Do you remember what you did?"

"Equal length," Yetunde chimed in as I held the back of my hand between my chin and my shoulder. This meant medium-thick braids falling from a center part to just below my chin.

"I have a lot of customers today," the owner said. "But I'll start you after my friend here." She gestured to a woman whose corn rows were being used as the base from which lengths of straight hair about a foot long would be sewn into place. The hair you'd been given by nature placed no limit on the look you could take away from here, and enormous changes were wrought by the skillful hand of this woman who clearly enjoyed her job.

My own transformation took about four hours, since only one person was free to work on it. Yetunde brought me a "take out" of rice and beans and a bottle of Sprite to keep me going.

"I'll send you a picture," I told the owner as I looked in a mirror at the finished effect. "So you can put me on your wall with all these other styles."

Two days later, I pulled my suitcase out from under my bed and noticed that the small combination lock was open. It was the one I had not been permitted to use at Newark Airport. So I must not have closed it properly the last time I took a batch of African bills from the suitcase. A five-hundred-naira bill had been introduced into the currency since my last visit, a sign of the "new, improved" Nigeria. So carrying naira around was not the problem it had been when the highest denomination had been fifty. But this new bill was worth only about four dollars, so it was better to take out small amounts every day or two. I had been careful to lock my suitcase each time I took money out, or so I thought.

After counting the remaining bills, and doing some subtraction, I realized that four thousand *naira* were missing. This is a little less than thirty dollars, an amount that would pay for dinner in a nice restaurant in my neighborhood. But given the uncertain status of my transportation back to Lagos, I knew I needed to watch every penny. It hadn't been smart of me to show Foley the envelope with my ticket in it and those tempting hundred-dollar bills, and I had to wonder if I was unconsciously trying to turn my short trip into a disaster for which I, who had never been vigilant when it came to money, would have only myself to blame. I was glad I had hidden my third hundred-dollar-bill in my waist bag's secret pocket.

At first, I was too angry to say anything. What was the point? It was a short visit—eleven days including travel time. So I'd be out of there in four more days—"Forever," I told myself in a burst of anger that subsided after a night of fitful sleep. The next time Foluke and her brothers barged into my room, I screamed at them to leave me alone. Their startled faces made it clear that they had no idea why I was upset. So I counted my money again and turned my wallet and suitcase inside out. Finally, I decided I had no choice but to speak to Idowu, who was sitting on the living room couch. He was in charge of the household and spoke the best English, so he was the best person to talk to about a matter this serious.

"Are you sure?" he asked at first. "Have you looked everywhere in your room?"

"You can look if you want to," I said. He followed me into my room, but nothing showed up. The sun was setting when he summoned everyone to the porch in front of the house, bringing wooden chairs from the living room to add to the two benches already there. Sunsets are brief near the equator, so it was dark when Yetunde, her children, and two of Foley's cousins were all sitting on the benches or standing in front of the portrait of Jesus. Facing them next to Idowu, I was glad I'd gone public with my accusation even if I never found out who took the money.

I gave him paper and a pencil, and we began to go over my expenditures. I had not been alone from the time the children woke me up till I got tired of reading with my book lamp, so I had plenty of help remembering each outlay. There was the money I gave Yetunde for everyone's food, and for my extensions and taxi fares to buy them. Then there was the hairdresser, the food I ate there, and taxis and sodas for Yetunde and me. Foluke remembered a pineapple and biscuits from the stand where our road met the highway into town. No one could remember any other purchases, so Idowu and I totaled them. My two hundred dollars had turned into twenty-six thousand *naira*, and when I did the math again, the difference was four thousand *naira*—an amount I might spend in a day without thinking back in New York.

"That's the exact amount that's missing," I announced, surprised that the math had come out so neatly. No one asked who the culprit was, but it felt good to have brought the matter out into the open. I decided at that point to take my hidden hundred dollars back to the States with me. Why spend more money on people who did things like this?

"Why didn't you lock your room?" Femi asked.

"There's no way to lock it," I said. "There's just a bent nail holding it shut. You know that. Anyway, I didn't think I would need to. I'm staying with my family, aren't I?"

"You should always lock something up," Yetunde said. "This is Nigeria."

It was indeed.

I stood up and walked slowly into my room. When the children later banged on the door, I said I was using my computer myself and didn't want company. I certainly had no wishing to let them see how disappointed and angry I was, alternately with my African family and with myself.

The next morning Baba Sunday, my rescuer on my previous visit to Osogbo, appeared at our front door. "I heard you were here," he said, "and I want to ask you a favor. Let's go to my house, and we can talk." I knew he was going to ask for an invitation, but I was glad to get out of the house. As we drove to his gallery, he asked when I was leaving and offered to drive me to the airport. He remembered that I liked tea, and I was touched that he had the requisite powdered milk and sugar on hand. I saw the man, who was some ten years older than Foley, as an ally who was also enough of an insider to give me a key to Foley's lengthening absences, to the truth that would set me free. Sitting on the balcony above his gallery, a cup of tea in my hand, I had an idea. "I'm taking an empty suitcase home," I said to him as I looked out onto a group of thin-legged children playing tag on the dirt road below us. "It was full of Christmas presents when I came. Why don't I fill it with carvings and take them back to the States for Foley to sell?"

"Where do you want to get these carvings?" he asked.

"From the Morimoyo Gallery," I said. This was the second address, along with mine, on the business cards I'd made for Foley after his falling out with Nike that had him so determined to set up an enterprise like hers, with a workspace and a showroom. "Better than Nike," he always said when talking about his future. When he first spoke that way, I had seen us as partners committed to our own separate artistic aspirations in ways that required an unorthodox marriage like ours. "Could we not just go over there?" I asked when Baba Sunday hesitated.

Baba Sunday shook his head. "I know Foley talked about setting up a gallery, but he never did it."

"...You mean the Morimoyo Gallery is a lie?"

"I wouldn't call it a lie. He wants to set up something like that. He just hasn't done it."

"How come?"

"I don't know. Money, probably." The usual answer.

"So there's no difference for you all," I asked after a few minutes of silence, "between what is so and what you want? That's not a lie?" Baba Sunday shrugged. Foley had told me that he wanted to be the heir of his family's tradition. But perhaps he had said this only to impress me, with no real idea how to get there. Perhaps Nike, who'd had exhibitions in the West, had told him that this information would open doors to visits to my country, and beyond that to marriage and a green card to boot. Well, she'd certainly been right about that.

On my first visit, I had watched him cut into a large piece of wood "from the bush," sitting in Nike's workspace. But since then I hadn't seen him with a chisel in his hand. Perhaps what he had seen of the States took away his confidence that he could be great. The few clippings from Nigerian newspapers, and my two books with his picture in them, were now the only proof I had that he had once been moving toward that dream.

Then there was Tom, the Fulbright scholar who'd set up the exhibition in Queens for the two of them and then called Foley a liar. Perhaps not all those carvings were Foley's. Perhaps he'd sold them, never paid the people whose work they were, and lied about that. That would explain why he had stopped carving with his fellows. But Tom must have been impressed with Foley's skills, or he would never have studied with him or set up the exhibition. There had never been anyone in Foley's world to whom I could talk about this, though Baba Sunday had given me a clear, if painful reality check. I was reluctant to promise to send an invitation when I got back home, but with so much betrayal around me I felt that I needed an ally, and Baba Sunday, who had come to rescue me from Nike's, was the closest thing I had to a reliable observer on his side of the Atlantic. "I guess I'll leave my suitcase here," I said to him. "You can use it to bring things when you come."

"I'll bring it to you," he said. "You can count on me to do that."

"And one other thing. Make sure Nike and the Commissioner don't find out that I wrote an invitation letter for you."

"No chance of that," he said. "Nike and I are not speaking. But why do you say this?"

"They ratted me out to the president of my university," I told him. "And I could have gotten into serious trouble. In fact, tell everyone that I can't write invitations anymore."

"I told you," he said, "Nike is a very wicked woman."

Back at the house, I tried to act, in front of Idowu and his brood, as if nothing had happened. But what Baba Sunday had said about lying brought crashing down the belief I'd clung to whenever I heard something bad about my husband: that his enemies lied because they wanted to hurt him, but he did not lie. Now I could feel the marriage I'd always imagined, the one promoted by the God we both worshipped, collapsing around me like a tent whose center pole has just broken, taking with it the future self I had been so happy to imagine: the married English professor with a home in a West African country. I wanted to cry out to the same Baba Sunday whose observer perspective had been so on the mark when he drove me home from Nike's party. What was he really thinking about me, I wondered, and what was behind his support? And what about all the people I'd imagined as a community welcoming me into their midst, the ones who had chanted "iyawo Foley" when they saw us together? The ones who told me that Kehinde would be fine about my bringing Funmi to the States? Why had they done it? Was I nothing but a rich American so fearful of being unloved that I let myself become a willing target? I remembered Nike telling me that perhaps I would like to retire to Nigeria, and how it had struck me as a good idea at the time. Did I think that what I saw was true just because I wished it to be so? If so, I was really not all that different from Foley.

But at that moment I decided: If that tent was the marriage as I'd envisioned it, I was not going down with it. I needed to find out what was behind all the deception, and I was not going to walk away until I did. In the meantime, I'd let all of them know that I had a whole system of economic support behind me, from Rutgers and from my family, that they could not even imagine, let alone damage. But what was I going to *tell* everyone—my friends, my colleagues, my son and his wife—when I got home, about Foley and me? Then I remembered a

t-shirt that I'd left at home, one of the hundreds sold on the streets of New York after 9/11, that had Nietzsche's words emblazoned across the front: *Whatever Does Not Kill Us Makes Us Stronger.* Even Foley, wherever he might be, needed to get this message. Perhaps my mother's words were also floating into my consciousness. *Don't come running home to mother.* I'm sure she had followed her own prescription, but where had it gotten her? Did she and my father love each other? They certainly never engaged in any public display of affection. But they did stay married till death did them part.

These conflicting memories must have followed me back to the house with Jesus on its wall, and they filled me with a desire to show its inhabitants that they were no match for me. What had they ever done to deserve my admiration? Where was Thich Nhat Hanh, telling me that hurt people hurt people? Nowhere that I could hear his voice. So with Foley and one of my hundred-dollar bills three thousand miles away, and the contents of my suitcase seen as fair game by an unknown member of his family, I pulled my last hundred dollars from its hiding place inside my waist bag. There was more, they should know, where that came from. Money is power only when you spend it, and right then I needed a sense of my own power.

But behind the hidden money was something else, a shadowy presence that was with me even when I did not think about it. My mother had been my teacher long before I came across Thich Nhat Hanh. Her husband's infidelities had not been hidden. Everyone knew about them, and she knew that everyone knew. But she hung in there, kept the marriage going. No pain that her husband could inflict on her could be worse than being thrown into the outer darkness of a failed marriage. And all my determination not to have a life like hers did not prevent me, in that moment, from doing exactly what she had told me to do when things went wrong. I would *stay married no matter what.*

The first thing I did was to pay Idowu's overdue phone bill, which took only about twenty American dollars. To my amazement, the first person to call in on it was Foley. Sometimes it felt as if we had a psychic connection, and this was one of those times. I'm embarrassed now to admit how happy I was to hear his always cheery voice. After talking in turn to everyone present, Femi included, he got back on with me and asked if I was still willing to send Femi to a boarding school in Nigeria in preparation for bringing him to an American school in the States. The idea of putting him in a boarding school came from a friend who'd lived in Nigeria. "At least he'll have a chance to actually learn something," my friend said. "Otherwise he will flounder when he gets here. They're cheap, too," she added.

Foley had promised Femi before he left that he could come to the States, and everyone in his household was delighted when I told them I would get behind my husband's words. Femi was elated at this scheme that would, I assumed, connect him to a much-absent father.

"We can go tomorrow to Femi's day school and get information about boarding there," Idowu suggested, and I was happy to agree. If the definition of insanity is doing the same thing over and over again and expecting a different result, I could be called insane.

But that was not how I felt. I was simply doing everything in my power to turn this story toward the happy ending I wanted it to have. So with two days remaining before I left, I went with Idowu and Yetunde in one of Osogbo's rickety taxis to a building on the other side of the town. We walked through the wrought-iron gate and stood in a dark hallway with classrooms on either side. The rolling cadences of rote-learning came at us from right and left as Idowu explained to a woman in a white blouse and a knee-length navy skirt why we had come.

"You will want to speak to the principal," she said in a crisp English. "I will tell him why you are here."

We waited in silence until she came back and led us into an adjacent building. The principal's office was a small room with glass-doored bookcases along one wall and a framed photo of President Obasanjo above his desk. The principal's navy blazer, white shirt, and red necktie had me wondering whether the teachers there wore a uniform, too. He did not ask us to sit down, since there weren't enough chairs for all of us, but handed Idowu several printed sheets listing the school's fees and the items that boarders were required to bring with them.

"I think you will find the information you need," he offered. "If not, the school's telephone number is printed at the top." Given what happened later, I wish I'd brought those sheets and that number back to the States with me.

Having been to boarding school myself, I would have liked to talk to that serious-looking man about the school's routine and living arrangements, but Idowu and Yetunde were already going over the list of required items. They exchanged a few words with the principal in Yoruba, presumably explaining that I would be the patroness of the venture. Then we all shook his hand and walked back outside into the blazing noonday sun.

As we waited for a taxi to take us to the market, I took the sheets from Idowu. The fees came to about $200.00 per trimester. With Foley's abandoned van paid off, I could handle it. I was intrigued by the list of the items that Femi would need to bring, so different from what my mother had been expected to send with me. Boarding schools back home costing thousands of dollars more provided sheets, cups, plates, mattresses, and soap, but this school expected its students to bring their own. I was also remembering the envelopes that came regularly to my mailbox, bringing details of the precarious lives of smiling but impoverished children all over the "undeveloped" world to the attention of the world's fortunate. My connection to those children had been on paper only. But with Femi, my tie would be tangible and enduring. I saw this boarding school venture as temporary, so my financial commitment would probably involve no more than what I'd spent in a year on the children I'd supported by mail, whose lives I could know only in a highly mediated way.

Perhaps I should have summoned up Marcia's warnings about Femi not being another Kevin, and I now wish I had. My long relationship with her changed over the years as its context shifted. But by the time we sat together again, drinking tea at my kitchen table, I had promised to send Idowu, via Western Union, a trimester's tuition for my new "stepson" and to spend on him half of my once-hidden hundred dollars. Generosity felt a lot better than the anger that had been simmering since I discovered the theft from my suitcase. Going over the list of items that Femi needed, I let go of that anger, at least for a while

The noonday sun threw a glare over the rows and piles and boxes of the ubiquitous made-in-China goods that surrounded Idowu, Yetunde, and me as we moved through the market. I felt very much in charge as I checked off the items on the list and wrote down the prices of each. We needed all three pairs of hands to collect the metal pail, which came from a stall that sold auto parts, and the foam mattress, rolled up and tied with a string, that we left with the store's owner while we threaded single file through the narrow lanes between the stalls in search of sheets, a blanket, a pillow, soap, a soap dish, a tin plate and cup, and a book bag. We then retrieved the mattress and put it in the trunk of a taxi with the rest of our purchases.

Just as we walked in the door, Foley called again on our newly revived phone. When I described our outing, and he told me how pleased he was at what I was doing for his son, my hopes flew across the thousands of miles that separated us to imagine that he really wanted to put our marriage on a solid footing. The other children were probably jealous, but the smile on Femi's face as he looked at his new things went straight to my heart. Nevertheless, when Baba Sunday offered to take me to the newly launched and popular fast-food restaurant in Osogbo for my last full meal in his country, I thanked him but said I had nothing to celebrate. With all that had happened, I was glad to be on my way home.

Saying goodbye to the children was the only really difficult part of leaving. "I'll be back," I told them. And to Femi I made another promise. "I'll see you in the States when your father brings you with him."

"Thank you," he said, lowering his eyes, and I wondered what Foley had told him, and if he believed either of us.

My plane left at ten-thirty the next morning. Idowu and I had planned to leave Osogbo at five, to avoid an overnight stay in Lagos. But the car that pulled up in front of the house was not Baba Sunday's old but reliable Peugeot 404. Instead, a white jeep of uncertain vintage stood at our front door. Baba Sunday had apparently promised the Peugeot to someone else. Though I was annoyed, I climbed into the back seat of the jeep next to a friend of Baba Sunday's who was going as far as Ibadan. Idowu sat next to Baba Sunday's assistant, Sina, who drove.

The gas gauge registered almost empty as we pulled out onto the half-paved road to Ibadan. "The filling stations in Osogbo aren't open yet," Sina explained, and I knew we could not wait around until they were. I seemed to be the only one in the car who was anxious about this, but then I was the only one with a real deadline. Finally, just before we reached Ibadan, we saw an open station, and I handed Sina my last two five-hundred-*naira* bills to fill the tank. Not fifteen minutes farther on, steam started rising from under the hood. We waited another ten minutes while Idowu went in search of a gallon of water to pour into the leaking radiator, which got us to the taxi stand on the outskirts of our halfway point.

Standing by the side of the road outside Ibadan in the early morning light with nothing but a credit card I could not use until I reached Heathrow, I was kicking myself for being so willing to spend my money just to make myself an indispensable part of the family I had just left. I should have remembered that trips to the airport are almost never disaster-free. Cars run where I come from, and when they stop running, people get one that does. Here most cars are geriatric, with exhaust fumes billowing out of their tail pipes, a sign of their determination to hold on for as long as they can.

At that point I had to insist that I really had no more money. Idowu disappeared to borrow some *naira*, and when he returned half an hour later, he and I took off in a taxi at top speed, certain that this vehicle wouldn't break down. Miraculously, the roads were somewhat clear, so we escaped the worst of the crippling traffic jams that choke Lagos almost to the point of paralysis.

When we got to the airport, so many people filled the space between the Plexiglas entrance doors, where a member of the military personnel demanded to see Idowu's passport as well as mine, and the row of check-in counters some fifty feet away, that I was sure I'd never get onto my plane before it took off in two hours. Whatever patience was still with me when I left Osogbo had long since been replaced by panic, but luck appeared again when Idowu found a shorter line and summoned me to it. Perhaps it was because I had no luggage to check, but to my surprise no one objected when we jumped ahead of hundreds of fellow passengers, each with a cart piled high with boxes and bulging suitcases. I realized by then that I'd left my winter coat in Osogbo, but Idowu assured me that someone would bring it to me with my suitcase.

I'd forgotten that planes always take off at least an hour late from Lagos, so I need not have worried that mine would leave without me. On top of this, we had on board a bag for which no corresponding passenger could be found, so we waited inside the plane for two more hours while the bags were reloaded and the errant one removed. Then my connecting flight from Heathrow had a problem too, and though one is always thankful not to be flying with a door that won't lock or a bag with a bomb in it, I was almost at the end of my rope when, at five in the morning American time, I made my way through Newark Airport after the most exhausting plane trip I've ever taken.

The temperature had dropped to record lows that January morning—not a good time to arrive coatless in New Jersey. I was nevertheless thrilled when twenty-dollar bills promptly emerged from the mouth of a waiting ATM. My driver turned up the heat in his cab, and I was grateful to him for the warmth and the speedy ride home. In the coat closet in my hall, I found a down jacket of Foley's with a broken zipper but snaps that kept it closed. Then, after spending most of the next two days asleep, I took a train down to Kevin and Mitzi's, where I planned to stay before and after the antiwar march that I hoped would be huge. Did either of them notice our role reversal: the bedraggled antiwar protester being welcomed by the stable suburban couple? The next morning, I headed out into the early morning Metro and the freezing Washington streets. Thanks to Mitzi I was wearing four layers on top and three on the bottom.

The demonstration was as big as I could have wished, and I felt happy to be with several hundred thousand like-minded people who had come on busses, one of whom was Marcia. I glad to have my family nearby so that, when exhaustion kicked in, I could simply get on a steep escalator at the nearest Metro stop rather than wait for my bus to take me home. I'd bought a *No Blood for Oil* button and picked up a sign that said *Empty Warhead in the White House* that I carried with pride to Vienna, the last Washington Metro in Virginia.

"Granny doesn't like President Bush," Kevin said when Henry asked what my sign meant.

"How come?" he wanted to know.

"He wants to start a war—" I began, but Kevin signaled me to stop, so I changed the subject. His protectiveness toward his children meant that he never let them watch the news.

I returned to New York wearing a new winter coat that I'd bought with Mitzi and went straight to the bank and then to Western Union to send Femi's tuition. I stood in a line of my neighbors, most of whom spoke Spanish and were probably sending money to a relative in their country. The husband of Foley's sister Julie was an auto mechanic in Nigeria, and the wives of Idowu and Kunle were teachers, but no one else seemed to have a paying job. Young women in West Africa cross the Sahara and the Mediterranean to work as sex workers in Europe, so they can send some of their meager wages home. Or they are married off to a much older man who will presumably relieve their families of the financial burden of taking care of them. Desperate parents give their boys to men who claim to have work for them someplace far away from home. The money sent from outside is a huge part of the economy of developing countries. What did my two hundred dollars mean in the face of all that?

*The Big Tree, 2003–07*

# 13

Back in the States, I watched in disbelief as the leaders of my country claimed to find weapons of mass destruction in Saddam Hussein's Iraq. Despite my efforts and those of thousands of others, the invasion began on March 20, 2003.

A few weeks before this ominous date, I had gone to see my accountant, Sara, and had come away with the phone numbers of Kathryn, who became my lawyer, and Skip, the private detective who helped me piece together the rest of the story.

Then came the annoying phone call from the collection agent who gave me Foley's address, and the following Saturday found me standing in front of Apartment 1404, unable to knock on the door and see who was behind it.

I remember looking around for a few more minutes at the doors set close together before picking up my briefcase and ringing for the elevator, which once again took its time coming. No one joined me as I retreated, much to my relief, and it seemed safest to leave the way I came. Outside it had started to rain. But as I made my way past a guard sitting in a cement bunker that borders on the street, my stark surroundings gave me an unexpected burst of relief.

Up to then I'd been asking myself what I could have done, what sort of person I could have been, that would have made my husband want to spend more time in my book-lined, plant-filled world. Perhaps I was not as generous as he thought I ought to be. But seeing those burgundy doors, and sensing the bustle and the shared language behind them, I understand that they offered Foley something I could never provide: a life out here at the end of the A line that for him was familiar and manageable. In that "Nigerian" building, he would not have to improve his English, which never got beyond what he had picked up in Nigeria, just as I had never learned more than the series of greetings and polite questions that begin every conversation in Yoruba, the difficult, tonal language that everyone in that neighborhood probably spoke. Perhaps the people behind those doors enjoyed the wrestling and horror movies that Foley loved. The guard in his concrete cubicle, and the rows of small windows above and behind him, reminded me of a prison, but perhaps they made Foley feel protected.

Outside, it had started to rain, not heavily but enough that I wished I had brought an umbrella. Standing on the sidewalk, I could hear the rattle of an arriving train on the tracks above me. But then I knew something I could not have found out had I not made the trip: My husband had left me to live in a small apartment surrounded by others who had come here from Nigeria for the same reasons that he had. He came to live here surrounded by cement and barbed wire, with not a tree in sight.

But how did he support himself? What could he do here that he could not have done living rent-free with me on the Upper West Side? Perhaps he was living off the multiple credit cards that came to him at my address, believing that they produced free money. The possibility of drug dealing briefly crossed my mind, but I'd never met a drug dealer, and the image I had was of a ruthless gang member; mild, non-verbal Foley just wasn't the type.

Taking a last look at the formidable gray walls that separate me from the life he had chosen, I suddenly found myself filled with a sense of freedom. I could stop feeling angry or hurt each time I came home to no Foley and no message on my answering machine. I might even stop the repeating thoughts that would not let me focus on the novel I was teaching the next day. Hearing his voice on the phone, or seeing him walk through my door with his usual smile, would wipe out the feelings of failure and abandonment that welled up, drowning out everything else when I saw myself losing him. My mother's belief that women who are married are loved is printed on a place in my soul with an indelible dye. But standing there, I felt a crack in that belief, the crack that lets the light in, as Leonard Cohen put it. If Foley *chose* to live here, how could that mean that I had failed? Something beyond my control had to be going on.

Looking back at the building, I found myself wishing, in spite of myself, that Foley would appear out of nowhere, take me with him into this world so remote from my own, and let me know that I really belonged there. Was this not what I'd married him for?

Still, I knew I was no Gladys Knight, who declared that she'd rather live in her man's world with him than in hers without him. I was the one with a steady income, after all. I'd always seen myself moving back and forth between the Upper West Side and his vibrant Nigerian world with its drumming and dancing, its power outages and erratic plumbing. He, I had blithely assumed, was interested in a similarly divided life.

But here in Far Rockaway, as in Nigeria, I would always be a visitor from a distant world. I would never master Yoruba, and could not even adopt the offbeat English he shared with others from his country. In Nigeria, as in Far Rockaway, I was often the only white person wherever I was, and this gave me a sense of myself as special. But what would make Foley feel special in New York? I assumed he would enjoy himself in the States and feel lucky to be here thanks to me. Is not the American way of life admired all over the world?

Stopping for a Sprite at the pizza parlor near the subway entrance, I had to ask myself what had made me so confident that the marriage would work out. I think the fact that I come from Canada gave me a naive faith in our ability to speak a common language—the shared legacy of growing up in different parts of the former British Empire. I am very much an Anglophile, my sentiments enduring in songs my British nannies taught me. In my boarding school we sang of the land of hope and glory, with no doubt about which land God had made mighty, and would make "mightier yet." Like others from that once-mighty empire, Foley and his friends spoke what English they knew with a particular flavor of a British accent that was, and still is, music to my ears.

But Foley also said things that fed my belief. "Marriage is forever," I remember him saying to me more than once. But these words, like so many we thought we shared, called up different things to each of us. "Thank you for yesterday," he liked to say, lying next to me in the morning after we'd had a good time together the day before. I assumed it was his way of telling me he loved me. And I've sometimes used it since as a brief but heartfelt prayer when I get up in the morning.

"Did you find the place you were looking for?" the woman at the token booth asked as I came toward her. I nodded, and wondered if the help given by two women I did not know from a community I'm not a part of says something about the world I was leaving: the sense of concern its residents extend even toward strangers. I can still see the "Nigerian" building from the outdoor subway platform that would take me back to a world familiar to me but too far from my husband's to let him feel at home there.

With that long ride behind me, I called the lawyer first. Telling this stranger about my situation, I heard in my tentative voice a description of a marriage that was doomed from the start. When I told the same story to my friends, I had seen myself charting new marital territory, a bold combination of independence and connectedness. But now I sounded like a person unwilling to face an obvious truth. "You must think I'm crazy," I said to her. "A man more than twenty years younger than I am . . . ." I didn't add that Foley doesn't know his age, though his passport gives his year of birth as 1960, making him five years older than my son.

"I always say," she answered cheerily, "that you pay your lawyer and your therapist not to judge you. And anyway, believe me, I've dealt with much crazier situations than yours." I was tempted to ask for examples.

A week later, we met in her office in the East Twenties.

"That looks like your son," I said to her once I was seated across from her, eyeing a framed photograph on her desk and several more on her wall, one wearing a Cornell t-shirt

"Yes, she said. "That's Tommy at different ages. He's my one and only."

"I only had one as well," I told her. And with this connection established, we got down to business. Before I left, I gave her a deposit, then noticed signs of spring on the street outside as I made way home, glad to have done what I did.

Over the next few weeks, her efforts to serve a summons on Foley were coming up empty. My level of frustration was heightened by the fact that American troops had invaded Iraq on March 19 despite my fervent hours of leafleting my nearest subway entrances during the month before that decisive date. People sailed past me as I tried to accost them with a leaflet. "It will be over in a matter of weeks," they shouted over their shoulders. How could this be? I asked myself. The Upper West Side is known as a leftist enclave. Nevertheless, even the presence of my warmly wrapped body at two huge antiwar demonstrations, the one in Washington and another in New York a few days before the actual invasion, had made no difference whatsoever. So there was nothing to do on either front but wait.

"What will happen," I asked Kathryn, "if we never find Foley?" The person to whom my private eye, Skip, had talked told him that he was "not around" just then, though he did show up at that apartment from time to time. But his call must have tipped someone off, because the door to 1404 was never opened when Kathryn's process server knocked.

"You can still get a divorce," she said. "We will have to prove to a judge that we've made a reasonable effort to find him. Putting notices in the paper, things like that. It will be slower and cost more, but it will still go through."

"You have to go through something similar," I said, "when you try to adopt a child from Nigeria."

"You did that?" she asked.

"Tried to," I said. "Oh, yes."

Ever since my conversation with Baba Sunday on his porch in Nigeria, I'd been wrestling with the knowledge that it was not just other people who were lying to hurt both of us. My husband, too, was a liar. What besides his gallery was he lying about, and what were those lies hiding? I had not forgotten the card I'd found in his wallet the night I spend under Nike's roof in Lagos, the one that read Komolafe Infant. Nor did I know the source of his income in Far Rockaway. Whatever truth might be waiting for me out there, I wanted to keep our connection long enough to get the whole story.

Nevertheless, I had to reckon with the possibility that I would simply never see him again. I called his friends who were still in New York. But even Stella, the woman who'd connected me to my babysitter Leah, did not tell me anything. Then I'd rehearse what I'd say when I next heard his voice on the other end of the line. In the grip of that repeating loop, I felt as if I was losing my mind. The engine I'd come to count on to keep me moving toward the future was sputtering for lack of fuel, refusing to go on in the absence of "my man." Where were Thich Nhat Hanh and the calm I had felt after Foley had not shown up on Thanksgiving?

Sometimes I wake up with a line from a song or a hymn in my head that lets me know how I'm feeling that day. One of my favorites is about how it's always seems darkest in the moments before dawn, from an album by the Mamas and the Papas that came out in the Sixties while I was I college. It's a cliché, but it is so for a reason. And help had already begun to arrive by the time I'd made my connection with Kathryn. A flyer with the legend *Spiritual Recovery* in bold appeared on the bulletin board of a health food store in my neighborhood. "Find calm at the center of the storm," it read, along with "gentle, powerful healing, awakening, and freedom."

I called its number as soon as I got home, and that evening I walked fifteen blocks down West End Avenue to one of the last single-room-occupancy buildings on the Upper West Side that had not been turned into expensive co-ops. This kind of low-cost living space had once been common in many parts of the city. Thinking back on my first years in New York as a rolling stone, I sensed that I could have ended up in a place like it had I not met Kevin's father and joined the world of family life from which the building's residents seemed to be in flight.

A small TV set was on behind the reception area, so while several residents asked for their mail, I tried to catch what CNN was saying about the war that was supposed to be "over in no time." A sign on the wall warned that, *in view of recent events, the management has decided that non-occupants of rooms will not be allowed ingress unless accompanied by an occupant, or suitable arrangements have been made with the management.*

Apparently, no such arrangements had been made for me, so Rory, a soft-spoken man with a salt-and-pepper beard, had to come down and get me. I followed him into the elevator and then into a room where three other women were sitting on a couch under a painting of a cross-legged deity with the words *Om namah shivaya* inscribed across the bottom. Candles flickered, and flute music was coming from a CD player near the window. The half dozen people who had already arrived had taken off their shoes and left them by the door, so I did the same. Rory hung up my coat and motioned me to a surprisingly comfortable chair. You could meditate in a comfortable chair? You did not have to sit cross-legged on a hard wooden floor? Finding that posture uncomfortable had always been my excuse to avoid meditation.

Following Rory's instructions, I closed my eyes and focused on my hands on my lap, my feet on the floor, and the sounds of the cars on the street below, and after a while I felt myself sink into a space with no dimensions. Years before, driving across the country with Kevin and a male friend, we'd stopped in New Mexico at the Carlsbad Caverns that extend for hundreds of miles below ground all the way to Mexico. The first miners to explore those caves, wearing on their heads only a tiny, flickering light, had no idea how far the darkness around and below them extended. That's how I felt, at moments, in the presence of that group of shoeless people.

At the end of the session, I told Rory I would start coming weekly. He did not ask what in particular had driven me toward him, but I wanted to tell him. "My marriage is in shambles," I said, "and I feel like I'm losing my mind."

"Here you lose your mind intentionally," he said gently. "We all need our minds, and they can do amazing things. But in a situation like yours, they're the source of our misery."

"I've always had a hard time letting go of mine," I said. "In fact, I've probably spent most of my life filling it with things that would make me interesting—"

"We all do that," Rory interrupted. "But here we don't need to prove that we're interesting in someone else's eyes." The other women nodded and smiled at me as he said this.

"My first husband always told me I had an interesting mind," I said to them all. "I really think that's why I married him. We were graduate students, and being smart was what mattered. Whatever others might think of me, he thought I was smart. That meant a lot to me."

Before I left, I pointed to the painting and asked, "What does *Om namah shivayah* mean?"

"It means something like, *I bow to my inner self, which is Shiva*," Rory said.

"And Shiva is who?"

"He's the supreme embodiment of the deity in Hinduism."

I looked at the picture again, but smiling, cross-legged deities had never struck a chord with me. "Could my inner self be Jesus?" I asked.

"Sure. Whoever it is for you. I grew up Catholic," he added. "Very strict Catholic."

"I was raised Episcopalian."

"Whatever helps you to move beyond the difficult times we all go through," Rory said. "That's the point of any religious practice. At least that's what I think."

I did not turn a corner that night. But I did walk down West End Avenue once a week to these sessions, and gradually my feelings of abandonment became less intense. A favorite image of Rory's was the ocean. "On the surface," he'd say, "the waves look turbulent. But at the ocean floor there's stillness." Waking up in the morning alone could still bring back my years of singleness after my first marriage ended, when I asked the I Ching the same question over and over: Will I ever find someone? But now I drew a few mindful breaths before putting my feet on the floor. And once I started moving, I'd notice the buds on the trees outside my bedroom window, the softness of my blue fleece bathrobe, the warmth of my morning cup of tea. And gradually the weather, both inner and outer, felt less severe.

Though I did not change my religious practice, as I gathered that Rory had, I began to see its emphasis on inner peace as a missing component of the Christianity to which I'd returned after years of being alienated by its insistence that we are all sinners first and foremost. "Perhaps I can figure out a way to include features of both systems," I said once to Rory.

"I don't see why not."

Then, just as I was becoming used to my new, fragile equilibrium, I came home from a meditation session one Tuesday night at the beginning of June to a flashing light on my answering machine. It brought the voice I'd been missing back into my life after five months, with a number to call. When I did so, Foley picked up on a cell phone with weak batteries, his voice fading in and out. He gave no information about where he'd been or why he had not called or shown up. But he did say something I was glad to hear. "You have always been very good to me, Kate. You are not the cause of my problems."

"Thank you, sweetheart. Where are you calling from?"

"I'm in Miami."

"What are you doing there?"

"Landscaping," he said. "But I'm coming to New York now. I'll be with you on Monday next for sure."

"What shall we do about our marriage?"

"For me, marriage is forever," he said, the phrase I had heard from him before. Nigerian men don't end marriages. They simply take on new wives, as Nike's and Abike's husbands had done. Nike often said that Foley was not like that, though she'd said the same about the Commissioner, who was Muslim, a religion that allows for four wives. Christianity is supposed to require monogamy, but in Nigeria it sometimes looks the other way, as it had with Foley's father and his many baptized wives and children.

"Then we need to talk," I said, though I was not sure we could really manage that.

"I will see you Monday." As always, I was relieved by the sound of his voice, and by the thought that some connection between us had alerted him to what I was doing. He might be far away, but he was still a part of my life.

"I'd be so angry with him," said Marcia, the first friend I spoke to after this exchange. "Look what he's put you through."

"But I really like who I am now, and maybe what he's put me through, as you call it, is what brought me to that place. Maybe nothing else could have done it."

"What do you mean?"

"Well, all my life I've wanted to handle being alone better than my mother did. She had nothing but alcohol to fall back on, and I have so many other resources."

"You've always *had* other resources," Marcia said. "You're giving Foley credit he doesn't deserve. *You* got yourself to where you are now."

Marcia was the woman I spent the most time with when Foley was not around. She has never married, and I saw her as an example of the kind of woman who could find validation in the life she had rather than focusing all her energy on the one she did not have. When Foley was around, we sometimes went to a concert or a movie I knew he wouldn't enjoy, while he headed to a Nigerian party that lasted into the next morning. I saw this as a plus, and I assumed he did, too. As long as we spent one weekend night together, it seemed fine to spend the other one on our own.

"Well, I'm not frantically looking for someone new to replace him. Isn't that progress?"

"Maybe you're just tired of doing that."

"I wish I'd been able to do it less when I was younger."

"I know what you mean. . . . When is he supposed to show up?"

"In a week. I'm not sure what I want, but I'm glad I didn't change the locks on my door like everyone said to do."

"I never told you that."

"I know."

"But really, Kate, if it were me, I would have ditched this guy by now. And I honestly don't understand why you haven't done that. He's supposed to contribute to your support, not detract from it."

"I'd like to be more like you, Marcia, but I'm not. I'm very attached to being married."

"I see that."

"And I like to spend my summers and winter breaks in Nigeria. I didn't like spending them in New York."

"Kate, you're an able-bodied woman. You can travel anywhere you want."

". . .You're right," I said. "I'll think about it."

The conversation ended there, but it kept going in my head. Of course I was lucky to be able-bodied. In fact, I was lucky to be alive, to have enjoyed everything that had happened to me since that terrifying night in the lobby of my building so many years before. My son had grown up and made me a grandmother. I had started singing. I had gone to Africa.

But the issue of spending my summers and winter breaks from Rutgers there touched on a sore spot. I had told Marcia about my struggle with depression. She knew that it had taken me, in the early Sixties, to a private mental hospital on Long Island, and had once told me that she, a black woman, could never have let anyone take her there because she feared that she would never get out. And given what I now know about state mental institutions, I suspect that she was right. But depression is a black hole where no willed motion is possible, and I don't think we had ever talked about my fear of returning to that state. Perhaps it's a fear you can't understand if you've never been captured by it. But for me traveling to Africa actually worked as a kind of anti-depressant. It gave me somewhere to go when I wasn't teaching. It gave me a welcoming family at the other end of the journey. And it gave me something interesting to say about myself when people asked me, as people do, especially those in academia, what I had done during those intervals. The good answer was that you were doing research for your next book. But being in a post-colonial African country was perhaps even better. So much as I hate to admit it, I was using him as much as he was using me.

Foley actually did arrive when he said he would, and though I really was working on becoming the new person I described to Marcia, some of the joy that the old person used to feel came rushing back when he walked in the door. I hugged him as if he had been gone for a matter of days, not months. "Are you hungry?" I asked him, and when he nodded I immediately began heating up water for spaghetti, the only food I had on hand that I knew he liked, with sauce from a bottle that belonged to one of my roommates. While he was eating, I brought up my problem with filing a joint tax return that contained nothing about his income for two years in a row. "Do you have any documents now for this past year?"

"No."

"How come?"

"This man won't give me anything just for myself. He says it's a contract he gets for several people."

"He could just write something on a piece of paper."

"He won't do that."

"But I'll get into trouble with the IRS if I'm filing as a married person when I have nothing on paper to show that my husband is around. . . . You know I've been looking for you since January." He looked surprised. And yet, now that he was back in the place I called home, I couldn't stop imagining ways to extend that situation into the future. "It's not working like this," I said. "I can't be married to a man who won't tell me where he gets his money."

"What do you mean?"

"We have to get a divorce. I have a lawyer who will do it. You can stay here now that you're here, but I have to go to school early tomorrow, and when I come back we can go and see her. You okay with that?"

I took his silence for a yes. He looked tired, and when I got up to wash his plate he walked toward the bedroom, expecting to sleep where he always had, on the right side of my platform bed. I don't think he noticed that I'd put away all the pictures of him and of the two of us, though not of Gbenga. My sexual feelings were completely shut down, and his obviously were, too. Stripping down to his boxer shorts, he glanced over at the clothes tree that had always been his, and asked about the hip-hop pants I'd given him for Christmas.

"I gave them to Brian." Brian, the younger of my two roommates, was a tall, thin African-American who looked great in the pants. Foley didn't pursue the matter, and in his usual fashion had nothing to say on the subject of his lengthy absence. I was starting my summer school class the next morning, so, in my usual fashion, I didn't bring up the status of his permanent green card. And I didn't offer to retrieve the pants from Brian.

My first day at summer school ended early, and I was back on my side of the Hudson by the middle of the afternoon. I called Kathryn from Penn Station and told her that Foley was willing to go along with my plans for a divorce.

"Can I send my assistant to your house to serve the papers on him then?"

"Let me call you as soon as I get home," I said. "Just to make sure he's still there."

I let myself in and was glad to hear Foley's voice when I called out his name over the TV in the living room. I told him again that we needed to clear the decks and figure out what, if anything, we wanted from each after we'd disentangled our finances. I was so committed to this scenario that I wasn't even hoping he would ask me to stop the process.

When Kathryn's assistant arrived, he handed Foley a document laying out the standard grounds for divorce: refusing to have sexual relations with me for over a year. Foley stared at it for several minutes, then signed it with the process server's pen. "Now I'm a free man," he said.

Taken aback by his confident tone, I answered quickly, "And I'm a free woman."

That night we went out to dinner at a cheap Indian restaurant where they served free wine with dinner. He told me about his troubles with family members back home, and about Femi's future in the States with me. "I bought land in Osi," Foley said, "but that wicked Idowu sold it. So he's in jail now." Aha! I thought. People there prey on each other, not just on me.

"Idowu has been sending me lots of emails," I told him. "Always asking for money. He told me that Femi's school had no phone, but I know Femi never went there as a boarder."

"Did you send the money to him or to the school?"

"I didn't have a way to send it to the school. I did send him the first semester, since I'd said I would. I guess he just kept it."

"That's Nigeria," said Foley.

"But now that I think of it, I haven't heard from him in a while. I guess they don't have computers where he is, huh?" Foley didn't laugh when I said this, but I sensed a lowered tension between us as if, for a moment, we were once again allies facing a new common enemy.

I felt relieved again when I called Kevin the next day to let him know what had happened. I was worried that he might say "I told you so," but he did not.

"I know things were not always so easy for you, but you looked like you were pretty happy most of the time," was what he did say. "So I didn't see the point of voicing my doubts." He had clearly sensed that something was very wrong over Thanksgiving, but he had waited till I was ready to tell him what it was. I've brought a person into the world who has become a real grownup, I said to myself after hanging up the phone. A truly sensible, compassionate human being.

Out at school, my secretary friend Wilma saw things a bit differently. "So little emotion from him," she said. "Didn't you want him to get upset?"

"Maybe, but I knew he wouldn't. I don't know what he feels. Maybe I never did."

"Do you know what he's doing now?"

"He says he's going back to Miami to finish a job. He's promised to come back in three weeks to sign the official divorce papers at my lawyer's office."

"Well, I'd be more pissed off than you are."

"You know, I can get furious at Foley when he's not around and I talk to other people about him. But I still can't do it when he shows up."

"Well, keep working on it. You're a smart woman. You shouldn't be putting up with this nonsense from him." I got the same no-nonsense message from Marcia.

I promised both of them that I would take their advice, but it was Sean and Brian who broke into my trance, a dissociated state that had me believing that this break with the past could be a way of preparing for a real new beginning. After teaching my two classes in New Brunswick, I came home that night from a singing rehearsal to find the two of them watching a TV movie in the living room. "Is Foley here?" I asked them.

"I think so," said Sean, who stood up when I walked into the room. He is Irish, like his name, and short, with muscular shoulders from working in a restaurant as an aspiring actor. "But can we talk to you about this? We're kind of uncomfortable about the whole situation."

"Sure. What exactly is bothering you?"

Sean continued to speak for both of them. Lanky Brian remained stretched out on the couch, but I could tell that they had been talking before I came home. "Well, we really don't like the fact that you've let him back in here."

"What exactly is bothering you?"

"What's he doing here? Do you have any idea where he's been?"

"He said Miami—"

"Holy shit! What would someone who can barely speak English be doing in Miami, the drug capital of the country?"

"He said he was doing landscaping, but I guess he could be doing something like that."

"Well, congratulations, Kate. Welcome to the real world. You're lucky he hasn't cleaned you out already and taken off."

"That's why I closed our joint bank account. That's why I had a process server come yesterday."

"So you're getting a divorce?"

"He's supposed to sign the final papers in a few weeks."

"Then why the hell is he still here?"

"He's going back to Miami tomorrow—"

"Kate, you're goddam crazy," said Sean, whose bursts of Irish temper I had learned to enjoy. "You're putting yourself in real danger, and I don't think you know that."

"You're putting *all* of us in danger," Brian said. "Didn't you say something about collection agencies calling him? And if he's involved with drugs or something, we definitely don't want him bringing that stuff here."

"Okay, I hear you. He's outta here tomorrow. I promise."

Foley woke up when I walked into the bedroom, but I did not tell him what had happened. "Sleep well," I said as I stretched out next to this body I had no desire to touch.

"You, too," he said, and turned his back to me. When his breathing told me he was asleep, I carefully went through the pockets of his clothes. But I could not find any slips of paper that might have told me what he was up to.

The next morning, he promised to come back from Miami in a two weeks to sign the papers that would make our uncoupling official. I was too conflicted to count on it, but when I called Kathryn, she assured me that the process was firmly in place no matter what he did. She also reminded me how lucky I was that he was not contesting it. "As it is," she said, "he's not getting a dime from you, and he could have been legally entitled to a lot more."

Foley actually showed up a second time when he said he would, two weeks after he first appeared at my apartment after an absence of five months. But even that small victory was fraught with the missteps that had been woven into our relationship over its ten-year lifetime. A message on my machine said he would arrive "Monday at twelve." Perhaps because I pictured myself at home when he arrived, I took this to mean midnight. That Monday, I left early to teach my summer school class in New Brunswick. I came back to Penn Station and went straight to an anti-Bush demonstration in midtown. Someone gave me a sign showing a picture of Bush and containing the legend *Leaves No Millionaire Behind*.

Setting the sign between my feet, I called Marcia on her cell phone. "Are you here?"

"No. I'm on my way to teach at Medgar. Are there lots of people there?"

"Yes. And lots of cops, too."

"How did your meeting with the lawyer go?"

"She said I was lucky that he wasn't contesting the divorce."

"How come?"

"She didn't say. But I'm sure we would have had to spell out our incomes. That's what happened when I did it the first time, and I think he would be legally entitled to half of mine."

"Looks like the force is with you, Kate," said Marcia, raising her voice over the sound of an approaching train. "I'll talk to you soon, okay?"

My final destination that day was a "sing" in the church in the Village where the first choral group I had joined rehearsed and performed. It's an evening where people show up and pay fifteen dollars to sing a major choral work with a conductor, accompanied on a piano. After singing the Brahms *Requiem*, some of us went to a restaurant near the church, where I was happy to fill in the time before Foley arrived. The old me had spent too much time waiting anxiously for him to walk in the door, a posture I was determined not to resume. Though I doubted that he cared, I wanted to remind him, and perhaps myself, that I had important people and interests in my life.

But I was so successful at having a good time with my old conductor and fellow singers that it was well after midnight by the time I got home. That morning I'd put a sign in Yoruba on my front door to welcome him, but my main worry was that he might not show up at all. The sign was not on the door when I opened it, and Foley was in bed fast asleep.

"How long have you been here?" I asked guiltily, leaning over his reclining body. "I've been singing."

"I got here around noon. That's what I said."

"And you've been here ever since?"

"Yes," he said, and I was all apologies as I walked over to my side of the bed. I also knew that, had the shoe been on the other foot and he'd shown up more than twelve hours after I expected him, I would not have fallen asleep the way he did so easily. I would have been contemplating the divorce we were about to complete. Foley had never been curious about what I was up to when I was not with him, nor did he get upset when I lost my patience with his "Nigerian" sense of time. That night I saw evidence that he'd gotten some Chinese take-out, watched wrestling on the channel that was still on in the living room, taken a shower using my towel, and gone to bed.

The next morning I called Kathryn, who said we could come by after I got back from Rutgers. Since her office is not far from Penn Station, it made sense to meet Foley there. "There's a police stand across from the big board that tells you when trains are departing," I told him. But since Penn Station has several areas labeled *Police*, it took us a good twenty minutes to find each other.

I finally caught sight of my soon-to-be ex wearing a T-shirt that was too big for me, one I had been sent in return for a donation. I'd offered it to him that morning, contrite over my lateness the night before, and it looked marvelous on him. *Don't Trust The Corporate Media,* it warned in white letters on navy blue.

We got to the law office late but in good spirits, to be ushered into a conference room lined with legal reference tomes. Kathryn's assistant, the same man who had served the summons three weeks earlier, brought us each a multiple-page document filled with words like "witnesseth" and mouthfuls like "in consideration of the premises and mutual promises and undertakings hereinafter set forth, and for other good and valuable consideration."

Foley and I could now live apart, it said. We could not "in any way molest, disturb, trouble or interfere with the peace and comfort of the other, or compel or seek to compel the other to associate, cohabit or dwell with him or her by any action or proceeding for restoration of conjugal rights or by any means whatsoever." No longer were we liable for the other's debts, nor were we required to contribute to the other's support. "Each party hereto waives, renounces, grants, remises and releases to the other forever and for all purposes whatsoever, any and all rights against the other's estate including dower, curtsey, and community property rights and interests." I recognized the archaic legal language and found it amusing. Foley could not have understood a word of it.

"Does this mean that we were legally allowed to demand all these things while we were married?" I asked Kathryn.

"Of course."

There remained one other matter, a mystery that had lurked in the back of my mind since the Commissioner had accused Foley of bigamy in Lagos—the plastic card I had found in Foley's wallet with *Komolafe Infant*. When I learned, just before I traveled out to Far Rockaway earlier that year, that apartment 1404 had been rented under the name Komolafe, I remembered the Commissioner's words and asked Skip to check the Brooklyn birth records for the mid-Nineties. He called a week later to tell me that Kehinde gave birth to a son in September 1996. "Who signed off as the father?" I asked him. "I think my husband's name should be on that birth certificate."

"You'll have to ask your lawyer for that information," Skip told me. "You can only get it if you need it for a lawsuit."

I'd called Kathryn, and she'd promised to send her assistant down to the court. The Commissioner had mentioned May as the birth date, which would have put the date of conception around the time when Foley returned from Zimbabwe to Nigeria, if he had in fact gone there. But *this* date meant that the baby had been conceived in December 1995, when Foley was in the States with Emmanuel and me after our wedding. If he was the father, Kehinde and Funmi must have been here too, and would have used the visas and passports I'd paid for to get here. Could they have been a couple during the time that I was preparing for the wedding in which all four of us would wear matching outfits? If so, who else was aware of this liaison? Could it have been Kehinde's friends, the ones who had been so keen on my bringing Funmi to the States, the ones who'd called me "*iyawo* Foley" and Funmi "*omo* Katie"? Did Nike know about this when she proposed Funmi to me in the first place? It had never occurred to me, in all the years since Foley told me about Funmi's father's refusal to let his daughter leave the country, that there could be so much lying about a plan that everyone involved appeared to be supporting.

"Do you have any information about the other matter we talked about?" I asked Kathryn when she popped her head in the door to the conference room.

"Why don't you go into my office and wait for me there?"

"I just have one little thing I need to ask her," I said to Foley, who was still examining his copy of the divorce decree. His placid, accepting response gave me a pang.

"I can't get the birth certificate unless I go before a judge," Kathryn said, closing her office door behind us. "And I have no reason to go before a judge, since your husband is not contesting the divorce."

"So there's no way I can get this birth certificate?"

"I'm sorry," Kathryn said. "Samir, my assistant, went to the court this morning, and that's what he was told."

"But I need to *know* this," I said. "For my own peace of mind. Why would the law make it so difficult for me?"

"It's a right of privacy," she said. "It protects people. Why are you so concerned?"

"It's too complicated to explain. I suspect that my husband had something to do with the birth of this baby, and someone who doesn't like me has told me he's the father."

Kathryn raised her eyebrows. "Look," she said, "maybe there are some things that are better not known. Maybe he fathered this woman's child, maybe he didn't. He's being marvelously cooperative now, so that's the tradeoff."

"Okay," I said. "I guess you have a point." I thought back to time just before our Nigerian wedding, when I noticed that Kehinde had disappeared and no one would tell me where she was. I never occurred to me back then that she might be saying goodbye to her family in preparation for a long stay in the United States on my dime.

As we emerged onto the rush hour street, I wish I had said goodbye to Foley then and there. I had not expected Kathryn's news about the birth certificate, and needed some time alone to come to terms with the suspicions that Kathryn's silence had only reinforced. But as we walked toward the subway, Foley told me that he had left a bag at my house, so we traveled uptown. "I need to go downtown tomorrow," he said, "to see about my permanent green card."

He went into the bedroom while I waited in the hall, and as I stood by the door I suddenly I felt very hungry and decided that we would have a last meal together and part in a civilized way, as friends. Why not? "Shall we *jeun*?" I asked him, using the Yoruba word for eating.

"That will be good," he said. "I will pay for you." What had brought on this sudden magnanimity? I wondered. But as we waited for the elevator, I noticed that he had not brought his bag with him. We made our way up Broadway, and I caught one or two admiring glances thrown our way. He really was a catch, I said to myself. *Just as my handsome father had been for my mother.* For ten years I'd taken in those glances. Felt special because of them. And now they were coming to an end.

We found a table in the outdoor café part of the restaurant, and when the waiter offered him a menu, he said, "You have hamburger?" The waiter nodded and turned to me.

"I'll have the cobb salad. You know I like leaves," I said to Foley.

As we ate, he spoke again about how Idowu had cheated him, and that he still wanted to bring Femi to me in the States. He must be delusional, I thought. That made two of us.

His offer to treat me held until he saw the bill. "Prices have gone up in this neighborhood," I told him. "I'll pay for me. How's that? I can only eat half of this, so I'm going to get the waiter to pack it up so I can have another meal tomorrow."

"Thanks," he said. My guess is that he didn't leave a tip.

Back in the lobby of my building, we were greeted warmly by his doorman friend Donovan. I turned the key in the door of my apartment, knowing that this would be the last time I would do this with him. Foley of course dropped off to sleep almost immediately while I lay awake, as I had done in Osogbo, asking myself why I had turned a blind eye for so long to what others could see so clearly.

Foley took off early the next morning. "Where are you going?" I asked him without getting up.

"Back to Miami."

# 14

Four years later, in 2007, I traveled once again to Queens, this time in the middle of a very cold winter, to visit Foley in a federal detention center, two weeks after I received a call from Foley's younger brother Lawrence—"same father, different mother"—who lives in New Brunswick, not far from Rutgers. He also lives not far from Emmanuel, who has a different mother from both Foley and Lawrence. I'd last seen him when the two of them came over for Christmas dinner just before Foley disappeared. We three still call each other family, and it's important to me that we do. Sister Sledge's "We Are Family" is a song I still like. It brings back happy memories of the time I spent in Max and Felicia's organization, though we haven't spoken since they came over to my house and enjoyed my brownies the night that Foley and his friends first arrived.

"So whassup?" I asked, recognizing his voice and imitating it.
"Foley is in jail."
"... *Where* in jail?"
"It's in Queens. Kehinde called to tell us."

"Do you have any idea what he's there for?"

"I don't know," said Lawrence. "Kehinde didn't say nothing about it."

"What do you think?"

"I don't know, but I'm thinking drugs."

"Me, too," I said, and I marveled that this had not occurred to me when I took that long subway ride on the A train in search of Foley's new home.

Of course the Far Rockaway projects, those towering, barricaded buildings, were a perfect setting for this way of making "big money" even as it jeopardized the green card he'd been so determined to have. The Commissioner got his money that way, Foley always said, but I never thought he would see himself following in the man's footsteps. It looked like they were allies now, perhaps actually working together but certainly drawn together by a common goal. "Can you call someone who's in jail?" I asked Lawrence.

"No, I don't think so," said Lawrence. "Me and Emmanuel haven't heard from him long time. E-man had a big fight with him and he called us both bad people."

"Last I heard, he was going to Miami," I told him. "That's where lots of drugs come into this country."

"Kehinde says you should call her. She will take you to see him at the jail. We don't like her," he added, almost as an afterthought.

"Give me her number." I had no desire to call this woman. But I was curious enough about my now-former spouse in his new situation that I wrote her number down.

What could either of them do to me now? Foley being in jail felt like an action propelled by "a divinity that shapes our ends," or at least a twist in the story far beyond anything I could have imagined, even in my angriest moments. He had gotten what he deserved, not at my hand but at the hand of some larger force.

Meanwhile, I had gone back to school, starting in 2004, a year after Foley disappeared from my life. Ever since my first trip to Africa more than a decade earlier, I'd been puzzling over questions about my religion and the God at its center. And since I had nothing but happy memories of my time at Columbia, I decided to dig around my WASP roots by visiting the Episcopal Seminary, founded in 1817 as "the first seminary of the Episcopal church," on what was once the estate of Bishop Clement Moore of "'Twas the Night Before Christmas" fame. A brochure for its MA program asked if I was looking for a community where I could "discuss issues pertaining to my faith in a structured setting, but had never found a way to be part of such a community."

How did they know? "I guess I'm not very good at marriage," I told Marcia. "But I'm good at school, and I like doing things I'm good at."

"I know what you mean. Maybe you can find a community there with other folks who are into religion. You thought you'd become part of one in Nigeria, part of a big family. And that kept you from seeing what was really there, didn't it?"

"Yes, it did. I didn't see what I didn't want to see. Obviously there was a lot of lying, but I was there when it happened.... I wasn't *just* a victim, you know."

"Sure, but don't beat yourself up about it, okay? Women do stupid things all the time. And I include myself in that group."

So I continued to teach, but I also became a student again, facing the world of term papers and grades, mid-terms and finals. I did make some friends there, but I also wanted to get back to the roots I'd tried so hard to cut away when I left Toronto. I saw the church inaugurated by Henry VIII as the invisible thread that ran through my family's history, the one I'd learned about from my cousin's research and the photographs I have of our common ancestors. I wanted to study it and write about it and figure out how much of it I really believed. Everyone in this lovely space believed in the same God that I had returned to after my shooting, a fact that contrasted sharply with the world where I continued to earn my living.

Because I'd stopped going to my department's monthly meetings and showed up only twice a week for my classes, I had to tell Richard, my undergraduate chairman, how I was spending my time. "You're not creating what the university administration calls academic capital," he told me. "They'd probably think you were going to be handing out Bibles in the mail room, or something like that," he added, reminding me that, in academia, religious believers are seen as weak-minded and unable to face the fact of their own mortality.

But I enjoyed moving between these two worlds, crossing the Hudson River to be a teacher at Rutgers and then coming back to be a note-taking student, writing papers and taking exams. It gave my life a shape and a goal, something I had looked to my marriage to provide. If my colleagues had asked, I would have told them that my sojourn on the student side made me a better teacher because it gave me insight into one side of my students' lives. Like me, they had taken on heavy course loads, and most of them had jobs as well. I went to the seminary only part time, and sometimes it felt as if I had taken on more than I could handle. Nevertheless, going to Africa had started me questioning the claim, with which I had been brought up, that Christianity is the one true religion. How could that be when most of the world's population were not Christian and are not Christian now? Religions that see themselves like that are happy to justify violence against unbelievers. Going to Nigeria got me thinking about all of it, so becoming a seminarian felt like a continuation of that journey.

After that phone call from Lawrence, I had written down Kehinde's number and kept it by the phone, but I let a week go by without calling her.

The one time I'd seen her in the States was when Foley and I had traveled to a distant part of Brooklyn to the naming ceremony of a baby of Bodunde and Grace. Bodunde was the friend who tried to get Foley into the "dollar van" business, and I'd gone to their bare apartment once or twice so that Grace could braid extensions into my hair. Seeing the two of them together was always a reminder that a Nigerian marriage could be a real partnership. Knowing that the party following the naming ceremony would last into the next morning, as Nigerian parties always did, I planned to leave Foley behind and head home around midnight.

When Foley and I arrived at around eight, Grace and Bodunde were their usual welcoming selves. As I expected, I was the only person there who was not from Nigeria.

The first faces I saw after greeting my hosts belonged to Kehinde and Funmi, by then quite tall and thin, and a boy several years younger. All of them were wearing American clothes. I went toward them but she pretended not to recognize me, and the three of them moved quickly into the bedroom, where they remained out of my line of sight while the ceremony went on in the sparsely furnished living room.

"What's going on?" I asked Foley. "Why is Kehinde acting this way?"

"I don't know," Foley said, and my hosts were equally evasive.

After that I could not enjoy the party. So not long after the ceremony, of which I have no memory at all, I told Foley I wanted to leave. Since it was quite late in a deserted part of Brooklyn, he walked me to the nearest subway station. "Will you be all right?" he asked.

"I'll be fine." Even at that hour in that area, I was not afraid to travel alone. Nor did it occur to me to be suspicious of what he would do after I left. I had no interest in cheating on him, and I assumed he was enjoying a similar freedom to be with his friends who spoke a language I did not understand.

Since then I've wondered if my mother had friends like mine, friends who would tell her that it was not because she was inadequate as a woman that her husband strayed. She did have a "girls' night out" when she went with some of them to the Toronto Symphony's monthly performances. My father thought that classical music was "girl stuff," and nothing could have persuaded him to go to those concerts with her. The husbands of her friends presumably felt the same way.

When I finally dialed the number Lawrence had given me, Kehinde offered to meet me at the same subway stop that had been my destination on that rainy March morning when I tried to find out where Foley was living and left without knocking.

In fact, she greeted me with a surprisingly warm smile as I came down the subway stairs. The Commissioner's words about Foley having a wife in Buffalo Rockaway rang in my mind as we left the subway station on one of the coldest days of January for the bus stop that would take us to an intersection in Queens and, from there, in a crowded "dollar van," to a deserted warehouse area in some remote part of Queens where the jail was located.

An icy wind from the nearby Atlantic cut into my face and coat, and I wondered why Kehinde was willing to put up with this kind of physical discomfort to take me to see Foley. She'd made the trip several times, she said, so she was clearly a more regular visitor than I was willing to be. Perhaps she simply enjoyed his company to a degree that I, with all the baggage I'd brought into the marriage, could not. I wondered what he had told her about the two of us and how she felt about what she knew. Perhaps they didn't talk about it at all.

I thought she might be ashamed that I had now figured out what she must have been planning when Nike proposed Funmi as a candidate for my adoption: to have me buy their passports, then use them to come to the States behind my back. But sitting next to her in the crowded van in the late afternoon, I saw no embarrassment in her placid face.

It was dark by the time we reached the jail, where the guard told me I was not on a list of visitors permitted to see Foley. "I will tell him to call you," Kehinde said as we walked back to where the bus had let us off. "He will put you on the list." On the bus ride home, I closed my eyes, claiming fatigue as we made our way in silence back to the subway.

A few days later, Foley did call. He sounded like his old, cheerful self, like he could have been calling from anywhere. "My lawyer wants to speak to you," he said, and gave me the man's number. Always eager for clues about what my now-ex-husband was all about, I promised to call the lawyer and to return to the jail once I'd spoken to him.

Here was a chance to see these larger forces carrying out their mission. I assumed that Foley thought I'd tell the man good things about him, just as he had with the woman who'd called me.

I met him in his small, nondescript office whose window overlooked the park at the bottom of Madison Avenue. When I told him that my husband's secretiveness about money was the grounds on which I'd been unwilling to continue the marriage, it was clear that I would not help him build a case for Foley's defense.

I wanted to appear cooperative, though, at least until he asked for a copy of my memoir, *Crossing Borders*, which Foley must have told him about. Working on it had filled many blank spaces in my life as Foley's disappearances grew longer and more frequent. Its cover shows Foley and me, our noses and foreheads touching, me wearing an African outfit, he in an American shirt. It might have been useful to the lawyer in depicting his client as a naive and struggling artist. I'd inscribed a copy for Foley when it came out, but like other things I'd given him over the years, he had probably lost it or passed it on to someone else.

"I gave him a copy," I told the lawyer. "If he doesn't have it any more, that's his problem."

Of course the lawyer could have bought the book himself, but I doubt that he did. And now it looked as if that happy image on its cover, of two vastly different cultures coming together, was just not true.

It was only an image of what I had hoped to make happen, a bridge that could be the beginning of something new. The barriers that stood in its way were part of a long history that no one person can dismantle on her own. If I wanted to tell the whole truth, I would have to write another book about how my plans had fallen apart, and why.

We shook hands when I left, but not before he asked me if I recognized the name and number of a man from India in a notebook that Foley had kept.

I had looked though this book a few times, but the names were scattered randomly and I had never seen any identifiably female ones. "I don't recognize that number," I said.

The lawyer also showed me a photocopy of a Nigerian passport, with a picture that looked a bit like him. "Did you ever see this?"

"No, but I'm not surprised that he has it."

"Nor am I. Your husband is not the first Nigerian client I have represented."

I took the long subway ride out to Far Rockaway the following Saturday, and caught a bus and a "dollar van" back to the anonymous building where Foley was. A guard searched me, and after a short wait he let me in. I'd read a newspaper report on the horrible health care in these private prisons where "illegals" before being brought to trial, and was expecting the worst. But Foley, on the other side of a sheet of Plexiglas with a cluster of holes through which we could talk, let me know right away that being there was "no problem." In fact, he showed no sign of damage to his smiling self. "I have a place to sleep and three meals a day," he said, "and I don't have to do anything but exercise." He was probably comparing the jail to the Nigerian one he'd been in. It was clear to me that he was serious, this cheer-filled man who had not changed a bit since I first met him in Nigeria. It was this trait that had first drawn me to him, but now it looked like there was more to it than I'd seen more than a decade before. I'd always admired Nigerians for their capacity to enjoy themselves in the face of adversity, but perhaps there could be a down side to this ability.

"But you'll have to go back to Nigeria when you get out," I said. "That's the law."

"Who told you that?"

"Your lawyer," I said, though this wasn't literally true.

"Don't believe what he said," said Foley firmly. "He has no power over me. Only the judge has power."

"Okay," I said, wondering why he felt so confident.

He was less worried about his future than he was angry at Emmanuel and Lawrence, who had not traveled in from New Jersey to the edge of Queens to see him.

"They're just frightened," I told him.

"Don't talk to them," he said. "They are bad people."

On the long trip home, I recalled the Commissioner's words about Foley being a criminal. Perhaps what he'd said was true then. Or not. Either he knew more about Foley than I did at the time or his words had an uncanny power of prediction.

A month after hearing from Lawrence, I was getting ready to spend the morning at my seminary and then to take a train out to my classes at Rutgers when the phone rang. I picked it up and heard a female voice I did not recognize. "I'm calling you," she began hesitantly, "about Funsho," the correctly pronounced version of his name that collection agents could not get right. But she sounded American, not Nigerian.

"How do you know him?" I asked, not sure if I wanted to hear her answer but too curious to back away.

"He's been asking me to call you," she said, "but I wasn't sure—"

"How long ago did you see him last?"

"It's been a while," she said. "That's why I'm calling. I hope it's okay."

"It's fine that you called. But why did he want you to do that?"

"Well, you guys were married, right?"

"Yes. For abut ten years."

"Oh, my gosh. He said you were only married a year."

"He lied to you there, then. Did he tell you anything else about me?"

"He says you and he have a business together. He gave me one of his business cards that has your number on it. That's how I got it."

"I had those cards made for him years ago. I'm amazed that he still has them."

"So you haven't seen him recently? He said he spoke to you the other day."

"No, we haven't even spoken in quite a while."

"When was the last time?"

"Let me see. It must have been before I enrolled in my seminary three years ago."

"You're going to become a minister?"

"No, I'm just interested in understanding how different people think about God."

"Well, good luck to you," she said with a laugh.

"Thanks. But why did he want you to call me?"

"He's been asking me to marry him."

I took several deep breaths. Why would he imagine that I would give this woman a good recommendation on his behalf? "So what would you like to know?"

"Well, my friends all tell me there's something fishy about him. And my daughter, she doesn't like him a bit. She calls him shifty. So I guess he thought you'd say something different."

"It depends what you want. If you want someone who is going to be there for you, in a steady way, I'd say you've got the wrong man."

"You know, he keeps making appointments with me and then not showing up. He's always got some excuse but I really don't get what's going on with him."

"Sounds like the story of my marriage," I said.

"And you put up with it for ten whole years?"

"Sounds crazy, doesn't it?"

There was silence on the line for a minute or two. "It's just what we women will do," she said, "for some admiration and attention from a man."

"Yeah, that's it, isn't it? It *is* crazy."

"So you don't have a business with him that is making lots of money?"

"Absolutely not. He has a lot of financial problems, actually. Do you know where his money is coming from?"

"He says he's a security guard," she said. "But he says he has lots of money in Nigeria, and a big house there."

"Well, he talked a lot about building one there. But I was always a bit suspicious about it. I wouldn't believe everything he says about Nigeria."

"Have you been there?"

"Many times. It's a place with lots of problems, but there's something about it that I love in spite of everything."

"The last time I talked to him, he said he was going to go there soon, and then when he comes back he's going to buy a house here."

"How long ago was that?"

"I don't' know. He's kind of disappeared lately. That's why I'm calling."

I was about to say maybe that's for the best, but instead I said, "Look, forget about him buying a house for you. He can't even open a bank account, let alone get a mortgage. All I can say is, I'd be careful if I were you. Don't do as I did, do as I say."

"Okay, thanks for talking to me."

I was glad to be off the phone so I could be with my thoughts. I knew that Foley was a liar, but this nonsense that he was spilling to her was really over the top.

I also saw that, like this woman, like my mother and millions of women everywhere, I had put up with incredible deception in return for male attention, many years of writing and teaching about feminism notwithstanding. I had made my life interesting to my fellow New School students and future readers by telling them about "my husband." Then there was Nike, who had set up a school to help women to be self-sufficient, then married the Commissioner, who had destroyed her school, and perhaps her life as well, out of a belief that she needed the protection of a powerful male.

A few minutes after I hung up and made myself some tea, I punched up "the number of your last incoming call" and rang the woman back. "I'm sorry to bother you," I began. "But you need to know that when you marry a person you are responsible for that person's debts." The collection agencies that still called occasionally had not gone this far, but Sara had given me this information and I was happy to pass it on.

"Oh," she said slowly. "Perhaps that's what it's about."

"I don't know that for sure," I said. "But I thought you ought to know."

"Thanks. And let me say just one more thing. I hope you someday find the love you were hoping for all this time."

"Thank you. I hope you do, too."

Marcia shook her head when I recounted the conversation to her. "He thought you would give him a recommendation to this poor woman he was planning to lie to even worse than he lied to you? I sure hope you're glad he's not in your life anymore." I told her I was. But after that, the conversation I'd had with Baba Sunday about the Morimoyo Gallery began to make sense to me. The truth was not confined to what was so. It included the way you wished things to be. And that's different from lying. It's magical thinking pure and simple. I did it too, and in fact we all do. It's really the core of faith, including religious faith, "the substance of things hoped for," as St. Paul puts it—the belief that God has kept you alive for a reason, even if you can never prove that this is so. I had come face to face with the side of Nigerian culture that lies as a way to survive. But was its spiritual side that had first drawn me to that country, before I heard any talk of "that carver." It happened when I walked to the church behind Nike's house and saw people dancing up and down the aisles as they sang. Back at my seminary at home, nothing like this was even imaginable. So now I needed to find out what that was all about and bring a piece of it back home.

Soon after that phone call, I handed in an application for a grant, offered by my seminary, to go to Nigeria and record the singing I'd heard in the church behind Nike's house. Here was a chance to do what I'd always wanted to do, to find out why Nigeria was the way it was, why there was so much corruption alongside so many churches, large and small, and mosques as well, wherever you looked. I didn't know if that singing went on elsewhere, but I had a hunch that it did. I also wanted to reconnect with Foley's family, knowing that they still considered me one of them. Lawrence has a younger brother—same father, same mother—named James, who lives in a house in Osogbo built with money sent to him by his now-American senior brother. I knew that Lawrence would be happy to arrange for me to stay there with James, and I could not have done what I wanted to do without this help from Foley's extended family. So when winning the grant presented me with an opportunity to go back to Osogbo on my own with a project connected to these new interests in my life, I jumped at the chance.

# 15

As I would soon learn from my hosts, my plane that summer was the last to land at the Lagos airport before it closed down for almost a week. I might have wondered, as I pulled my suitcase through the almost liquid heat toward the checkpoint where my documents would be stamped, why the place was so empty, why no one was waiting for an outbound plane, why only one or two of my fellow passengers was white. Instead I worried, as I always did when I landed at that airport, that my luggage had not made it with me. On past trips it had always shown up, but tales of suitcases hijacked as they came off planes had been in my head since my first visit, and the fact that the airport had installed clean bathrooms since my first visit fourteen years earlier did not entirely block those stories out.

Lining up with the two or three other foreigners, I produced my passport, my invitation from James, and a letter from my seminary about my month-long project.

So there I was on a sweltering day in June 2007, with a camera that promised good sound, to capture the singing and dancing music I'd heard on my first visit. I imagined myself an amateur ethno-musicologist recording ways in which an imported religion had, after the nation's independence from British rule in the Sixties, embraced the best of its surrounding culture and brought it into its churches.

I was also happy to be making my own connection to a country that still intrigued me and to the people who were still my relatives even though our legal ties had been broken. Nevertheless, gaps in the story of this marriage lingered, and I was hoping that, freed from the wish to keep it going, I would find the pieces I needed to make sense of it.

I wanted to learn what Femi was doing, for instance, since what Foley had said about being his father was obviously a lie. I had always given Foley's mother a hundred dollars when I came with him, so I wanted to do that again. But she still lived in his birthplace, Osi, a two-hour drive from Osogbo. Waiting for what felt like forever for my green suitcase to bounce up over the lip of the carousel and begin its slow journey toward me, I saw a sign above the exit that read, in large block letters, *Welcome To Nigeria, Home Of The Happiest People In The World*. Was there some sort of survey that said that? I knew that my country had never come in very high on those surveys.

I'd never met James, but Lawrence assured me that I would recognize him easily, and I picked him out right away from among a smaller-than-usual cluster of happy Nigerians waiting outside the entrance to the airport. He reminded me of Foley when I first met him, which would be about right since James was a "junior brother" by about fifteen years. They were both my idea of handsome, with smiles that signaled a confidence that always felt protective. "What's going on?" I asked him after he had grabbed my suitcase and handed my backpack to the male friend he'd brought as company for the three-hour drive.

"It's a strike," he said, "over the price of fuel."

"How much is it now?" I asked. I'm terrible at math, and figuring out the ratio of *naira* to dollars has always been a challenge.

On top of that, fuel, a two-syllable word in Nigeria, is sold in liters, so I've had to rely on people more skilled at conversion than I am. Had my mathematically brilliant son been with me there would have been no problem. But he was in Washington taking care of three children, the oldest of whom had inherited his father's genes in this area, and who can now do in his head operations for which I need paper and pencil, and sometimes more than that.

"The union wants it sixty-five," James said. "But the government wants seventy-five. We have enough to get home," he added, "but after that it will be hard. Maybe only black market."

Men rushed in on us from every side, waving handfuls of *naira* and shouting, "Change money! Change money!" James brushed them aside, telling me, as I slipped a hundred-dollar bill into his hand, that he would change my money at a place he knew, and I was grateful, as I always am, that a male member of this family was there to shepherd me past predatory offers of help to a foreigner. Westerners have been robbed passing through that airport. A few have even been killed.

"No problem," said James, giving me the familiar mantra. Perhaps this attitude was how "the happiest people" became that way and stayed that way.

We put my suitcase in the trunk of James's battered navy blue Peugeot 404 and I got in the back, while his friend climbed in the front next to him. "A seat belt, I see," I said to them with a smile, remembering when my complaint about their absence in Nigerian cars was met with assurance that they were "not the Nigerian way."

"Yes, we're quite up to date," said James's friend, flashing a smile.

From the back seat I leaned forward to answer James's question about why I had come. "I want people back home to see something good in Nigeria," I said. "They see too many bad things. Corruption, bribery, you know." I did not mention homophobia, though that was what my fellow seminarians back home were worried about.

"Yeah," said James. "It's true."

"But the services I want to record with my camera are so joyful, if they're the way I remember the one behind Nike's house in Ido-Osun. So I want to go to one of them every Sunday with my camera."

"I know that one," said James. "I can take you there. But we need fuel."

"Oh, dear," I said, suddenly wondering if I was going to be able to do my project at all. "I need to find three more like it. "I have a letter from the bishop of Osun diocese. I was hoping he could help me."

"I know that bishop's house," said James's friend. "It's on the other side of Osogbo."

"And how's Nike?" I asked, as casually as I could.

"She mostly stays in Lagos," said James. "I think the Commissioner is sick. He falls asleep all the time."

"Maybe I can call her. She was the one who brought Foley and me together, you know."

"So you still love Nigeria?" James asked.

"Oh yes."

As we pulled out onto the highway that connects Lagos, on the Atlantic, with Ibadan, in the middle of the country, I saw why James spoke of the strike in such an ominous tone. Like abandoned carcasses in the midst of an ongoing war, oil trucks lined the shoulders of the road on both sides. I could only pray that our Peugeot would not join them, with some rattle or burst of steam coming out from under the hood. I did not remember driving as a problem on my past visits, though there had sometimes been long lines to get fuel in that major oil-producing country. This time I was relieved, as well as tired, that we made it to Osogbo, where James lived with his wife and daughter. The dirt roads leading to their house were so deeply rutted that I wondered how any car could survive the knocks and the revving of engines needed to navigate them.

Our destination was a one-story structure surrounded by a thick cement-block wall edged in pieces of broken glass, a form of protection that I thought was confined to the rich when I lived with Nike, but which encircled each of the buildings in this modest Osogbo neighborhood. James honked as he pulled up on the grass outside the wall, and a young woman came through the heavy wooden gate that would be padlocked at night. She was wearing a wrapper of Nigerian fabric tied at her waist and a short-sleeved white t-shirt. "You remember me?" she asked. I did not, but I reciprocated her hug and waited for James to address her by name, Funke.

"I remember you, Mama Kate," she said shyly. "We met at the gallery."

I left my shoes outside the front door and stepped onto the unevenly tiled living room floor. The room was furnished with the usual sofa, upholstered chairs, and a TV set. The owner of the house, Foley's brother Lawrence, had come to the States and married, fathered a child, and gotten himself a green card—perhaps not in that order. He now held down two jobs in New Jersey in order to be the sole support of James, his wife, and their four-year-old daughter, Mary. My room, the nicest in the house, officially belongs to him and was kept ready for him when he came to visit. A row of windows looked out onto an alley leading to the kitchen in the back of the building, where Funke would prepare our dinners. The small refrigerator in my room was working, though it would depend on an irregular power supply. So I entrusted to its erratic care the three hard-boiled eggs and an orange I'd brought from the States to tide me over. But my prize item, one that I would leave behind when I packed to come home, was a mosquito net that floated down over a wooden hoop suspended from a hook that James twisted into the ceiling.

He had changed my first hundred-dollar bill on our way home. The rate of exchange was 130 *naira* to the dollar, almost twice what it had been on my first trip, so I got an even bigger pile of bills. After spreading the double-bed sheet I'd brought from home over my mattress, I gave him two five-hundred-*naira* notes, asked him to buy some bottled water, and stuffed the remaining bills into the wallet I kept in the fanny-pack that wrapped around my waist.

News of my arrival must have traveled fast, because our first visitor, the son of Foley's sister Julie, arrived before I had even started unpacking. I had not seen Tunde since my last visit five years before. He was now a handsome teenager who wanted to try out my laptop, so I let him open it and hunt and peck his way through the English words he knew. I also gave him one of the t-shirts I'd brought with a picture of the Empire State Building on it. He put it on immediately, and we all admired him.

"What did you bring for me?" Funke asked. It was a question I was used to hearing, both from people who knew me and people who did not. No one in my part of the world would say such a thing, but here it was quite normal. I pulled from my suitcase a cotton dress I had bought off the rack from a street vendor in my neighborhood, a one-size-fits-all garment of which I own several. She, too, put it on right away. For James I'd brought a Blackberry cell phone with directions that struck me as hopelessly complicated, but which Lawrence insisted that his brother wanted. I still had two more t-shirts to give away, along with two outfits for their four-year-old daughter. But by then I wanted nothing more than to climb under my mosquito net for a nap on the bed that would be mine for the next month. I put my fanny pack beside me on the bed and fell asleep immediately.

When I woke up, it was beginning to get dark outside, and no one was around. I was feeling in need of some tea, but I knew that I would have to wait for the tea bags, powdered milk, and sugar lumps to make the beverage that punctuates my day at home, but which no one in Nigeria regards as a daily necessity.

James had left a dozen bottles of water at the foot of my bed; having no idea when my hosts would return, I peeled my orange and drank some water. In anticipation of going to the market to buy what no one else considered necessities, I opened the wallet in the fanny-pack I had taken off before lying down, to check on the money I had just changed. It was empty.

My other American money, nine hundred-dollar bills, was still in the pouch I had strapped to my waist under my clothes on the flight over. I'd calculated enough to feed James and his family for the month that I was with them, and to reimburse each of the four churches where I hoped to find the kind of singing I remembered. I wanted to give a hundred dollars to Foley's mother, who still lived in Osi, two hours from Osogbo.

Fuel was obviously going to be more expensive than I'd expected as well, which meant that other things would cost more, too. "Why did I come here?" I asked myself as I waited for the sound of James's car outside the gate. It wasn't the first time that money I'd thought was safe had gone missing. Why could I never learn, and even if I did learn, could I ever be vigilant enough? In any event, I was there on a grant and needed to do what I'd come to do.

James and Funke appeared forty-five minutes later, bringing Mary and a few items from the market for our dinner. Mary immediately rushed into my room and climbed under the hanging mosquito net that would become her favorite place to play for the rest of my stay.

"Careful," said Funke. "You'll tear it if you do that. I don't think Mama Kate wants you playing with her net."

"She just needs to be careful," I said. "If you want to get under it, Mary, that's fine, but don't jump up and down on the bed. You will just pull everything down from the ceiling if you do that." I knew this would not be an easy rule to enforce, but her impish, four-year-old face looked so adorable peering out through a cascade of white tulle that it didn't feel right to put the bed out of bounds altogether.

"Well, it's your net, Kate," said James. "Just don't let her ruin it."

"I won't. But I have something else to show you." I opened my wallet and told him what I knew had happened. James tore it out of my hand and let out a horrified shriek. *"Tunde!* Of course it was him doing it. How dare he do such a thing! And to you, Mama Kate, when you give him a nice t-shirt from America. Twelve thousand *naira!"* He repeated the amount several times, along with repeated pleas that I not tell his brother about what might look to Lawrence like his fault for leaving me alone with

Tunde.

"Do you think he would confess?" I wanted to know.

"I'll go to find him," said James, and he was out the door. Outside the gate, he revved his car's engine and took off.

While he was gone, Mary brought me a rubber ball, and we played catch in my room for a while. She also went through my suitcase with great curiosity, and climbed inside it, pulling over her head a pillowcase that matched the sheet already on my bed. I'd forgotten that Nigerians don't sleep with pillows, a reality I would have to get used to again.

"Does Mary go to kindergarten?" I asked Funke, to make conversation.

"Yes," she said, sitting down next to me on the edge of my bed. "Lawrence pays the school fees, and we're grateful to him." From previous visits I remembered clusters of children in checked blouses and solid-colored skirts or pants in a country where free schooling is virtually nonexistent. Mary's purple-and-white shirt was tucked into a short purple skirt.

When James came back with Tunde in tow, Funke and Mary went into the living room. Mary could not yet read, but I could hear her naming letters. I stood next to James while he questioned his nephew, but Tunde adamantly denied everything.

"Just don't tell Lawrence," James said after he left, still visibly upset. "We promised we would take good care of you, and he will think we weren't doing it. Promise you won't tell?"

"Of course I won't. But why would he think that? This is not your fault."

"Yes, it *is* my fault," James insisted. "I should not have left you alone with Tunde. I know he is a wicked boy."

"Well, okay. But I should have been more careful," I said. "It's happened before, so I should know better. But I won't say a word to Lawrence or Foley or anyone."

"What of Foley?" James asked. "How is he?"

"Well, I haven't seen much of him lately," I said. "He has been traveling a lot." I had promised my ex-husband, before I left the States, that it would not be from me that his family learned where he was. "But as for the money I brought, I think I'm just a target for theft here. So I'm going to give it to you, and I want you to keep track of it as you spend it, okay?" It was a drastic solution to a difficult situation, but I saw it as one that would take some worry off my shoulders. Of course James assured me that there would be no problem.

The following day was a Friday, two days away from my first "recording session" of a Sunday service. James put in a call, on his newly charged cell phone, to the bishop who had sent a welcoming letter to me in response to one I'd written to him on seminary letterhead, and a time was set up to meet later that day. It looked as if the strike would not be over soon, which meant that I would have to keep traveling to a minimum. James had driven Mary to school earlier that morning, promising to get some fuel that would take us to the bishop's compound on the other side of the town of some quarter of a million residents.

The bishop's house was at the end of a dirt road that began at a very wide wrought-iron gate. The gatekeeper let us proceed past a school, a chapel, and a long, white administrative building. Given the fuel situation, I would have to confine my project to churches in and around Osogbo, so I was dependent on this bishop to recommend services under his jurisdiction that included the dancing and congregational singing I remembered. In truth, I was flying blind, but I had been sure when I applied for my grant that I would find something worth recording. The archbishop of Nigeria claimed to have authority over the largest number of Anglicans in the whole Communion. His church is large and growing, in contrast to its slow decline in the West. There had to be a reason for that, and I imagined it might be the singing and dancing that I'd been so taken with on my first visit.

Arriving late at the bishop's white-walled stucco house, we waited for another half hour in a long, carpeted room lined with upholstered sofas. Above these, framed photographs of a good-looking man at different stages of his clerical life marched in an orderly file. When he finally did appear and sat down on a sofa across from us, wearing the red cassock of his office, I saw right away that he was a no-nonsense person. He immediately understood my project and assured me that all Anglican services in his country now included what he called "lyrics," sacred singing in the Yoruba language. "I will give you the names of the churches where I will be in attendance while you are here," he said. "You can come and do your recording at any one of them."

Using some paper and a pen I gave him, he handed James a list of the names and locations of four churches. "Tell me your name again?"

"James Bamidele."

"James—that's my name, too," the bishop said with a smile. "I will see you next Sunday."

"I'd like to come and talk to you too," I said. "I'm a student at the General Theological Seminary in New York." This was an institution that had recently allowed gay faculty and students to share a room with their partner. They had nothing positive to say about the Anglican Church of Nigeria, whose primate, Peter Akinola, had just set up a process to ordain clergy who broke away from the Anglican Communion because it had ordained a gay bishop.

The project for which I got funding involved filming the singing and dancing that I so loved in Anglican services in Nigeria, so much more alive than the prayer book-driven services held in the seminary and in Episcopal churches across the United States. I'd read about the establishment of the Anglican church in Nigeria by the Church Missionary Society, founded in England at the end of the eighteenth century. I'd also read Chinua Achebe's *Things Fall Apart,* whose hero commits suicide when he sees his community taken over by Christian missionaries and his son converts to Christianity.

"Fine," he said as he walked us toward our car. "Just call to make sure I'm here."

The next morning, Saturday, James and I drove along the narrow road behind Nike's house where, fourteen years earlier, I had taken in the early morning sounds of a small village waking up. It was on that road that I had begun to imagine a way to connect to the country on a regular basis.

The pastor, who lived some hundred yards behind the cemetery of the white wooden church with its steeple and bell, was not at home. But the church door was open with a new sign next to the main door that read *Please Turn Off Your Cell Phones*, a new development that had ushered in huge changes in this country since my last visit. From inside we could hear people practicing, in a nearby building, the "lyrics" I remembered.

"I hope I can do this," I said to James on the drive home. I've read the directions for my camera, and I know how to record sound. But I see now that it's the dancing that makes the music come alive, and I'm not sure how to get that."

"I have a friend who works in a photography store," he replied without missing a beat. "Maybe you would like to hire him as your cameraman."

James's friend Seun turned out to be a godsend, a young African man who understood the services and could walk through the church as they were happening: a mobility essential to what was now an audiovisual project, but which I, the only white person in gatherings of several hundred at services where the bishop presided, could never have attempted. That night Seun came to see us, and after examining my small Sony for a few minutes, he assured me that he knew everything he needed to know about it. He also agreed to come with us on all four Sundays. The next day James changed the second of my hundred-dollar bills. I handed Seun five thousand *naira,* and we were in business.

That evening, Foley's sister Yemesi came to visit with her husband, Bayo, who wore the uniform of the Nigerian military. We exchanged greetings, but then James turned on the TV, and rather than watch one of the movies he had rented, I went into my room to read a book for a course I would be taking at my seminary in the fall.

I was taking notes on my computer when James knocked on the door and entered with a grim expression on his face. "Kate, may I ask you something?"

"Yes, of course." I saved what I'd written and set my computer on the floor. Just then the power went off, and my room, with its one small window, went dark. There were no chairs in the room, so James sat down beside me on the bed.

"It's about Foley."

"Okay. What is it?"

"Is he in trouble? Yemesi's husband says he has heard something very bad."

"Yes, he's in trouble."

James nodded and paused. Then, turning to me, he asked, "Is he in prison?"

Foley must have assumed that no one in Nigeria would have this information, and I'd seen no reason to be the one to dispel their ignorance. But word had clearly gotten out, and it didn't feel right to lie. And my loyalty lay more with James and Yemesi by then than with Foley: My legal tie with him had been severed for four years, but they were still my family. So I looked at him and answered, "Yes, he is."

"Since how long?"

"Since January. Lawrence told me about it. I don't know how he found out."

"What did he do?"

"He hasn't said, but we know it's drug dealing."

James let out another of his howls. "Why would he do this?"

"I don't know. He pretty much disappeared after the last time we were here."

"But you are *oko* and *iyawo*."

"We're separated," I said. Telling them the whole story, or at least the part I knew, might have risked my membership in the family, and why be the bearer of more bad news to these people than necessary?

"Come out and talk to Yemesi and Bayo," James said, and I followed him into the television area. The three of them spoke in Yoruba for a few minutes, and Yemesi put her hands over her face. "You know how we would have handled this in Nigeria," Bayo said after I was firmly seated on one of the upholstered chairs. "The family would have gotten money and bribed the judge."

"Yes, but Nigeria is not the States," I said, trying not to sound too smug or too appalled.

"You know, when Foley married you, Kate," James said, "a woman from America, we thought he would be a big tree that would lift all of us up. We depended on him to help us from America," he went on, and my high school Latin reminded me that the Latin root of "depend" is "to hang from." So it would be my outstretched arms from which the family would hang. That need for rescue put pressure on anyone in the States to bring the "big money" that one got by simply being in America, a conviction that neither Foley nor I, nor his two brothers now living in the States, could dislodge.

"What will happen to him," James wanted to know, "when he gets out of that jail?"

"He'll be deported."

"Perhaps he can get another passport," Bayo offered.

"I think he has one of those already. They fingerprint people pretty carefully now, since 9/11," I said. "It's a different world now. Really different." The looks on the faces of my three listeners told me they wanted me to say more about this, but I didn't know what I could add.

"He has no house here," Bayo said after a moment of silence. "His mother had no other sons, so he had no brothers who could help him build it, and the people he trusted cheated him."

"You're talking about Idowu, right?" I asked, reminding myself that I was not the only member of the family who was a target of theft.

"You know Idowu?" James asked me.

"I sure do."

"He was a wicked man," said James. "He went to jail, you know, for the money he took from my brother. But Foley was a good brother. I didn't hear from him long time, but this should not happen to him."

What would they do now that their big tree had been felled,

cut off from the strong roots they thought it had? When the tree fell, many felt it, though none of us had witnessed its slow descent. The mystery I was hoping to solve was not just mine. And when the hopes of Foley's family came down with a crash, the fall was not just his either.

# 16

I was glad that Foley was safely behind bars on the other side of the Atlantic when I stayed with his brother. It would be another year before he would be taken from jail to a plane bound for Nigeria, his hard-won green card confiscated permanently. With him out of the picture, I grew quite attached to James and his family in the course of making my movie. His friend Seun was an ebullient cameraman, and James did all the driving. The strike ended during my stay, but for most of it we had to buy black market fuel. Because it had been watered down, our car sputtered and stalled whenever we reached a hill. I went into my usual hand-wringing mode, but James kept insisting, "No problem," and just kept going. He would stop, wait till the car cooled down, then rev up the engine to get it started again. I simply could not believe, as we made our way along pot-holed roads, that we would ever reach our destination. But we always did, entirely due to James's calm presence behind the wheel. Like his older brother, he was an expert behind the wheel.

Finally I said, "James, I have to ask you something about this 'no problem.' You say it only when there *is* a problem, right? If there really were no problem, you wouldn't need to mention it."

"Yeah, you're right," he said. And for the rest of my visit, every time he said those two words, we would give each other a big smile, or sometimes a high five.

Seun was invaluable, too. Without his contribution, I would have returned to the States with little to show for my grant money. He really loved doing what I never could have done: moving up and down the aisles of our churches, holding my camera over his head or zooming it over the crowd of seven or eight hundred people and in on the bishop in his full, embroidered regalia. He zoomed in too often on me, the only white person in the church, dancing in an African outfit and a wide-brimmed, floppy white hat from the States, surrounded by women with spectacular head ties who cheered my efforts to fit in with them. He ignored my pleas to ignore my efforts, but I knew I could edit myself out once I got home. I'm from the part of the Christian world where the body is considered sinful, and moving it the way I was attempting to do simply felt weird.

The services were a week apart, however, and I spent the intervening time with Funke watching television in James's living room. James rented these DVDs for a few *naira*, and sometimes joined us. They are made by a lively low-budget film industry that has taken the name Nollywood, turning out romance stories about betrayed wives and straying husbands who are either forgiven by their weeping spouses or else receive their just deserts through the power of spirits, omens, and curses. Some were set in "the olden days," with actors living in thatched mud huts and wearing minimal clothing. A baby stolen from a king's palace would be raised as a slave, only to have his origins revealed in time for him to marry his true love, his owner's daughter. Nigeria has a public TV station too, but it presents local news only. If *BBC World News* came to Osogbo, it came only to houses with large satellite dishes rising above their roofs.

It began to dawn on me, after watching several of these dramas with Funke, that she spent a lot of her time alone like this, and when I asked her about it she nodded but did not elaborate. James, it seemed, "went out" without telling her where he was going. It had always upset me when Foley did so, but he never showed the slightest interest in changing his ways to please me. Of course the shadow of infidelity always hung over these absences, such as the time when a bunch of us went to Osi and discovered that Foley was "not around."

But Foley had never struck me as being all that into women. Some of my friends even thought he was gay and in the closet. The closet in Nigeria is a dangerous place to be, and from time to time I caught a glimpse of it. But this was not at all true of my sense of James, or the two other brothers of Foley's that were now in the States. So I worried about James's absences for Funke's sake. But hanging around the house was not, it seemed, what Nigerian men did.

"I don't like gossiping," Funke told me one day when I was particularly annoyed at James's absence and asked her if she might not "go out" as well. "I would rather stay here than go out and talk, talk, talk with people I don't really know." She'd grown up in Ibadan, so she did not have members of an extended family dropping in.

"I know what you mean. I spend a lot of time alone, too," I told her, though Foley's absences had at least allowed me to pursue my long-held interests: reading, writing, choral singing, going to demonstrations, and spending time with the women friends who had been so important to me in my years of singleness. That's why it took so long for Foley's absences to upset me. "I have all the benefits of being married," I liked to say, "and all the freedom of being single." Maybe no one believed me, but that's what I'd always wanted, and not just with him. Above all, I simply believed, despite his erratic behavior, that he loved me, and why would I turn away from that?

However, I did fill in one missing piece of the story I was hoping to complete, having to do with the "secret" that Foley had told me the last time we were in Nigeria together. One night halfway through my stay, I was waiting with James in the darkened living room for the power to come back on while Funke prepared our dinner of rice with hot pepper sauce on a kerosene stove in the kitchen at the back of the house. "I want to ask you about Femi," I told him.

"What about him?"

"Is he Foley's son?"

"I never heard that, but I don't think so His mother is here in Osogbo with Soji. But Femi and Foluke are in Osi, and they're both being taken care of by Foley's mother."

"Well, the last time we were here, Foley told me that Femi was his son. We were going to bring him to the States as our child and send him to an American school."

"That would have been nice for Femi. He goes to school in Osi, but it's a bad school, so he doesn't learn anything."

"Well, I sent money to Idowu so that he could go to school in Osogbo. Of course he never went, but he's a sweet kid, and I would have loved to bring him to the States."

"You can see him," James said, "when we go to Osi."

This meeting happened when we combined filming the third church on the bishop's list with a visit to Foley's mother, who bowed in her usual deferential way when I gave her the money I had always brought for her. We spent the night, as we usually did, on thin straw mats on the upper floor of her house. Femi and Foluke, both several inches taller than the last time I saw them, gave me warm hugs, and I had one last Empire State Building t-shirt that I gave Femi. "I'll bring you one in your size the next time I come," I promised a disappointed Foluke. But neither Femi nor anyone else said a word about his once-anticipated destination: the city where that t-shirt had come from, and I didn't bring it up either.

In addition to offering permission to film a service on three of my four Sundays, the bishop and I had a brief but friendly conversation, sitting with James on wicker chairs on the front porch of a one-story white house on the bishop's property. Given how helpful he had been, I felt I could not raise with this kind African man the main issue that I had brought with me: the absolute condemnation of homosexuality that was shared by every Nigerian I knew.

But then, as we all stood up at the end of the conversation, he said something that I registered as the pearl of great price I had come to his country to hear. I had been saying that dancing always lifts my spirits, though I had never done it, and probably never could, in a church back home. "Yes, it does do that," he said. "It changes you. And if you go to church and nothing changes in you, you have wasted your time."

"That's what I want Americans to hear, Bishop Popoola," I said. "If I can come to the service where you will be next Sunday, can we find a way for me to film you saying those exact words?" I'm not sure he understood why I thought his comment was so important, but it captured some of what I find so alive about religion in Nigeria. There, strangers tell me how much happier they've been since they accepted Jesus as their savior. It's not only their public proclamation of faith but the joy accompanying it that I don't hear much about back home. Perhaps this is the truth behind the claim that Nigerians are the happiest people in the world.

"You be there," he said, "and we'll find a way to do it."

The grant from my seminary required me to focus on their Church, which, its bishops love to announce, is the fastest growing church in the whole Anglican Communion. This was only a part of the huge revival scene that is going on throughout the global south, in Africa especially. But I tuned into it via television and got to understand some of the secret of its growth at a time when Christianity in the northern hemisphere is declining. It came to me near the end of my stay, during one of the long, drawn-out weekdays when I had little to do but watch Nollywood films with Funke and wait for another Sunday of filming. She and I were watching a televised service called *Winning Ways*, broadcast from a huge, stark megachurch on the outskirts of London. I was watching it only because I was bored, sitting with Funke in her living room, both of us waiting for James to show up. I wasn't happy that neither of us had any choice but to spend a large part of our days like this. But waiting with her, I came to know, in my bones, what I could not have learned in any other way: what it is like to depend for your survival on money from remittances because there is no income for you in your country. As long as I was still teaching, I had a busy life, and I needed it, knowing that waking up with close to nothing to do can bring on a cloud of depression. But Nigerians rely so much on remittances because unemployment is so widespread that having no job probably felt like reality to her.

"A Worry-Free Life" was the title of the first program I saw. The preacher, Matthew Ashimowolo, is Nigerian, and he held forth from a huge, warehouse-like building in a part of London that's off my radar. Bible verses poured out of him, and he preached without a script, as far as I could tell, for at least an hour, just as the preachers I heard in the past weeks had done. He wore street clothes: a dark suit from a good tailor, and a white shirt but no tie. When the camera panned over the congregation, I saw a few white faces. But most of his audience of several thousand looked to have come from Africa or the Caribbean, men and women, young and old. They looked happy to be there.

"Worry," he announced, "has us unable to see anything clearly, even ourselves. We can't see the beautiful creature God made us to be. We let others tell us we're not worthy of the love that God offers every day. But the person God sees is bigger than the person you see," he said with a sweep of his arm, pacing in front of the offstage TV camera. God had a plan for each of us that He will reveal if we ask Him in prayer. "Bring your worries to Jesus," he told us. "Only Jesus can set you free." Why didn't I think of that? I asked myself.

At one point he had us all repeat after him: "I am not my circumstances," and I joined the mostly African congregation gathered in their unadorned church in outer London.

"Say it again." And we did, including me. Twice. The startled look on Funke's face told me she must have thought I had taken leave of my senses. "I'll explain this later," I told her, but I never did. What were "circumstances" anyway? Everything around you that makes your life the way it is? I don't know how she took what we heard, but on several occasions when I felt frustrated, I remembered the preacher's mantra, and it let me escape momentarily into a place not bound by the waiting that defined our days together.

I also had a particular reason just then to feel worried. I had left a new relationship behind in New York. It had begun suddenly and had been going on in intense fits and starts for about four months when I took off for a month in Africa.

I had met him through my voice teacher, and we shared a love of singing, he being a fine tenor who could also play piano and bass. When I mentioned him to James and Funke, they were fascinated by my "new boyfriend," though they were also disappointed, since they'd hoped that I would forgive Foley and resume the marriage.

The sexual part of this new relationship was wonderful, and I wanted more of it. He adored my body and had told me he loved me just before I left. After such a long stretch of disappointment with Foley, I hated to think of losing him now. We had been emailing each other while I was in Nigeria, this man and I. But I did not have a good history of getting what I wanted from the men in my life. So, like Funke, I had an absent someone on my mind.

All I could do was worry, and worry I did. With each new email from him, I became euphoric as I answered it, only to have my elation disappear after a day or so. Then I'd be seized with anxiety waiting for the next reply. Why could I not have faith in a "higher power" that would bring about the best outcome for me? The fact that the man was about the same age as Foley was part of it, but I knew that, whatever happened when I got back to New York, I would have to come to terms with some deeply embedded fears about men that I'd inherited from my mother and had never been able to fully dislodge. And when I thought about my hopes for this man in my life, I sometimes remembered the woman who had called me at Foley's behest, a woman I never met, whose name I will never know, who hoped that I would find the love that neither of us could ever have gotten from him.

After that sermon, I listened to the preacher as often as I could find him, and he helped me through those blank weekdays when I had nothing to do but wait for another email and another round of filming. I could not go anywhere by car because we were watching every liter of fuel. I couldn't walk anywhere because James, worried about his promise to his brother Lawrence to take care of me, would not let me go out alone. After all, Lawrence was paying for the comfortable place where I was living. "We don't want you to be kidnapped," he told me. And though I found it hard to imagine it happening, I did what they asked. So I read and wrote in the journal I keep on my computer. But the high point of the long weeks between Sundays was a TV program I would have scorned at home, if I could even have seen it there.

The next time I went to our local internet café, I read one of the messages to me that were always signed *Love, Paul.* Then I called up the website of the church, located on the outskirts of London; it appeared with a burst of loud, explosive music. It claimed to be the fastest-growing church in Western Europe, and mocked the belief that religion is dying out. *Who told you church was boring?* it asked. *Let the revolution begin!* You could click to contribute to a church building fund, though nothing was said about where the unfinished building in the picture was. Or with another click you could buy a DVD that promised *100% Life Improvement.* Perhaps the money went right into Matthew's pocket, as it does with some preachers who preside over huge congregations. But did that really matter? What he said in his long sermons rang true for me. As did the church's mission statement:

> *It Is Our Vision To Be A Place Where The Hurting, The Depressed, The Frustrated, The Confused, Can Find Love, Acceptance, Hope, Help, Forgiveness And Encouragement.*

Why is this not the mission of every church? I asked myself as I copied those words into my journal. I identified absolutely with each of those states that they mention   Things are better for you when God is at the center of your life, the website insisted, no matter what else is going on.

My final recording session took place on my last Sunday in Nigeria. The two-hour drive took us into a part of the country that I did not know existed, with views of a wooded mountainside spreading above and below us at every turn of the narrow road. The spectacular drops so close to the road reminded me more of the California coastal highway than of the flat Nigerian landscape of bush and palm trees with which I was familiar. The strike had ended by then, thank goodness, so we did not have to contend with watered-down fuel. We drove through the town market, past rows of tomatoes spread out on burlap sacks on the sidewalk in front of houses with wooden balconies dating from colonial times.

At the end of the service, the bishop processed down the aisle and out the door behind a cross and a red and gold banner, as the congregation sang a hymn I knew, "The Church's One Foundation." As he passed my pew, he signaled me to follow him outside. With a noisy crowd gathered around him, he stood in front of my small camera in his full regalia, miter, and cope, and spoke about the need for church attendance to change you, the words I had come to record.

"Thank you, Bishop Popoola," I shouted over the surrounding bustle. I wished I had brought a microphone, and could only hope that his words would come though clearly.

"Good luck to you," he said and shook my hand, then drove off in a white van with the logo of the Anglican Church on the side.

Before I left, I bought a quilt made from the *adire* fabric that Nike had taught her students the techniques for dying. I bought it from another one of James's friends, promising to send a money order for three hundred dollars as soon as I got home. In my mind, it replaced the one that was supposedly stolen from the gallery ten years before, the one I'd once imagined as the centerpiece of the Nigerian home that never materialized. It's a light covering, so I only use it in the summer, when it brings the still-loved world of

Nigerian art right into my bedroom.

"Will you come back to us?" James and Seun wanted to know on my last full day there.

"I hope so. Christianity in Africa fascinates me, and I've loved Nigeria ever since the first time I came here." The two of them mumbled about me always being "one of them," and a project came into my mind that had not occurred to me before.

"Maybe I could make this into a full-length movie," I said.

"What sort of movie?" Seun wanted to know.

"The thing that most interests me about what goes on here in church is the way people use their bodies as part of worship. Where I come from, the body is seen as a source of sin. But here that idea doesn't seem to have caught on, and I wonder if that's so elsewhere. So I would go to other African countries and film what they do in church."

"Then James and I could be your assistants?"

"Absolutely."

I got back to the States with three rolls of unedited film in my backpack: about five hours altogether. From the airport I called Foley's lawyer to see if my no-longer husband's trial had begun. If so, I planned to go straight from JFK to the court in Brooklyn, bringing my suitcase with me, to see what the larger forces were up to now. Before I left for Nigeria, the hearing had been scheduled to begin two days before I got back to the States. But I would not miss much, Foley's lawyer assured me, since jury selection would take a day or two and had to be finished before anything else could happen.

"There's not going to *be* a trial," he snapped over the pay phone at JFK. "Your husband has chosen to plead guilty."

"Guilty? How come?"

"Beats me," the lawyer said. "There'll be a hearing at some point to determine the sentence, but that's it."

"Will you let me know when it is?"

"Sure. It hasn't been set yet. Call me in a couple of weeks."

When I called, he gave me a date in September. "Same place

as the first one, the Brooklyn Federal Courthouse on Cadman Plaza. Eleven-thirty, Judge Cantrell."

That hearing, too, was postponed until November, but I did not visit Foley during this delay. I am no fan of the INS and its deportations, justified by a need to hunt for "illegals" and the so-called war on drugs in which Foley had become a minor combatant. But I thought he deserved his fate—not for drug dealing, but for lying to me. It felt like justice that someone who'd been given as much financial support as I'd given him should be punished this way for going after more—a lot more, if I took his bad credit card debt of some twenty thousand dollars into account. This was what those collection agencies had been calling me about, and I found out about it by forging his social security card and getting his credit report: a very Nigerian way of dealing with things. Where had all that money gone? And what chaos were banks trying to create when they showered an unemployed African man with all these cards and with such high credit limits?

I also wondered where he got the idea that he would not be deported. The lawyer had surely told him that it was the law. Someone else, perhaps a fellow inmate, must have told him that he would be spared if he confessed, that a lone judge would be easier on him than twelve American jurors. I thought back to Bayo's comment, in James's darkened living room, about bribing the judge. Nigeria is a country where the idea of the rule of law is imposed from the outside. It has so few laws that judges have total discretion. Foley must have known that bribery was not possible in his case. But the judge had treated him with courtesy, so why would he not be on his side? And why would Foley's word not be definitive?

On the morning of the new hearing I called the lawyer to make sure that it had not been moved ahead again. "Just the time," he said. "Not eleven-thirty, but two o'clock."

I arrived in plenty of time at a modern building, all marble, glass, and steel, with a metal detector in the lobby. Three floors up, floor-to-ceiling windows next to the elevators looked out onto a park whose trees were in their final autumn glory. I found Kehinde sitting at the back of the small, wood-paneled court room, dressed in a Western-style skirt and blouse. During my meeting with Foley's lawyer, he had referred to Kehinde as Foley's girlfriend. On the fourth finger of her left hand she wore a ring with a pink stone in it, no doubt a gift from him.

"I've been here now since ten o'clock," she said. Her impassive face gave me no clue of what she was feeling, about me or about the situation in general.

"I called the lawyer this morning to check on the time," I told her. A few days earlier, I had given her the man's number, but I probably felt more comfortable calling him, a fellow American with some supposed power over Foley's fate, than she did.

The hearing finally began around 2:30 and was over quickly. Wearing the same clothes he'd worn when I saw him in prison, Foley was led into the courtroom in handcuffs and stood with his back to us the whole time. If he saw Kehinde and me sitting together as he walked in, he did not register it, and he spoke only a barely audible sentence or two when the judge asked if he had anything to say. Could this stoop-shouldered man be the same guy who had changed my life in such a dramatic way? The entire event could not have been more anticlimactic.

The only issue was the length of his sentence. Three years was the usual minimum, but it might be reduced to two, of which he had already served one. The prosecuting attorney argued that Foley's involvement was not limited to the transactions for which he had been caught. Foley's lawyer countered that, even if that were true, he'd been only a marginal player. The judge sided with Foley's lawyer and gave him two years, with one to go. I have no idea what Kehinde was feeling as we said goodbye in front of the glass doors of the courthouse. I was disappointed that the prosecution had not prevailed, though really, what did it matter?

A few days later, I asked Foley's lawyer if I could see the records of the court proceedings. He said no over the phone, and I was tempted to stop there. Now that I knew where Foley had been when he disappeared, what else did I need to know?

But I'm glad now that I reached instead for the number of Skip, the private detective Sara had brought into my life. I left him a message, and he came through with a large pile of Xeroxes.

Among these were five pages containing the proof of Foley's fatherhood that neither he nor Kathryn had been able to get for me, coming at last from Kehinde herself. Her testimony told me that Foley, the father of her son and daughter, had lived with her off and on for five years in the "Nigerian building" to which I'd come alone on that cold March morning in 2003.

The document described his arrest. On January 30, 2007, two agents of the Bureau of Immigration and Customs Enforcement had shown up at Apartment 1404. When they asked for Foley's identification documents, she had produced his passport from a black duffel bag. Clearly this was where he was keeping it when I'd asked for it to get my visa to go to Nigeria. The agents thought the bag might contain a weapon, the transcript says. What it did contain was, not one, but two scales, and when they searched more thoroughly, they found the day planner that Foley's lawyer had shown me in his office, with the phone number of a man in India.

Kehinde had signed a form and let the agents take Foley's bag with everything in it. He was at work, she said, so they had returned later that day to question him. Their case against him involved two envelopes from India, intercepted at JFK airport, containing 110 grams of heroin between them. The agents had taken his cell phone and found two recent calls from the number in his day planner. In Kehinde's mailbox they had found two more envelopes with the same handwriting as those they already had. These, too, had contained heroin. So Foley had been taken back to the prison in Queens.

I don't know what he expected when he first came here. I imagined him going to one of the trade schools I see advertised on the subway, where you can learn remunerative skills like automotive repair, plumbing, and electrical work of various kinds. The Nigerians I know in Santa Fe have prospered, either by going to school or learning from others. Perhaps Foley was fearful of schooling because he'd had so little of it growing up. Drug dealing is an obvious source of riches for people who live in inner-city projects such as the "Nigerian building" in Far Rockaway. Since then I've learned, mostly by reading, that Nigeria's oil wealth, along with the diamonds, timber, coltan, and other minerals that fuel conflicts in other parts of the continent, have created a new "scramble for Africa." The first one had taken place between 1881 and World War I, with European countries dividing up the continent. But on a more local level, the absence of trust that Foley was always telling me about, the belief that others will harm you if they see your success, brings its own kind of harm. *The person who is making you suffer is suffering, too.*

Reading those court documents in the safety of my living room, surrounded by my plants and books, and with the familiar sounds of wheels and the brakes of a Broadway bus stopping outside my window six flights below, I thought back to the day I'd stood in front of the door numbered 1404 and realized that Foley *wanted* to live there. But now I knew why. He moved there to live with a woman I never could have been, a woman who knew that he was dealing drugs, who let him to use her apartment as a base for his operations and saw this way of life as no problem. But as a drug dealer, he could be the man, the provider, that he could not be with me.

Having put this together with the birth date that Skip had found for me, I now see that Nike was making use of me right from the start, and that Foley was simply her bait, a way to insure a continuous flow of invitations or whatever else she and her husband were fishing for.

I remember being surprised, when I mentioned the word "adoption," that Nike had come up so quickly with baby Funmi as her candidate. Now I realize that this had to have been part of her plan all along. Her students must have known this as well, which is why they assured me that Kehinde would have "no problem" with the arrangement. I think she simply used Foley as bait to get the invitations she wanted, and he knew it.

So this was the life I would not have had if I had not been shot, if I'd been killed in that head-on collision on the highway in Nigeria, if I'd shared the fate of Natasha Richardson. Forgiving Foley for bringing Kehinde here and becoming a drug dealer in order to become the man his culture told him to be was the easy part. Forgiving myself was much harder, and it happened, I realize now, only after I'd started writing this story and showing it to other people. I learned things about myself that I could not have understood had I not been trying to put this material onto paper. I don't know how this works, but a friend who is a Vietnam vet told he used to wake up screaming every night. But then he wrote about his time over there, and since then he sleeps like a baby.

There is still a lot that I don't know, and never will, about Foley, Nike, the Commissioner, and their country. The credit reports I got through forgery listed Foley's credit card debts. Most were for around $800.00 but one had a credit limit of $6,000.00 and a debt of close to that much. The latest notice to come from one bank to my mailbox offered him a discount payment of $1,965.46 on his balance of $3,926.91. Debt collectors still call my number every once in a while, and I wonder if they have any idea what lies behind the sums they are trying to collect. Did Foley think that the bounty that came with those cards would never run out? His Nigerian travel agent has records of a number of brief round trips, so he probably worked as a drug courier some of the time. I've been told that being a courier is such a dangerous way to make money that people will do it only out of desperation.

Did he have the Commissioner at his back? That's a missing piece of the puzzle that I'd love to get my hands on, though maybe someday he will tell me. I can't step into his shoes and give his side of the story. All I know is that bringing money home from America was what he was expected to do as a man.

As for me, Leonard Cohen's "Hallelujah" still runs through my head, along with another one that I danced to during my first marriage, the Stones' assurance that you get what you need even if it's not what you want.

Seen through my mother's eyes, my marriage was a failure and a source of shame. But my friends didn't see it that way, and neither do I. They were angry that I stayed in it for so long when it was so obvious to them that Foley and his boss were taking me for a ride. My mother's friends probably felt sorry for her because they knew she had no other option but to stay with her womanizing husband. But mine were puzzled and annoyed when they saw me acting like her rather than on the advantages I'd worked so hard to make possible, not just for myself but for all women. Why did I do it?

It was looking for the answer to that question that had me take a look at the role of our ancestors in shaping who we are. Research in the field of epigenetics has mapped the impact of our social environment, not only in our minds but in our bodies, even in our DNA, transmitted back through multiple generations. One researcher has found high levels of mistrust among the descendants of West Africans now living in countries from which most slaves were transported. In this environment mistrust would enhance your chances of survival, and those were Foley's ancestors. I thought of the times he insisted that others were trying to hurt him "because I have success." They didn't trust him to pass his good fortune on to them. I had brought him to the country, where he and all his friends wanted to live. But it is a country still divided by economic inequality and a centuries-old gulf whose troubled waters were too wide to cross over. And as one of my favorite folk songs puts it, "The water is wide, I cannot cross over. And neither have I wings to fly."

A part of me still believes that marriage will fix problems that began in early life, even though I know it doesn't. My mother, and a long line of women who had to stay married no matter what, are part of my heritage, but the earliest ancestor I know of is the guy who left Holland by himself and came to Upstate New York when he was about the same age I was when I left Toronto for New York. Why he left his life in Holland behind, I don't know. But did not most Americans leave a known world of famine, poverty, and persecution for an unknown one with all its risks? We're a nation of survivors. I think my father's announcement to my mother that he had fallen in love with someone else, and the silence with which she waited for his decision, can be seen as a trauma that she passed on to me as a baby. But other ancestors had their say as well.

As for Foley, one year after the hearing he was put on a plane, without his precious green card, and sent back to Nigeria. Perhaps Kehinde sends him money. He probably has gray hair now, which in Nigeria makes him an old man. He knows that I had crossed the fifty-year line when I met him, so we are both getting on. But he is not the only Nigerian from the gallery who has been deported. A good half dozen of his friends from the gallery have also been, including some who came to the States using my invitations to pursue "big money" here through various venues: not just drug dealing, but identity theft. "They could have done that to you, sweetie," Marcia said when I told her about this last. "Then you would have been in *really* bad trouble. Did you ever think of that?"

"No," I had to confess to her. "It never crossed my mind."

*Epilogue, 2016*

One morning in the dead of winter, I picked up the phone, and an unfamiliar voice that sounded Nigerian but came through the static on the line asked, "Is this Kate?"

"Who's this?" I answered, a bit apprehensive.

"It's Gbenga."

"Gbenga! Oh, my God! *E ku ojo meta.*" This was one of the only phrases I still remembered from my Yoruba lessons from Florence years before. It means "long time no see." And this was certainly an understatement. The last time I had seen him was in 2002, when he was living in Nigeria with his mother, Sade, and Foley and I were still married. Gbenga had been seven years old then, so he was a young man of twenty. "What can I do for you, Gbenga?"

"I want you to help me."

"I know you want to come here," I said. "But I hear that the Embassy won't let you." I had written him an invitation letter at Emmanuel's request a year or so before. He must have lined up for hours, perhaps days, with desperate Nigerians trying to get visas. "But look. I want to see you, and I will come there. Let me speak to Lawrence about that."

It's not clear how much of this he heard, because the phone cut out and I had to hang up. Many Nigerians have cell phones now, but they buy minutes only when they want to use them. So I called Lawrence, and he assured me that it would be fine with James for me to come and stay with him again.

"It'll have to be in the summer," I said. "That's when I'm not teaching."

But the presidential primaries began, and as the fight became more intense, I got completely involved in the Hillary Clinton campaign. I also read pieces in the *Times,* not just about the attacks in the northern part of Nigeria by Boko Haram, and the alternately brutal and ineffective efforts of the government to control them. "Militants are roaming oil-soaked creeks in the south," said the *Times* in July, "blowing up pipelines and decimating the nation's oil production. Islamist extremists have killed thousands in the north. Deadly land battles are shaking the nation's center. And a decades-old separatist movement at the heart of a devastating civil war is brewing again." Conditions of starvation had been created by Boko Haram, I learned to my horror. And the worldwide plunge in oil prices had produced fist fights at the long lines for fuel as vans allegedly belonging to some government entity jumped those lines. President Buhari, the former general brought to power in the most recent election, couldn't seem to do anything about these multiplying crises. Maybe going there would not be safe. Maybe the world in which this entire story was unfolding no longer existed.

When school started again in the fall, I called Lawrence and suggested that we all get together for dinner after one of my classes that ended at 7:30. But pulling that off was not so simple. We made a date for a Monday night, but when I waited for him at the train station, he did not show up. I didn't have his number on my cell phone, and when I got home and called him, he said that he'd had to work and didn't have my number with him either. "That's okay," I said. "We can do it another time."

I called him again numerous times but only got the his answering machine recording. Could something have happened to him? He had a second wife and at least two children to support, but where were they now?

I finally felt so frustrated and concerned that, after I finished with my classes at Rutgers, I took a cab to the address I had for him. "Wait here for me," I told the cab driver. "I don't know if the people I'm visiting are home." We had arrived at a cluster of two-story buildings with white aluminum siding and shutters next to the windows, and I rang the bell of the apartment number I had for him. "It looks like no one's home," the driver said when I returned to him.

I went back to the train station and took the next train home. When I walked in the door, the red light on my answering machine was blinking. It was Lawrence, apologizing for not answering so many missed calls. "I work at night now," he said. "And during the day I'm usually sleeping." I had assumed that he worked during the day and called him only at night. But now I could see why it is common wisdom that immigrants work at jobs that Americans do not want. He had no control over when he worked. When I called the next morning, I heard his voice again. "What do you say we get together for Thanksgiving?" I asked. "There's an Ethiopian restaurant in New Brunswick that I've been to. Maybe we can go there."

"I'll Google it," said Lawrence, "and see if it's open on Thanksgiving."

"Are you telling me you have a computer?"

"Of course."

"Well, you're a real American now," I said. "Give me your email address and I'll let you know about that restaurant. And I'll ask a friend who lives in New Brunswick if she has any other ideas." He gave me his address, which incorporated the name of his and Foley's carver grandfather: Arowogun.

A few days later, I heard from Emmanuel, who said that Sade was working on Thanksgiving, so could we get together on another day? When I told him that Gbenga had called me, he was suspicious. "Maybe someone who knows you love Gbenga is calling you and wants money from you. I will tell him to email you so you can see it is the Gbenga you know."

"Okay then, I'll be in tomorrow night. Can you call me then and we'll settle on the day?"

He promised to do so, but the call did not come, which reminded me of one of the reasons why Foley and I did not really connect. Watches, clocks, and cell phones have come only recently to most Nigerians. Only the industrialized world needs the kind

311

of precise relationship to time that we take for granted.

Lawrence did answer his phone, and I told him I wanted the gathering to take place in New Brunswick. "There are so many of you, and only one of me," I said. "So it doesn't make sense for all of you to come to New York when it's so easy for me to come there." We agreed to get together on the Friday after Thanksgiving. I would pick the restaurant, and he would relay our plans to Emmanuel.

When I told Sara about this upcoming gathering, I expected her to be critical of my efforts to stay in touch with this family. But she said just the opposite. "Look, everything we do has a down side and an up side. You took a big risk getting involved with this guy and his family. But look how it turned out. He was the loser, and you're a transformed person. You left Toronto in search of a different kind of family. And now you have one. How bad is that?"

Over the next few weeks I left several more unanswered messages, but on the morning of the day we were going to meet, Lawrence called to say we were on.

The restaurant, Old Man Rafferty's, is a block from the New Brunswick train station, so I walked there. They arrived together, the two men plus Sade; two small children belonging to Lawrence named Michael and Rachel, ages four and five; a teen-age daughter, Sade, from his previous marriage; and Emmanuel's Sade and their son, Segun, who was born here ten years ago. "My wife has to be at work today," said Lawrence. "Her name is Sade also," he said when I asked him.

We settled in to a table for eight, with me sitting between Emmanuel's Sade and Lawrence's Michael, who looked the spitting image of his father. Little Rachel, with her large brown eyes and multiply-beaded braids, must take after her mother, I thought, the Sade who was not with us. The children immediately began coloring the picture of the back of their children's menu. I intended to pay, so I urged everyone to order anything they wanted. Sade pulled out her smartphone while we waited to be served, and I asked her what she did for work. "I look after old people in a nursing home near where we live," she told me.

"That's pretty hard work, isn't it?"

"Yes, it is," she said. "But it's a job. And I want to get a license to be a nursing assistant. It's expensive, but it's what I want to do." Her hair was cut short, just below her ears, fluffed out, and dyed blond in the front. She wore a dark lipstick and mascara, and obviously spent time in a beauty parlor. "Here's a picture of Gbenga," she said, putting her phone in front of me.

The picture showed a tall, thin young man with a serious face. "He must be—"

"He's twenty," she said. Clearly there was a whole story there—how he'd grown up in Nigeria, raised by some relatives, while his parents were both here. They would have seen a lot more of him if I had adopted him, but that's not how it had gone.

"You people are all way ahead of me," I said, handing her back her phone. "I've had the same number on my land line for more than thirty years, so I hang onto it and just use my little cell phone for calling out. Here, let me put your number and Emmanuel's into my list of contacts."

Much of the conversation around the table was in Yoruba, I being the only one who didn't speak, or at least understand, that language. So I assumed that Yoruba was the language spoken at home. But the adults all spoke clear English as well. And as is always true when you're with Nigerians, there was a lot of laughing, especially between the two brothers, who still had the same round faces and winning smiles that characterized the Bamidele clan, though now their hair was beginning to go gray. "Like Obama," I said, and they laughed. They looked so confident, in fact, that I asked them the question that had been on my mind whenever I thought of them. "Are you here legally?"

"We're citizens," they said in unison.

"Good for you. So let's talk about going to Nigeria," I said, turning to Emmanuel. "I need to go in the summer, when I'm not teaching. Is that when you're thinking of going?"

"Yes," he said. "I have a beautiful house there now. Air conditioning. A generator." I thought about the private generator that Nike and the Commissioner had in Lekki Beach.

"So you'll always have a home in Nigeria, Kate," Lawrence chimed in.

"That's great," I said. "The main thing is, I want to see Gbenga."

"He's coming here," Emmanuel said. He then rambled on a bit about moving back to Nigeria and setting up a gallery there. "My job here makes me so tired."

"What do you do?"

"I drive a truck. I work for a paper company."

I then asked about Nike, but he didn't know much. "And the Commissioner?"

"He's very sick," he said, without giving any details.

"But with the oil prices so low now, there's a lot of sabotage in the Delta and long lines for fuel. And people are fighting over land," I added, thinking of the pieces I'd seen in the *Times*. "So I'll need you to protect me. I read about a white woman being kidnapped."

Emmanuel laughed. "You can't be kidnapped," he said. "They only kidnap someone if there's people with money back home that they can get. They want someone bigger than you."

"Well, you have a point. But I need you to meet me at the airport and go everywhere with me. Maybe we can even go on the same plane."

"...You really love Nigeria, don't you?" said Sade.

When the meal ended, I asked for the check, but Emmanuel took it out of my hand.

"This is *my* treat," I said, reaching for my pocketbook and credit card.

"No, Kate, please," he said, and I knew from the look in his eyes that he would be hurt if I insisted. "You know, you came and took us out of the garbage," he said solemnly. "And you washed us off and brought us here. When someone does something good for you, you need to give something back to them. Foley was not like that. He didn't do that."

"I know."

"He's not a good person," said Emmanuel. But me and Lawrence is good." With that he pulled out his wallet, counted out nine twenty-dollar bills, and handed them to our waitress. "Will you take our picture?" he asked, offering his Smartphone. "A family photograph, right?"

Yes, I said to myself. A photograph of a family I'm still part of. I thought back to what Sara had said, the day she gave me the numbers of Kathryn and Skip, about my life being a series of risks that hadn't turned out according to my plans. I also remembered what Marcia had said, standing next to my hospital bed. I'd had a life I couldn't have had if I had not been shot. And I had helped a bunch of real people—the ones who are in Santa Fe as well as these two brothers of Foley's, who seemed to be thriving.

"Okay," I said aloud to him as we gathered behind broad-shouldered Lawrence and tiny Rachel and smiled as the flash went off. "We can take turns paying. My son and I do that."

As we started collecting our coats and getting ready to leave, Sade handed me a Christmas bag with some hand lotion and a set of battery-operated candles.

"Gosh, thank you all. But I don't have anything for any of you."

"That's okay," said Lawrence, putting his arms around his two children "There's an awful lot of us."

"Yeah," I said, returning their infectious smiles. "You're right about that."

*Visit Kate Ellis at kate.ellis240@gmail.com*

www.ingramcontent.com/pod-product-compliance
Lightning Source LLC
LaVergne TN
LVHW011415080426
835512LV00005B/62